The
BEST TEAM
MONEY
CAN BUY

The Los Angeles Dodgers'
Wild Struggle to Build
a Baseball Powerhouse

Molly Knight

SIMON & SCHUSTER

New York   London   Toronto   Sydney   New Delhi

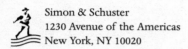 Simon & Schuster
1230 Avenue of the Americas
New York, NY 10020

First Simon & Schuster hardcover edition July 2015

SIMON & SCHUSTER and colophon are registered trademarks of Simon & Schuster, Inc.

For information about special discounts for bulk purchases,
please contact Simon & Schuster Special Sales at 1-866-506-1949
or business@simonandschuster.com.

The Simon & Schuster Speakers Bureau can bring authors to your
live event. For more information or to book an event contact the
Simon & Schuster Speakers Bureau at 1-866-248-3049 or visit our
website at www.simonspeakers.com.

Interior design by Ruth Lee-Mui

Manufactured in the United States of America

10   9   8   7   6   5   4

Library of Congress Cataloging-in-Publication Data is available.

ISBN 978-1-4767-7629-3
ISBN 978-1-4767-7631-6 (ebook)

This book is dedicated to all the women who fought to be allowed to report from locker rooms. Without them it would not exist.

Contents

The
BEST TEAM
MONEY
CAN BUY

PROLOGUE

I didn't think Clayton Kershaw would lose.

Though we'd spoken many times for this book during the Dodgers' crazy 2013 season, I waited until before Game 5 of the National League Championship Series—when his team was one loss away from elimination—to ask him if we could sit down for an extended interview about everything that had happened after the World Series was over. He agreed.

The Dodgers won later that day to force the series back to St. Louis and keep their season alive. Kershaw had the ball for Game 6. And though Los Angeles trailed in the series three games to two and would have to beat a tough Cardinals team in hostile territory even to sniff a Game 7, everyone around the club assumed that with their ace on the mound victory was a foregone conclusion. After winning the National League's ERA crown the previous two seasons by posting numbers in the mid 2's, the twenty-five-year-old lefty had somehow made himself even tougher to hit. When he finished the 2013 regular season weeks earlier with a microscopic 1.83 earned run average, he erased any lingering questions that he was the best pitcher on the planet. There was no such thing as a sure win in baseball. But sending Clayton Kershaw to the mound in an elimination game was as close as it got.

And then it all went sideways.

Kershaw was torched for seven runs in four innings in a game that defied explanation. There would be no Game 7 after all. The Dodgers were out, having lost to the Cardinals by the same score as if they had forfeited: 9–0. Kershaw took it hard, showing no interest in appreciating his role in taking the Dodgers the closest they had been to a World Series berth in twenty-five years; he preferred to blame himself for their failure to get there because his wiring didn't allow him any other choice. Two weeks later, the Red Sox beat the Cardinals to become world champions. Two weeks after that Kershaw won the National League's Cy Young Award for the second time in three seasons. I wondered if he could ever enjoy a plaque he would gladly trade to get just one game back.

I decided to wait a month to reach out about our sit-down, hoping to allow enough time for the sting of Game 6 to fade, even just a little. But then Thanksgiving rolled around, and in December he and his wife, Ellen, spent three weeks in Zambia to oversee the work their foundation did with orphans there. Christmas came and went and so did New Year's. With spring training approaching, I finally sent him a text message during the first week of January. Would he still be interested in getting together to talk for the book? Sounds great, he replied. And then he asked when I could come to Dallas, where he lives in the off-season. He told me he had to fly to Florida the following Monday, January 13, so we agreed that I'd come out from Los Angeles on Tuesday night and we'd meet on Wednesday.

When I landed at Love Field I turned on my cell phone and cursed. Social media lit up with news that Kershaw was about to sign a record contract extension to remain in Los Angeles. I'd been in sports reporting long enough to know that if there were any truth to that rumor, the last thing he'd want to do was meet a journalist for lunch. As I thought about cutting my losses and hopping on the next flight home, my phone buzzed with a text message. It was Kershaw. "Why don't you come by our house around 3 tomorrow if that works?" he asked me. It did. The extension talk must have just been another false alarm in a season full of them. The Dodgers had made no secret of wanting to lock up their star starting pitcher in blue forever, but negotiations early in the season had gotten weird, and the two sides had been locked in a standstill for months.

When I arrived at Kershaw's house at three the following day, he apologized for my having to park a block away. He and Ellen had just purchased a home across the street from an elementary school, and he forgot that he told me to come around pickup time, when minivans and SUVs snarled his street. (The traffic added an extra minute to my trip.) I thought I'd find the Kershaw residence by scanning the block for the biggest stately pile, but the two-story colonial-style home that wound up being theirs was the same size as every other house that flanked it. He and Ellen had met at a school they attended just around the corner as eighth graders. I rang the doorbell. Kershaw opened the front door wearing a backward navy blue baseball cap, a brown T-shirt, black basketball shorts, and flip-flops. His playoff beard was long gone. His eyes looked bluer than the last time I saw him, too, after the final game of the Dodgers' season in St. Louis, when defeat bled into them and turned them reddish gray.

The first thing I noticed when I stepped inside his house was the Ping-Pong table just to the left of the entryway. "I told Ellen she could get whatever furniture she wanted within reason if she just let me have my Ping-Pong table," he said. He showed me what Ellen had given him for Christmas: a tiny contraption that launched Ping-Pong balls toward him like a pitching machine so he didn't need a second person to play. "Who needs friends?" he said with a laugh. Then he grabbed a picture book of all his memorable moments from 2013 that Dodgers team photographer Jon SooHoo put together, another present from Ellen.

The book ended as abruptly as the season had. Its last page showed snaps from his Division Series–clinching win over the Braves. There was no photographic evidence of the St. Louis series.

We walked into the kitchen. He offered me a bottle of water and asked if I was hungry. A half dozen bananas and a vanilla-frosted Bundt cake sat on the counter undisturbed. Ellen had just left to run errands, so we were in the house alone. I told him that if he needed to kick me out so he could go sign a contract for half a billion dollars, he should feel free to do so. He laughed and shook his head. "Yeah," he said, tossing me a bottle of water and opening one for himself. "A lot of rumors, huh?" We sat down. Thirty seconds later his cell phone rattled against the kitchen table. He looked down at it and frowned. "Hmm, it's my agent," he said. "I actually do need to take this." He answered, without getting up from the table. Casey Close spoke from the other end of the line. "Congratulations. They met our terms," Close said. Kershaw scratched the top of his head with his right hand and smiled. Close told him that there was still some paperwork to sign, but that it was just a formality. After twelve months of negotiating, his mammoth contract extension was finally complete. "It's done, man," Close said. Kershaw nodded and thanked him. "It'll probably leak in the next twenty minutes," said Close. "But just wait until after the Dodgers announce it on Friday to comment." Kershaw thanked him again. The conversation lasted less than three minutes. Kershaw took a deep breath and hung up the phone. The room fell silent. I was now 100 percent certain he would ask me to leave. He didn't.

"So," he said. "Where were we?"

I was dumbfounded.

"Don't you have, like, a million calls to make?" I asked.

"Everyone who needs to know already knows," he said.

Was there a bottle of whiskey he needed to open or a touchdown dance he needed to do? "Nah, I'm good," he said. "Let's do the interview."

He was serious. I laughed out loud.

I first met Clayton Kershaw six years earlier when he was a wide-eyed nineteen-year-old rookie in big-league camp. I had spent the first three years of his career watching him make hitters much older than him look silly on television, and the last three trying to figure out how he did it in person. I'd committed the angles of his breaking pitches to memory, and heard teammates talk about how his freakish physical gifts were matched only by how hard he worked. I listened to him, time and again, as he stood in front of his locker after his starts and talked about whether his fastball was working that day or it wasn't, and how good his curveball felt as it left his fingertips. I talked to hitters who said his slider was invisible. I'd had a front-row seat to the truth but I missed it. At that moment I realized I was sitting across the table from a stone-cold assassin, a man so focused on completing the task in front of him, however mundane, that he didn't even postpone an interview to celebrate a phone call telling him he was $200 million richer.

Because he had, by choice, remained a bit of a mystery to the general public by keeping the press at a safe distance, once he made the decision to talk to me he was determined to knock it off his to-do list even though this news had given him an out. His astounding ability to focus and shut out any noise he didn't want to hear told a story that his pitching lines didn't. The idea of stepping into the batter's box against this man seemed even more terrifying. I flashed back to when his catcher and best friend on the team, A. J. Ellis, described Kershaw to me as a person who set his internal GPS at the beginning of each game and seldom altered course, regardless of the changing road conditions. Beyond his ability to make a baseball dance, I now understood why the opposition was at such a disadvantage. His life had just changed forever and he hadn't even flinched.

We began a wide-ranging interview that lasted an hour and a half. As he talked about growing up in Dallas his cell phone shook even harder. Four minutes after Kershaw hung up with Close, his little secret was splashed across Twitter:

Seven years for two hundred and fifteen
million, with an opt-out after five.

It was the largest deal for a pitcher in baseball history. One commenter pointed out that Kershaw would make seventy-five cents per heartbeat over the life of the contract—if he stayed in Los Angeles for the full seven years. In saying yes to the terms of the agreement, Kershaw joined Michael Jordan as the only other American athlete to earn an average of at least $30 million a season over the course of a multiyear deal. And, just as important to Kershaw's nagging itch to control his life, he was granted the ability to hit the eject button after five years just in case bad things happened that he couldn't foresee in that moment.

If he played out the entirety of his contract he'd hit the open market again as a free agent at age thirty-two. If he bolted after five years he'd be just thirty. Either way, this deal left him primed to sign another one just like it right as he was leaving his twenties, when the viability of the new Dodgers model would be more clear. After the incredible run Los Angeles went on to close out the 2013 season, its clubhouse was relatively stable. But Kershaw knew it took only one superstar ego to engulf the rest of the locker room in flames. The Dodgers' new owners were rich beyond belief, and that money allowed them to load their roster with all-stars. A handful of them were time bombs dressed as humans, which scared Kershaw, because what he wanted more than anything was to win championships. At the beginning of the season, the Dodgers wanted Kershaw to sign a fifteen-year extension, which, being longer than half of his life, was impossible for him to comprehend. Eventually they settled on a third of that.

In the end it came together quickly. On that Monday when Kershaw told me he was busy, he was in Florida for a private event thrown by Dodger ownership that had been on the books for weeks. He'd planned on flying home right after. But while he was still in the room, two of the team's owners cornered him. Since buying the Dodgers in

May 2012, Guggenheim Partners, a financial services firm out of Chicago, had added over $700 million in salary commitments to players. But they worried that if they let Kershaw walk, Dodger fans would never forgive them. The CEO of the company, Mark Walter, considered re-signing Kershaw as one of the Dodgers' top priorities. That night, two of the Dodgers' co-owners, Todd Boehly, the president of Walter's company, and Magic Johnson, the Laker icon, approached Kershaw. "What can we do to get this deal done?" they asked him. They had a jet. They were heading back to Los Angeles and wouldn't take no for an answer until he agreed to join them. So the three of them hopped on the plane at 11 p.m. and landed in L.A. in the middle of the night. Close ironed out the details of the contract with the club's front office. After a year of uncertainty, the impasse was over.

But first Kershaw had to take a physical. On Tuesday, the club stuck him in an MRI tube for what felt like forever. They did separate scans on both of his hips, his back, his throwing shoulder, and his elbow. Though Kershaw had never spent a day on the disabled list in his six-year career, $215 million was a lot of money—the most cash the Dodgers had ever promised an athlete, and by a long shot. The five MRIs took four hours. After they all came back clean, Kershaw flew home to Dallas Tuesday night. When I rang his doorbell the next day, Close was finalizing the deal.

I asked Kershaw if he wanted to turn on the news. He shrugged, got up from the table, and walked toward the small television that sat on the marble counter tucked in the far corner of the kitchen. "Isn't it amazing how fast it gets out?" he said. "Do you want to listen to this or no?" I did. When he flipped on the TV, it was already set to MLB Network. A red "BREAKING" banner crawled across the bottom of the screen with news of his contract details. He stood in front of the television alone and watched. His phone continued to buzz. "It's funny who texts you," he said. He didn't want to reply to anyone yet. "As soon as I get started I'll want to get through all of them." His iPhone kept lighting up. I asked how many texts he'd received.

"Twenty-nine," he said. Many of those came from the text chain used by his fantasy football league, which included a dozen of his Dodger teammates.

Another text came in from his childhood friend and current Detroit Lions quarterback Matthew Stafford. The two boys had played freshman football together in high school, with Kershaw hiking the ball to Stafford from the center position. Since Stafford had bought a home in Detroit and lived there in the off-season, Kershaw saw him around their old neighborhood only once or twice a year when he came back to visit family. "Congrats," Stafford wrote. "And you're buying dinner next time I see you. Well deserved." Kershaw also heard from his manager Don Mattingly's son Preston. A high school shortstop out of Evansville, Indiana, the younger Mattingly had been the Dodgers' supplemental first-round pick in 2006—the club's compensation for losing free agent pitcher Jeff Weaver to the Angels. Los Angeles took him thirty-first overall, twenty-four picks after they selected Kershaw. The two had played together in the organization's minor-league system, and remained close friends even though Mattingly never made it to the big leagues. I watched Kershaw watch with rapt attention as the analysts on television discussed his worth. When they began to show highlights, he made a face. "It looks gross to see yourself throwing so much," he said, as he turned the television off.

It had been three months since the worst game of his life. When Kershaw took the mound in St. Louis for Game 6 of the NLCS, he was supposed to dominate; he had given up just five earned runs total in his last seven starts combined. Kershaw said he had not watched tape of the game, and that he never would. "That was a tough one for me," he said. "It's still not easy to digest. We didn't score but I think if I had pitched better . . ." His voice trailed off. "If I had pitched better and we felt like we were in the game, we might have won. It's never one person's fault but it kind of feels that way for me. Who knows if we would have won Game Seven or not, but it definitely stings."

I asked him if the distance from that night had given him any more clarity as to what went wrong. But to him there was no mystery. "My stuff just wasn't very good that day," he said.

Was there a moment before the game where he felt something was off? "No," he said. "I usually feel the same. It's never like, 'Oh my gosh I'm gonna suck,' or 'Oh my gosh I'm gonna dominate.' Some days you'll go out there and watch my bullpen and you'll ask if I even made the high school team. I don't throw one strike," he said, shaking his head.

"But then once you get on the mound it's completely different. Sometimes it's just really bad for whatever reason. So you own up to it. It was my fault we lost. I pitched bad, bad time to do it."

We did our interview and then he showed me around his house. We walked back past the Ping-Pong table and into his office. It was littered with baseball memorabilia. One wall had a framed lineup card from his first major-league start: another game against the Cardinals. It turned out that the first big-league batter he ever faced was his future Dodger teammate and good friend Skip Schumaker. He struck him out. Kershaw liked to remind Schumaker every day that he was his first-ever strikeout victim. Schumaker always shot back that Kershaw owed him his career. Those days were over, though: Schumaker was no longer a Dodger. He'd signed with the Reds in the off-season. Kershaw's friend Nick Punto had moved on, too. Oakland had given him a two-year deal.

Next to the framed lineup card of Kershaw's first game was the lineup card for his first win. Another wall hoisted his framed all-star jerseys. The ball he hit for a home run on opening day in 2013 sat among other treasures behind a glass case. One of those mementos was a Don Mattingly autograph he acquired as a child, one of the first signatures he ever collected. He opened a closet with binders full of childhood memories his mom had put together for him, and pointed out a fancy desk he had never once used. On that desk sat a poster board Ellen was using to run a pool with her friends to pick the winner of *The Bachelor* television show. Life for Kershaw went on.

Though they didn't yet have children of their own, the Kershaws loved living across the street from that school. It was two blocks from Ellen's parents' home, and half a mile from his mother's. When the lot next door went up for sale they scooped it up, too, thinking it would make for a perfect yard for their future family. Kershaw pointed out a spot where they might add a pool. "All of my friends from home are single but in baseball everyone has kids," he said. Because he'd been in the league for six seasons it was often difficult to remember he was still just twenty-five years old. Sometimes Kershaw ventured across the street to shoot hoops on the school's playground. He didn't think any of the children knew who he was, or if they did, they weren't impressed. It was Dallas, after all. He had been a little boy here once, too, and had cheered his heart out for the Rangers. As an adult, he wore number 22 as an homage to his favorite player, former Texas first baseman Will Clark.

As he stood in his backyard and watched the kids play, the enormity of the contract he just signed seemed to hit him. In a few hours, Ellen would return and some high school buddies would come over and barbecue to help him celebrate. Twelve months later he and Ellen would welcome a child of their own, a daughter they named Cali Ann.

"I hope to never take for granted the amount of money I was given and hope I can help a lot of people with that," he said as he walked me out. "That's ultimately what you'll be judged for at the end of your career—how much of an impact you made off the field."

He continued.

"As far as on the field, nobody cares about how much money you're making if you perform," he said. "Mike Trout made five hundred thousand dollars last year and he's the best player in the game. Nobody really cares how much money you're making if you win a World Series. That's what the fans want, that's what we want, that's what ownership wants, and I think that's why I signed on. We have a good chance to do that."

I asked him how his life had changed since he woke up that

morning. He smiled. The money wouldn't change anything, he said. It wouldn't make him soft.

"Obviously it's a huge, huge gift and responsibility and I'm really excited about it," he said. "But at the end of the day it doesn't change the fact that I have to go out and dominate."

1

THE BILLIONAIRE BOYS' CLUB

When Clayton Kershaw hung up the phone $215 million richer on that January day, it was nothing short of a fiscal miracle. The Dodgers hadn't been to the World Series in twenty-five years, and, even worse, the club had spent most of the past decade owned by Frank McCourt, a man who forced the storied organization into bankruptcy. Though the Guggenheim Partners had paid $2.15 billion for the Dodgers twenty-two months earlier, what they got was a glorified fixer-upper.

Dodger Stadium may have been one of baseball's crown jewels, but it was in desperate need of repair. The fifty-year-old ballpark was the third oldest in the major leagues after Boston's Fenway Park and Chicago's Wrigley Field and it showed. Cracks in its thirteen-story façade seemed to deepen with each passing season, and when the warm summer breeze blew through the concourses, its concrete bones rattled and sighed. During playoff games when fifty-five thousand fans screamed and stomped, it often felt like the old press box, wedged right into the stadium's heart, would collapse on itself. Flickering bulbs on the video board made replays difficult to see. Overwhelmed conces-sion stands not equipped with twenty-first-century technology meant that during sellouts hungry customers had to wait in line up to forty-five minutes for a Dodger dog. Even the players suffered along with the masses. The tiny home clubhouse smelled of dirty feet and rot-ten tobacco, and the air-conditioning often kicked during the dog days of July and August. Manager Don Mattingly's office was the size of a broom closet. Even worse, the visiting team had no batting cage or weight room of its own, which meant rival players had to walk through the home clubhouse to share facilities with Dodger players before and after games. This led to awkward moments of subterfuge when any-one was working on anything he didn't want the opposition to know. "It was just really, really weird," Mattingly said.

After taking over, the new owners vowed to pour a hundred mil-lion dollars into stadium improvements right away as a show of good faith to fans. With that kind of cash in the hole, they thought they'd be able to dazzle patrons and players alike with state-of-the-art upgrades and fancy new fan attractions. (Or at the bare minimum, fix the cell phone towers behind center field so that it was possible to send a text message during a well-attended game.) But then they got reports back from the engineers who inspected the place. Their holy cathedral on the hill overlooking downtown Los Angeles had biblical sewage and electrical problems. "Dodger Stadium is historic—which is great—but when you use that word to refer to plumbing and wiring, *historic* is not a good word," said team president Stan Kasten. "I wanted to do all these things and they told me, 'Stan, if you plug in one more toaster the whole stadium will blow up.' " The Guggenheim group realized that despite its fancy high-tech ambitions the first round of renova-tions would have to go toward replacing lightbulbs and toilets.

But the new owners were in it to have fun. So after replacing the scoreboard and constructing bigger batting cages, weight rooms, and a centrally air-conditioned home clubhouse that was twice the size of the old one, they built themselves their own private bunker under the stadium and fortified it with liquor and flat-screen televisions. They planned to celebrate many championships there.

The town's beloved Lakers had won five titles in the past twelve seasons under the twinkling eye of the benevolent Dr. Jerry Buss, a man whose penchant for trotting out championship team after championship team led many to argue he was the best professional sports team owner ever.

Just winning, however, wasn't enough for Guggenheim. The Lakers had captured the attention of a city where actual movie stars roamed free in their natural habitat by showcasing the game's biggest superstars year in and year out. The "Showtime" era of the eighties and early nineties featuring Kareem Abdul-Jabbar and Magic Johnson gave way to the Kobe Bryant and Shaquille O'Neal "Lake Show." Supermodels, pop stars, and Oscar winners became courtside fixtures because nothing validates famous people more than being around other famous people.

Since the Lakers were already a global brand synonymous with the glitz and glamour of Hollywood, the new Dodger owners had the blueprint already laid out for them. To win over the citizens of the entertainment capital of the universe and surpass the Yankees as Major League Baseball's premier franchise they would first have to field a team with enough star power to impress folks in Hollywood. In doing so, they hoped to captivate a nation obsessed with celebrity and attract millions of new fans with their winning ways. And if becoming the loathsome Big Bad Wolf to millions more was the tax they paid on the path to glory, then so be it. They wanted to become the Lakers on grass. Only three miles separated Dodger Stadium from Staples Center, the Lakers' home court. Under McCourt, that gap would have taken light-years to cross. The Guggenheim group set out to bridge it immediately. But before the Dodgers had any prayer of competing with the Lakers, they had to dig themselves out of an even bigger hole.

●   ●   ●

When Walter O'Malley moved the Dodgers from Brooklyn to Los Angeles before the 1958 season, he was called a traitor in New York and a crazy person everywhere else. At the time O'Malley won the approval to relocate his team to L.A., the Dodgers' closest opponent would have been the St. Louis Cardinals, some sixteen hundred miles away. O'Malley convinced the Dodgers' archrival, the New York Giants, to move from upper Manhattan to California, too, and the two clubs launched Major League Baseball on the West Coast. Relocating the Dodgers three thousand miles away was a huge gamble, but O'Malley had long seen opportunity where others were tripped up by uncertainty. After all, he had been part of the group in 1945 that risked the franchise by signing Jackie Robinson. In addition to breaking the color barrier for generations of black baseball players to come, the iconic Robinson also went on to become a six-time all-star and National League MVP, and helped lead the Dodgers to their first-ever World Series title in 1955.

O'Malley's Los Angeles gamble paid off as well. Some seventy-eight thousand fans attended the Dodgers' first game at the Los Angeles Memorial Coliseum, shattering all-time Major League Baseball attendance records. For his efforts, O'Malley was put on the cover of *Time* magazine and christened the unofficial commissioner of baseball. His enormous success further perpetuated the fairy tale that the West was full of endless promise and possibility. The Dodgers' move to Los Angeles mirrored the flight of millions of displaced Americans who set out for California in search of better lives—or at least better weather. In 1950 the state's population was just over ten million. By 1990 that number tripled to thirty million. Even the Dodgers' traditional uniform colors now seemed to suggest the idea of the sky being the limit. Jaime Jarrin, the club's legendary Spanish broadcaster, once paraphrased the poet Pablo Neruda when describing what a jubilant home game celebration looked like after a Dodger victory. "Blue is the most beautiful color," he said. "It is the color of the infinite."

Angelenos were ready. They had tasted quality baseball with the

Pacific Coast League, and had been teased by the Cubs holding their annual spring-training camp on nearby Catalina Island, which was owned by William Wrigley Jr. himself. In 1958, Dodger games became a social event, with movie stars mixing with legendary athletes. Southern Californians no longer had to wait to read about yesterday's games in the newspaper. For the first time, they got to breathe the same air as Willie Mays, Ernie Banks, and Stan Musial. It was heaven.

The O'Malley family ran the Dodgers for more than fifty years until Walter O'Malley's children sold the team to Australian media mogul Rupert Murdoch's Fox Entertainment Group in 1998. At that time, O'Malley's son Peter was quoted as saying they had little choice but to unload the Dodgers because they felt that with player salaries skyrocketing, they would not be able to compete with the deep pockets of corporate ownership as the twenty-first century dawned. In Peter O'Malley's mind, nine-figure contracts marked the end of the golden era of family-run ball clubs. (A heartbroken O'Malley wound up regretting letting the Dodgers go, however. Fourteen years later he gathered some investors in an unsuccessful attempt to buy the team back. When his efforts failed, he bought the San Diego Padres instead.)

The truth was Fox never wanted to own a baseball team. Its main reason for buying the Dodgers was so its local cable television network, Fox Sports West, could continue to show the club's games. At that time, ESPN was rumored to be gearing up to build its own regional TV networks around the country. Compounding matters even more, Disney, ESPN's parent company, had just purchased the California Angels, some thirty miles down Interstate 5. If ESPN did launch those regional TV networks, then Fox would lose the Angels, making the rights to broadcast Dodger games even more critical. After all, they had to fill their airwaves somehow. But the idea of entering a bidding war with the sports programming giant for the ability to show Dodger games terrified Fox. So in a move that foreshadowed the thinking that would come to define the franchise and stun the rest of the league fifteen years later, Fox bought the Dodgers not so much for the team itself but for its media rights.

But when ESPN's regional television channels never materialized, Fox no longer cared about owning the Dodgers—not least because it had no idea how to run a baseball team, and the club was hemorrhaging tens of millions of dollars a year. When Fox sold the Dodgers to Frank McCourt in 2004, the team had been on the market for almost as long as Fox had owned it. Desperate to cut its losses, Fox created a bargain-basement clearance sale that allowed McCourt to buy the Dodgers without contributing one penny of his own money. In what would wind up becoming one of the most lucrative sports business deals of all time, McCourt financed his $430 million purchase of the Dodgers with nothing but borrowed cash. In fact, Fox wanted to get rid of the team so badly it lent McCourt a big chunk of the money.

Frank McCourt had also bought into the myth that to make his fame and fortune he needed to go west. A real estate developer from Boston, McCourt had tried, and failed, to buy his hometown Red Sox two years before he purchased the Dodgers. His local claim to fame was that he owned a large waterfront parking lot in South Boston, and his plan to buy the Red Sox hinged on tearing down hallowed Fenway Park and building a new stadium on his site. But he didn't appear to have the money to buy a ball club, much less run one. The same year he bid on the Red Sox, his company's chief operating officer, Jeff Ingram, sent an email to McCourt and his wife saying that they were in danger of running out of money in six to eight months. "Stock smelling salts in the office," wrote Ingram. "At this rate, I'm going to need them."

When McCourt announced his intention to purchase the famous franchise with no money down in 2001, he was laughed out of the city. Instead, financier John Henry bought the Sox. That transaction worked out well for Boston. Three years later under Henry's direction, the Red Sox reversed the famous curse of the Bambino and won their first World Series title in eighty-six years. After enduring one of the most inglorious championship droughts in the history of sports, the resurgent Red Sox would go on to hoist three World Series banners in Henry's first twelve seasons as owner.

McCourt's parking lot was more than just a piece of vacant land, though: it was his biggest asset, seemingly the crux of his empire. When he strode into Los Angeles as the new owner of the Dodgers, he touted himself as a developer who knew how to build from the ground up. But in divorce filings five years later, his estranged wife described him as someone who sued people for a living. Despite countless assurances about plans to construct waterfront complexes with shops and condominiums, his parking lot sat vacant for the entire time he owned it. Before buying the Dodgers with other people's money, McCourt's previous business highlights included nearly being thrown out of a high-rise window by a rival developer who claimed he stole that parking lot out from under him. While the idea of standing in front of a judge in court might make the average person squirm, McCourt seemed to thrive in litigation when his livelihood hung in the balance. "He was more stubborn than an army of cockroaches," said one Dodger executive who worked under him. But McCourt was as smart as he was obstinate. He put up his parking lot as collateral against the $145 million loan he got from Fox to complete the sale of the Dodgers. And when McCourt defaulted on that loan, Fox foreclosed on the lot and sold it to be done with him. In the end, McCourt traded a parking lot for one of Major League Baseball's flagship franchises.

It took him eight years to bankrupt it.

Frank McCourt looked harmless enough. When he stepped up to the podium on the day he took over the Dodgers, he bore all the markings of a man who was thrilled with his lot in life. Clutching a custom-made Dodgers jersey with his name on the back, flanked by a wife who seemed proud to be standing next to him, McCourt told the crowd of assembled reporters and well-wishers that after the impersonal Fox era, the Dodgers were returning to their roots of family ownership. Trim in the waist for a man approaching middle age, McCourt wore his Irish heritage in his curly gray hair and rosy cheeks. He showed up in Los Angeles in a suit and tie, with a softness in his gait and a huge smile on his face. But the years in Hollywood hardened him, and by the end of his time as owner he hid behind aviator shades and pink collared shirts as stiff as he was. His reed-thin lips were usually pursed into a frown, and when he spoke, the vowels that left his tongue were stretched haaaaaahd by a lingering Boston accent that hung on like a nagging cough. His Dodgers were the Daahjuhs.

A few years into his reign he installed his lawyer wife, Jamie, as CEO of the team. In a lengthy profile written on the nuclear dissolution of their marriage, *Vanity Fair* magazine likened the diminutive Jamie to a tense, skinny chihuahua. College sweethearts since they met during their freshman year at Georgetown University when Jamie was seventeen and Frank was eighteen, they eloped and married in her New York apartment in 1979. Her parents were so unhappy with her choice that they boycotted the wedding. But Frank and Jamie seemed to be a good match—at least on the surface. By many accounts, the McCourts had been happy for most of their marriage, buoyed by their shared Clintonesque relentless professional ambition. But after they moved to Los Angeles their aspirations morphed into an insatiable obsession with status and material possessions. By 2009 the couple turned on each other, with Frank testing the limits of the amount of money he could borrow, and Jamie instructing a Dodger executive to draw up a battle plan for her eventual ascendance to the office of president of the United States. "They were equally delusional but Jamie was better at parties," said another Dodger executive.

During the eight years McCourt owned the Dodgers, the club won the National League West division three times and advanced to the NLCS twice. McCourt clung to those statistics as he was thrown out for bankrupting the team, and even sent club employees a crystal clock with a list of his accomplishments as a holiday gift just months after the commissioner of baseball kicked him out for gross negligence. ("The best part is it arrived the day after Christmas," said the executive. "Frank obviously got a cheaper rate from UPS for December twenty-sixth delivery.") Though he liked to take credit, the Dodgers' success during McCourt's tenure was due to the strength of the club's drafts before he owned the team, and taking the malcontented superstar left fielder Manny Ramirez off Boston's hands for free during their 2008 playoff run. While the Dodgers' homegrown, cheap young players like Matt Kemp, James Loney, and Russell Martin stabilized the team's everyday lineup, McCourt cut funding for scouting in Latin America, choking off an international player development pipeline that had long been one of baseball's strongest. It was especially puzzling because the Dodgers had been pioneers in looking beyond American borders for talented ballplayers, from Mexico's Fernando Valenzuela to Japan's Hideo Nomo to South Korea's Chan Ho Park. In 1987 the club established the first American baseball academy in the Dominican Republic, the country that has since produced the most baseball stars in the world outside the United States despite being roughly the size of Vermont and New Hampshire combined. Even though the academy had nurtured future stars like Pedro Martinez, Raul Mondesi, and Adrián Beltré, McCourt decided it wasn't worth the investment.

During McCourt's time as owner, the Dodgers twice came to within three wins of making the World Series. But when the club's general manager, Ned Colletti, had agreements in place to add ace starting pitchers Cliff Lee and C.C. Sabathia to the Dodgers' rotation to push them over the top, McCourt cried poverty and nixed both deals. The organization's front office had built a team just one or two arms away from a potential dynasty, but with their young players approaching free agency all at once, their championship window was closing fast. McCourt's refusal to pay for the final pieces necessary to win it all dealt the franchise and its fans a devastating blow.

It wasn't as if the Dodgers weren't raking in the cash, either. The team played in the second-biggest media market in the country and led the National League in attendance during five of McCourt's first six years as owner. During the season before the McCourts filed for divorce, the club sold the most tickets in all of baseball. When McCourt bought the Dodgers, the club was fourth in MLB in player payroll at $105 million. Despite promising fans that he would keep the team's payroll in the top 25 percent of the league's, he slashed the Dodgers' dole to $92 million. He cut it even further the following year, to $83 million. Baseball, first and foremost, is a business. No one expected McCourt to put every last cent from ticket sales and advertising revenue back into the Dodgers and take nothing for himself. But when McCourt took the stand during his divorce trial, he admitted that the linchpin of his business plan as owner of the team was to significantly reduce player compensation. During the trial, a document submitted into evidence revealed McCourt's plan to cut the team's baseball operations budget by 21 percent by the third year of his regime. On McCourt's last opening day as owner, the Dodgers ranked an embarrassing twelfth out of thirty teams in player payroll, lagging behind such small-market clubs as the Minnesota Twins and Milwaukee Brewers.

Frustrated fans wondered where all the money went. As divorce filings later revealed, while the Dodgers were slashing spending, McCourt and his family spent extravagantly on nine multimillion-dollar homes, a private jet on permanent standby, daily home salon sessions, and a Russian psychic back in Boston whom they paid six-figure bonuses to "think blue." When the McCourts moved to L.A., they paid $21.25 million for a home on Charing Cross Road across the street from the Playboy Mansion—a move that must have been popular with the couple's four sons, who were between ages thirteen and twenty-two at the time. They spent an additional $14 million renovating it, including hauling their old kitchen across the country from their family home in Brookline, Massachusetts. According to divorce court filings, they purchased the house next door after deciding their main spread wasn't big enough for hosting guests or doing laundry. The McCourts also bought a Malibu mansion on Pacific Coast Highway from the actress Courteney Cox for $27.5 million. Then, when the family realized its beachfront backyard wasn't large enough to accommodate the Olympic-size swimming pool Jamie required for her morning lap swims, they snapped up the home next door for $19 million as well. The cash continued to roll in. As the Dodgers' chief executive officer, Jamie was the highest-ranking female in baseball. The McCourts were living the American dream, amassing their own personal real estate empire. It would have continued, if in the end the only thing they hadn't loved more than money was hurting each other.

Their marriage fell apart at the worst possible time for the franchise. After Jamie filed for divorce on the night before the Dodgers took on the Phillies in Game 1 of the 2009 NLCS, she alleged what many critics had suspected: that her husband had mismanaged the Dodgers' funds to within an inch of the club's life. Just before their divorce trial began, Jamie recalled a traumatic incident back when the family lived in Massachusetts: she had answered a knock on the door to find a sheriff sent to collect their mortgage payment. After describing that ordeal, she was asked when her financial anxiety had eased. "I never stopped worrying," she said. Jamie revealed that in spite of their family flaunting its lavish lifestyle, she lived in constant fear that one day the government would seize all their possessions. McCourt denied her allegations and countered with a press release firing Jamie as the Dodgers CEO and accusing her of destroying their marriage by having an affair with her driver, a man he had hired to squire her around town because her poor eyesight made it difficult for her to drive at night.

Since they had been married for decades, Jamie felt she was entitled to half the value of the Dodgers. Frank disagreed. Their divorce trial raged on. Because McCourt didn't have the cash to buy Jamie out, he released a statement saying the Dodgers were his and his alone, and that he had a signed document from Jamie to prove it. The certificate in question was prepared when the couple moved to Los Angeles to buy the Dodgers after their estate attorney informed them that California was a community property state. McCourt insisted that it gave him sole ownership of the Dodgers, and his wife exclusive custody of the couple's homes. In fact, he said, the division of assets was executed at Jamie's insistence since she was worried her husband's creditors would come after the family homes if his business deals soured, leaving her and their children with no place to live. Jamie, a former family law attorney, conceded she had signed the document, but said she hadn't read it and had no idea what it meant. For reasons still unknown, Frank and Jamie each signed ten copies of the agreement. But when the lawyers unearthed all the duplicates from a safe they noticed something strange: five of the copies included the Dodgers on Frank McCourt's list of separate properties, and five excluded the team. Jamie's lawyers cried foul. Her case hinged on the enforceability of a contract that had different signed versions. In the end, the estranged couple spent more than $20 million in legal fees fighting over a document that cost less than $10,000 to prepare. "Frank and I practically raised each other and put everything we had into the Dodgers," Jamie said. "The notion that I'd give that up is preposterous."

In perhaps the most pivotal moment in Dodger history since Walter O'Malley moved the team to Los Angeles, the judge ruled that the contract was unenforceable, which entitled Jamie to half of whatever the team was worth.

Since the two could no longer stand each other, running the Dodgers together was not an option. The only way McCourt could split the franchise in half was to sell it. But even though he was broke, and their salacious divorce trial had dragged the Dodgers through a prolonged national embarrassment, McCourt made it clear that he had no intention of parting with the team. According to court filings, the Dodgers owed $573 million to creditors in January 2012. In 2009, the Miami Dolphins had sold for $1.1 billion—a record for an American sports franchise. *Forbes* valued the Dodgers at $900 million. If the team sold for near that price, most of that money would be wiped out by debts and taxes, leaving the couple with nothing. But McCourt had an ace up his sleeve. The Dodgers' television deal with Fox was set to expire at the end of the 2013 season, and it was thought to be worth billions. If he could just hang on to the team for two more years, all of his financial problems would be solved, and then some.

Major League Baseball officials were not about to let that happen. Team finances are state secrets, but, much to the ire of MLB executives, the McCourt divorce trial had forced open the Dodgers' books for public consumption, and tawdry tales of the McCourt family's extravagant lifestyle had horrified the sport's commissioner, Bud Selig. The Dodgers were one of the cornerstones on which his league was built, and McCourt's driving the team into the ground threatened the livelihood of the game. Thousands of Dodger fans pledged to boycott as long as McCourt owned the team. From 2009 to 2011, attendance plummeted by 22 percent. The morale of club employees was in the gutter, too. "Every day going to that stadium was like showing up to a funeral and watching the congregation get smaller and smaller," said one Dodger executive. McCourt didn't care. Selig wanted him gone, but ousting him would be tricky. The league viewed owners like country club members who could be evicted if they offended the populace. McCourt saw the Dodgers as his private property that no one could legally repossess. Both sides dug in for a protracted fight.

Then, tragedy struck.

On opening day in 2011, a San Francisco Giants fan named Bryan Stow was leaving Dodger Stadium when he was assaulted by two men wearing Dodger gear. He was taken to a hospital with massive brain injuries and remained in a coma for months. Writers and columnists were quick to suggest that despite escalating acts of violence between the rival fan bases over the years, McCourt had been too cheap to pay for an increased security presence around the ballpark. The incident took place after dark and Dodger Stadium's massive parking lot lacked sufficient lighting. Off-duty police officers in uniform cost fifty dollars an hour, while undercover cops in polo shirts ran about half that. In 2009, the Dodgers started relying on the less expensive option. Their head of security resigned in protest.

As Stow clung to life and the hunt for his assailants intensified, the drumbeat for McCourt's ouster grew louder. Major League Baseball seized the opportunity to pounce. While Selig didn't exercise his power to toss McCourt out right then, by the end of the month he appointed an outside monitor to oversee all of the Dodgers' monetary expenditures. It proved to be a fatal blow to his ownership. McCourt protested, even going so far as to call the commissioner un-American. It also became evident how leveraged the team was—McCourt had been forced to take out a multimillion-dollar loan against future season ticket sales and charge the Dodgers $14 million a year to rent their own stadium. McCourt also raised eyebrows when it was revealed that the Dodgers Dream Foundation, a charity established to build ball fields for children in underserved areas of Los Angeles, had paid its top executive and main McCourt henchman, Howard Sunkin, more than $400,000 of its $1.6 million budget one year.

With the team's cash reserves dwindling, McCourt turned to Fox to try to extend the club's television deal in return for cash up front to float him. The Dodgers were earning about $40 million a year for their TV rights when Selig sent in the monitor. But when it expired in two years, McCourt was free to entertain offers from multiple networks and select the highest bidder. The Dodgers' next TV contract figured to bring in more than five times what the current deal was worth— maybe more. McCourt's desperation to hold on to the club was understandable: a mountain of cash lay just around the bend.

So McCourt had an idea. Why not borrow money from Fox against that future TV deal? Fox was more than willing to take the rights to broadcast Dodger games off the market to avoid a bidding war later, and the two sides agreed in principle to a twenty-year television deal worth $3 billion that would begin in 2014. Under the terms of the agreement, McCourt would receive $385 million up front. Of that money, $200 million would go into the team, while the rest would go to the McCourts and their divorce attorneys. Major League Baseball balked. With its monitor in place overseeing all financial transactions, there was no way it was going to let Fox toss McCourt a lifeline. Later that year, the league would allege in court filings that McCourt took $189.16 million out of the team for his own personal use, an activity Selig described as "looting." Without that loan from Fox, rumors swirled that McCourt would not have enough cash to pay his players when checks were to be handed out that Friday. MLB didn't care. It rejected Fox's loan to smoke him out. McCourt had one card left to play, and he didn't hesitate. On the morning of Monday, June 27, 2011, he plunged the Los Angeles Dodgers into bankruptcy.

That afternoon, televisions in the Dodgers' clubhouse played the grim news on a loop. Players called their agents to make sure their checks wouldn't bounce.

Though it ensured the end of his run as owner, filing for bankruptcy protection wound up being a brilliant move for McCourt. When an MLB team is sold, the commissioner's office is involved in vetting and choosing the new owner. Because the league operates somewhat like an old boys' fraternity, the winning bid isn't always the highest one. The league covets candidates it believes will toe the line, a sentiment that intensified after McCourt thumbed his nose at Selig at every turn. But since McCourt owed hundreds of millions of dollars to creditors— and the Internal Revenue Service wanted its cut—the authority of the bankruptcy court trumped MLB's typical selection process by ruling that McCourt was entitled to collect the most money possible in order to pay off his debts. The judge emphasized that creditors took precedence over the league's preferences for a new owner. And in a testament to how badly Major League Baseball wanted McCourt gone, it didn't fight his unusual, unilateral power to choose his successor. The league's acquiescence on this point was significant because it offered a way in for colorful outsiders like Mark Cuban, the outspoken tech billionaire owner of the NBA's Dallas Mavericks. (Cuban had tried to buy the Cubs a few years earlier but felt he had been blackballed because Selig didn't want him to own a team.) The Dodgers' sale offered an unprecedented opportunity for a Gatsbyesque character without connections to the commissioner's office to buy his way in.

Bids for the Dodgers poured in from across the globe. One investor who announced his interest in buying the team was Laker icon Magic Johnson, the man who, following in the footsteps of Dodger great Sandy Koufax, had made the number 32 synonymous with sporting glory in Los Angeles. After his playing days ended prematurely when he announced he had contracted the HIV virus, Johnson had proven himself to be somewhat of a business savant, coming to own stakes in, among other things, movie theaters, Starbucks coffee shops, and his beloved Lakers.

Johnson was rich by the average American's standards, but he had nowhere near the cash needed to buy the Dodgers. What people didn't yet know, however, was that Johnson had formed an alliance with Stan Kasten, the man who had served as president of Ted Turner's Atlanta Braves during their nineties dynasty. Kasten and Johnson had become acquainted when Kasten ran the city's NBA franchise, the Hawks, for Turner during that same time period. With fifteen-man rosters and a limited minor league, the NBA, Kasten explains, is a small world where everyone knows everyone else. Kasten and Johnson had almost joined forces back in the mid-nineties when the former flew to Los Angeles to try to convince the latter to coach the Atlanta Hawks. "But he turned me down, that son of a bitch," Kasten said with a laugh. "The truth is he didn't want to coach." Though the two remained friends, they could not have imagined the impact their relationship would have in shattering the economics of sports franchises some twenty years later.

Magic Johnson's smile had mesmerized Los Angeles from the moment the Lakers drafted him out of Michigan State in 1979. Thirty-two years later, that smile started a war. Despite the fact that he knew very little about baseball, six different prospective ownership groups courted

Johnson, each desperate to add his credibility with Los Angeles sports fans to its roster of moneymen. "It was like Earvin was going through the college recruitment process all over again," said his former agent and closest confidant, Lon Rosen, who would later become the Dodgers' chief marketing officer. "Groups were coming to him and making presentations." After his tenure in Atlanta ended, Kasten had moved to Washington, D.C., to take a job as the president of the Nationals the year after they relocated from Montreal. He stayed in that position for four years, and in 2010 he stepped down and planned to open his own consulting practice. Then Guggenheim contacted him. Would he be interested in joining their group to buy the Houston Astros? they asked. Kasten had heard the name Guggenheim before, but he had no idea who this group out of Chicago was. And when he went to search for information about the company's president, Mark Walter, on the Internet, he couldn't find anything. Walter seemed to be a ghost. Kasten was dubious. Sports franchise sales attracted so many hucksters and grifters pretending to be rich that the mystery surrounding Walter and Guggenheim did not help their cause. "There's a lot of bullshit in putting deals together for hundreds of millions of dollars, let alone billions," said Kasten. "There's a lot of groups that claim to have money and just don't."

But after a series of conversations, Kasten decided the group's money was real. And he became sold on Walter after Walter blew him off. A lifelong Cubs fan, Walter had kept his season tickets even though Chicago had been playing abysmal ball for years. On the day the first-ever phone call between Kasten and Walter was scheduled, Walter went to watch the Cubs play. "He sent me an email that said, 'Hey guys, I have to put the call off for a little while because we're in extra innings here at Wrigley,' " said Kasten. Walter stayed to the end and kept Kasten waiting for half an hour. "So that was great. I was like, 'I'm gonna do something with Guggenheim.' "

In the end, Walter decided not to bid on the Astros. But while the Houston sale was being processed, Kasten mentioned to Walter that because of the messy McCourt divorce, the Dodgers might be on the market soon. Walter had wanted to buy the Astros, but he was even more interested in the Dodgers. After McCourt filed for bankruptcy and it became clear Major League Baseball was going to force him to sell the team, Kasten called Rosen. He had someone he wanted Magic Johnson to meet, but the famously secretive Kasten wouldn't tell him who. Rosen and Johnson agreed to the meeting because they trusted Kasten. "We thought if Stan's bringing someone he must be legit," said Rosen. And so in November 2011, Mark Walter and Guggenheim president Todd Boehly flew to Los Angeles to meet with Johnson. When Kasten, Walter, and Boehly set off in a car from Guggenheim's Santa Monica office to Johnson's Beverly Hills office, Kasten realized he still hadn't told Johnson whom he was meeting with. "So I called [Rosen] and said, 'We're coming in a second, and here's who they are,'" said Kasten.

The drive from Guggenheim's L.A. headquarters to Johnson's office is just over five miles. It took the men two hours. Protesters had taken to the streets in support of the anti–Wall Street Occupy movement, grinding traffic to a halt. "We were like an hour late to the meeting, which couldn't be filling Lon with confidence," said Kasten. "It was horrible."

Johnson had already met with four prospective groups, but Walter and Boehly made a striking impression on him that day. The Dodgers were unique in that the team's stadium sat on three hundred acres of undeveloped land owned by the club that overlooked downtown L.A. The Raiders and Rams of the NFL had left the city twenty years earlier, but there had long been talk of luring one or both teams back with a fancy new stadium. Some thought the area surrounding Dodger Stadium would be the perfect location for such a structure. Each of the previous groups that met with Johnson had laid out its ideas for using the Dodgers as a foundation to build a larger sports and real estate empire. Johnson had grown skeptical of the motives of these rich men. So he looked at Walter and asked: "Are you doing this for the investment or are you doing this to win?" Walter didn't hesitate: "I'm doing this to win," he said, adding that he hoped to leave the team to his daughter one day. The meeting lasted an hour. As he walked out of the building, Kasten thought it went well. Johnson had one more group to sit down with, but he'd made up his mind. "I felt like I'd just met a guy who was just like Jerry Buss," Johnson said later, referring to the legendary Lakers' owner. "He's so into his family. He has a great passion for winning and doesn't care if people knew who he was." Kasten, Walter, and Boehly were just sitting down to dinner at the SoHo House on Sunset Boulevard when Rosen texted Kasten. Magic was in.

Days before the 2012 season kicked off, McCourt submitted his list of potential buyers to Major League Baseball. Selig's office then whittled it down to three finalists, who would be allowed to bid on the Dodgers at an auction held by McCourt. The first was Stan Kroenke, a real estate entrepreneur out of St. Louis worth an estimated $5 billion who owned the Rams, the Denver Nuggets, the Colorado Avalanche, and the English soccer club Arsenal. Observers joked that all Kroenke needed was a baseball team to complete the set. His interest in owning a ball club made sense for another reason, too: he had been named for Cardinals legend Stan Musial. Kroenke also held the distinction of being the only billionaire in the world married to another billionaire. His wife, Ann Walton Kroenke, was the daughter of one of the founders of Wal-Mart, Sam Walton's brother James. *Forbes* estimated she was worth even more money than her husband. The second finalist was Steve Cohen, a hedge fund deity from New York City worth an estimated $11 billion, much of it liquid. Cohen owned a small stake in the Mets, which he promised to sell if he won the auction for the Dodgers. The third finalist was Walter's secretive Guggenheim group.

The smart money was on Cohen. He seemed to have the deepest pockets, and the feeling was that Major League Baseball preferred him as the choice since they were already familiar with him as a minority owner of the Mets. So when McCourt issued a press release telling the world that Guggenheim Partners had bought the Dodgers for

$2.15 billion the night before the auction was supposed to take place, the industry gasped. No baseball team had ever sold for a billion dollars, let alone two. When John Henry purchased the Red Sox in 2002, he forked over just $660 million. After McCourt paid off his creditors and the IRS, it was estimated that he would walk away with close to a billion dollars in profit—not bad for someone who had put none of his own money into the purchase of the team eight years earlier. Underscoring just how wrong everyone was in their estimate of the Dodgers' worth, Jamie McCourt had struck an agreement with her estranged husband before he sold the team that netted her $131 million tax-free, plus ownership of the couple's homes. That settlement turned out to be a raw deal for her. After paying off his ex-wife, McCourt wound up with close to seven times what she got, a result she handled by suing him for $770 million on the grounds that he misled her in court about the Dodgers' real value. The judge denied her appeal to throw out the divorce settlement, saying that she chose the security of the $131 million and the homes over the risk of the Dodgers' sale. But what happened eighteen months after McCourt sold the team probably still keeps them both up at night.

After it was reported that the Guggenheim group outbid the next-highest bidder for the Dodgers by some $500 million, the gasps turned to snickering. But it wasn't true. When Mark Walter sat down alone with Frank McCourt in a Manhattan hotel conference room the night before the auction, McCourt slid a piece of paper across the table toward Walter. It was a signed offer from Cohen to buy the Dodgers for $2 billion. Walter told McCourt he'd give him $2.15 billion, plus an interest in the land surrounding Dodger Stadium should he and his partners ever decide to develop it. There was one caveat, however: Walter told McCourt it was take-it-or-leave-it. If McCourt left the room, the deal was off. McCourt agreed to the terms, and the two men shook hands. But members of the Guggenheim group worried McCourt would violate the handshake agreement and return to Cohen with Walter's bid to see if he could squeeze more money out of him. "You know Frank went back to Stevie Cohen and said beat this," said one insider familiar with the deal. If McCourt did in fact return to Cohen to give him a chance to best the Guggenheim offer, Cohen didn't bite. "It was unbelievable," said the insider. "The guy's got nine billion liquid and he wouldn't cough up another three hundred million to buy the Dodgers. And he's a baseball fan!" Had the team gone to auction the following day as planned, Kasten suspects the Guggenheim group would have been outbid. "We might not have won," said Kasten. "Both of the other groups were prepared—and we know this for sure for other reasons—that they were prepared to go a lot higher."

Cohen was not without regret. The day the Dodgers deal closed in Los Angeles, he flew in from New York and hung around the hotel where the contracts were being signed, just in case the sale fell through. It didn't. And it was a good thing for the city of Los Angeles that Cohen didn't end up owning the Dodgers on the heels of the McCourt debacle. The Securities and Exchange Commission had been investigating Cohen for insider trading for seven years before filing lesser charges against him for failing to prevent his employees from committing fraud, just four months after the Dodgers sale was finalized. The U.S. attorney for the Southern District of New York said that Cohen's firm had created a "culture of corporate corruption," something Dodger fans felt they were already acquainted with. Cohen pled guilty and agreed to stop managing other people's money. He was fined $1.2 billion.

The public never knew about Cohen's offer. Walter says he declined to set the record straight because he didn't care that people thought he had overpaid. He was content in his conviction that he had made a good deal. When a group led by Houston businessman Jim Crane had bought the Astros for $680 million in May 2011, an alarmed Kasten had called Walter. "I have some bad news," Kasten said. "The Astros just sold for seven hundred million. We might have to pay a billion to get the Dodgers." Walter laughed. Getting the Dodgers for a billion would be a steal, he told Kasten.

Walter knew that experts were wildly undervaluing the ball club because they failed to anticipate the tidal wave of cash that would pour into Chavez Ravine when the Dodgers signed their new television deal. Financial observers didn't grasp that baseball's TV revenue was surging toward heights that would dramatically alter the worth of franchises. Walter understood the salient point that fiscal gurus seemed to miss. And that was that no one watched television live anymore—except when they watched sports. The invention of TiVo, DVR, premium on-demand channels, and Internet streaming sites like Netflix and Hulu meant that time-strapped consumers never had to sit through another commercial again if they didn't want to. But people still wanted to watch sports in real time. Advertisers understood this, which is why they paid a premium for spots during high-rated games and matches they thought were least likely to be fast-forwarded through.

When first determining the baseline value of the Dodgers in his head, Walter didn't count how many tickets the team was selling each year or how their jerseys and caps were faring on the open market. He set the starting point on simple population arithmetic. Walter knew the real money was in the television deal, so he compared the L.A. and Houston markets. Houston had 2.1 million households. The Los Angeles metro area had almost three times that amount. The Astros had sold for $680 million. In Walter's mind, that meant the Dodgers were worth at least three times that amount on their media rights deal alone. The three hundred acres of land surrounding Dodger Stadium and the fact that the club often led the majors in attendance were perhaps worth another billion or two. The world thought he was overpaying. Walter believed he was getting a bargain. "Here was this baseball team, a global brand, a little bit tarnished recently, in the second-biggest city in America, in the entertainment capital of the world when its TV contract was up in two years at a time when rights fees were exploding," said Kasten. "All of those things at once and we thought, Wow. That has some potential that we've never seen in baseball."

Walter's instincts proved correct eighteen months later when Time Warner agreed to pay the Dodgers $8.35 billion for the rights to broadcast their games for the next twenty-five years. McCourt may have cleared a cool eight hundred million, but he'd been ousted a year and a half before he could have collected a signed contract for ten times that amount—a bitter pill to swallow for someone who could never stockpile enough cash to be satisfied. Had the McCourts buried their differences awhile longer, they could have split that windfall.

In many ways, Mark Walter was Frank McCourt's opposite. While McCourt hid from media behind PR lieutenants, in Walter's first season owning the Dodgers he greeted journalists like old pals and often divulged too much, to the point where Kasten begged him to begin his informal chats with members of the press by telling them that what he said was off-the-record. While McCourt never helped himself by appearing uncomfortable in his own skin, Walter was fully present, and hopped around the field during batting practice like a giddy child. He hugged stadium employees he hadn't seen in a while, and greeted most of them by name. Walter grew up in Cedar Rapids, Iowa, not far from the Field of Dreams, and radiated warmth, so much *gosh darn Midwest salt-of-the-earth nice* that it was difficult to imagine how he had the instincts necessary to run a company that managed $210 billion worth of assets. In considering this question, he smiled and shook his head. "I'm nothing special," said Walter. "Just the king of common sense."

Perhaps common sense isn't that common. After all, it was boring logic that led Walter to value the Dodgers at three times what *Forbes* did. Because the NFL is the most popular sport in America, many financial laymen believe that football franchises are worth the most money. But Walter didn't think that was true. The NFL broadcasts its games on national networks each week and splits that revenue equally among its thirty-two teams. *Forbes* estimated that the Dallas Cowboys were the most valuable franchise in the United States in the spring of 2012. But the Cowboys don't have the option of broadcasting their games on their own television network and reaping the benefits of the advertising dollars that would go along with that. In baseball there are no such limitations. When Walter took over in Los Angeles, MLB was as fiscally unregulated as the Wall Street financial institutions that caused the economy to collapse in 2008. While the NBA, the NFL, and the NHL relied on pooled profits and hard salary caps, Major League Baseball's evolution mirrored the staggering wealth disparity in post-recession America. The new Dodgers television deal would give the team an average of $334 million a year. The St. Louis Cardinals, on the other hand, made only about $25 million annually in media revenue. And the Pittsburgh Pirates pulled in just $18 million. For the Cowboys to be worth as much as the Dodgers during this TV revenue boom, Walter estimated the team would have to rake in one hundred dollars in beer and T-shirt sales per fan per game. To his credit, Frank McCourt saw this windfall coming a decade earlier. But Walter did, too. "We didn't have the dough to buy the team back then," said Walter. "No one did."

While his predecessor wore silk and linen to ball games, Walter, fifty-three, favored sneakers, blue Dodgers pullovers, and dad jeans with his cell phone clipped to his belt buckle. He and his wife, Kimbra, had met as undergrads at Northwestern University. They had one daughter, Samantha, who was twelve when her father bought the Dodgers. When Samantha expressed an interest in becoming a veterinarian, Walter bought a zoo in Tampa, Florida. After Walter purchased the Dodgers and she got a behind-the-scenes look at how professional sports organizations were run, she told her dad that she might want to be general manager of a team someday. So Walter bought the Los Angeles WNBA team, the Sparks, with the idea that she might run it when she was old enough.

Walter knew that Dodger fans had hated McCourt. He understood their wariness about another rich out-of-towner buying the Dodgers as a business opportunity, and not because he had deep roots in the community. So he went to work to win them back.

After his group took over, the first significant player contract to come up for renewal was Andre Ethier's. A right fielder who had been in the Dodgers organization since he was twenty-three years old, Ethier was a fan favorite, particularly among the women who whistled when his rakish mug was shown on the scoreboard. He had led the team with thirty-one home runs in 2009, the last year the Dodgers made the playoffs. But in the past two seasons his power had almost evaporated. In 2011, at age twenty-nine, he hit just eleven dingers—a lackluster number for a corner outfielder. On the plus side: Ethier was a career .300 hitter against right-handed pitching. Unfortunately, pitchers also threw left-handed. He hit only .230 against southpaws, leading commentators to point out he was best used as a platoon player. The Dodgers' front office was well aware of his limitations but decided that buying the goodwill of their fan base made more financial sense than paying Ethier what he would have been worth on the open market. Even though he was on the decline, and arguably the club's tenth-best player at that point, the Dodgers re-signed him to a five-year, $85 million extension that raised eyebrows around the league for its generosity. But the new owners weren't overpaying an aging outfielder as much as they were purchasing a citywide public service announcement letting fans know the bad times were over.

A few weeks later, the club made headlines again for another head-scratching investment by offering an unknown, out-of-shape, hot-headed Cuban kid a seven-year, $42 million contract after watching him take a few rounds of batting practice. Though other bids for Yasiel Puig's services were never made public, gossip around the league was that the dumb new Dodger owners had overpaid once again, offering the twenty-one-year-old outfielder more than double what the next-highest bid was. To outsiders, it seemed like the Dodgers had gone from bankrupt to bloated in a matter of months, and had found more expensive ways to lose.

2

BURN THE SHIPS

When Guggenheim bought the Dodgers out of bankruptcy, they inherited Ned Colletti as the team's general manager and Don Mattingly as its skipper. Colletti was entering his seventh season in the position, Mattingly his second. When Frank McCourt hired Colletti in November 2005 he became the eleventh GM in Dodgers history—but the seventh in the past eight years. In his first twenty months as owner McCourt had clashed with, and fired, the Dodgers' two previous general managers, Dan Evans and Paul DePodesta. So when McCourt set out to find his third GM in two years, the Dodgers' then second baseman, Jeff Kent, made a suggestion. Kent had ownership's ear because he had grown close to Jamie McCourt through charity work they'd done together to help Los Angeles police officers. He told Jamie that she and her husband should consider interviewing Colletti, a baseball lifer he had gotten to know well while playing for the San Francisco Giants.

Before joining the Dodgers, Colletti had worked as an assistant general manager under Brian Sabean in San Francisco for nine seasons. Prior to his stint with the rival Giants, Colletti had been with his hometown Cubs for twelve years, maneuvering his way up from press flack to negotiating player salaries for the club's front office. Intrigued by his pedigree and his familiarity with National League baseball, McCourt asked Colletti to meet with him about the Dodgers' GM vacancy. McCourt was said to be particularly impressed when Colletti didn't ask how much money he would be given to spend on player payroll during his job interview. After McCourt hired Colletti, Colletti returned the favor to Kent. Four months after he took over as the general manager of the Dodgers he offered the thirty-eight-year-old second baseman an eight-figure contract extension.

As the dysfunctional McCourt regime spiraled downward, the Dodgers became notorious for their revolving door of high-ranking executives. In addition to their general manager carousel, during their eight years owning the club the McCourts burned through four managers and three team presidents. Colletti somehow survived. Most baseball executives expected Walter to relieve Colletti of his duties when he came in, not because of his shortcomings but because each new ownership group tended to install its own brain trust to enact its vision—even when it didn't just spend two billion on a franchise. But the damage McCourt's tightfistedness inflicted on the big-league club and its farm system was so cataclysmic it was difficult for the new owners to evaluate Colletti. A general manager's number-one task is to stockpile as much talent as possible. But McCourt's thriftiness had limited Colletti's options. So the new owners decided they would keep him for a trial run, then decide if he was good enough to stay. "I didn't think the problems the franchise had were related to the front office," Stan Kasten said. Colletti remained the club's GM, but appeared about as comfortable on the job as a Bush White House staffer when Barack Obama's team came in.

For the first time in club history, the Dodgers were putting together a roster with no financial limitations. And the responsibility of loading the organization with expensive talent fell on two men: one who grew up in poverty, and another who had built his career on rarely splurging for stars.

In his thirty-plus years in baseball, Colletti had proven he had the moxy to hang within the upper echelon of the game. Major League Baseball can be a nepotistic crony fest, filled with sons of famous ball-players. But by his own estimation, Colletti grew up dirt-poor, and lived in a converted garage on the industrial outskirts of Chicago for the first six years of his life. His Italian-American father worked as a mechanic who was paid by the hour. When the family bought a home, paying the mortgage on time was a herculean task. It was seventy dol-lars a month.

Given his background, the fact that Colletti rose to become the general manager of the Los Angeles Dodgers is astonishing. It's easier to get elected to the U.S. Senate than it is to be named a GM: there are one hundred senators, and only thirty MLB general managers. And the game's analytics renaissance meant that Colletti didn't just have to compete with well-connected scions to hold on to his position. In the early 2000s, the Oakland Athletics' GM, Billy Beane, and his Money-ball philosophy inspired legions of MBA grads and computer science savants to seek out jobs in front offices so they could use their skills to do something more exciting than writing code for Silicon Valley start-ups. The new owner of the Houston Astros, for instance, had hired a former management consultant, Jeff Luhnow, to be the club's GM. Luhnow then brought in a crack team of Wall Street wizards, lawyers, and a NASA behavioral scientist to overhaul the organization. When Walter's group bought the Dodgers the club had an analytics depart-ment that consisted of one person. Colletti preferred cowboy boots to calculators.

The directive to overpay Ethier to keep him in Los Angeles must have been a shock to Colletti's system. Gone were the days of being allowed to add impact bats or arms in the middle of the season only if he could somehow do it for free. Colletti was finally able to pursue the roster he wanted, which better suited his confrontational style. Perhaps because of his humble beginnings, Colletti approached the game with a chip on his shoulder the size of Illinois, and refused to suffer coddled ballplayers. If players viewed him as a bully, which many did, Colletti was more likely to chalk it up to their lack of mental toughness than reflect on the wisdom of letting young guys know they were fucking nobodies who could be cut at any time. While organizations like the Cardinals routinely inserted rookies into the middle of pennant races, Colletti was loath to throw kids into big spots, often to the chagrin of his coaching staff. Regardless of the energy youngsters provided to an older lineup, Colletti worried that rookies didn't possess the guts required to succeed in October.

Colletti's emotions often got the better of him. He was so upset when right fielder J. D. Drew surprised him by opting out of his contract that he told reporters he would not rule out filing a tampering grievance against the Red Sox (where Drew went). He also hinted at his displeasure with ever doing business with Drew's agent, Scott Boras, again. Since Boras represented many of the game's best players, this fatwa, if adhered to, would put the Dodgers at a serious disadvantage. But in the moment Colletti didn't care. Or, maybe the problem was that he cared too much. One of his favorite sayings, to the amusement of his players and staff, was "I care so much that I don't give a fuck."

That passion extended to storytelling, too. On the first day of spring training before the 2011 season, when the Dodgers were neck-deep in McCourt muck, Colletti addressed the team with a barn-burning speech he hoped would inspire them into battle. In the early 1500s, famed explorer Hernán Cortés set out from Cuba to conquer Mexico for the Spanish crown. Colletti said that, according to legend, when Cortés arrived on the shores of Veracruz, he ordered his frightened men to burn their ships as a means of giving them confidence and scaring the Aztecs, the message being that Cortés believed his men would so thoroughly dominate that when the job was complete they would leave on their enemies' ships. Colletti told this story to the Dodger players who sat before him, and beseeched them to learn from Cortés and go out and burn the figurative ships. The men shot each other confused glances and shrugged. Three years later, Colletti sat the Dodgers down on the first day of spring training again for his annual pep talk. He told the same story. Only this time he got mixed up and replaced Cortés with Alexander the Great. Players looked at each other in disbelief. When Colletti left, the room erupted in laughter. Within weeks, the guys had T-shirts made that said BURN THE SHIPS on the front, with ATG for Alexander the Great scrawled on the back. During the 2014 season it was not uncommon to hear players yell, "Burn the ships!" before taking the field. It had become an unlikely rallying cry, but not in the way Colletti intended. What Colletti didn't know was that Cortés didn't burn his ships as a motivational tool; he did it so his terrified men couldn't retreat.

In spite of the Dodgers' financial limitations during the McCourt era, or perhaps because of them, Colletti did find his strengths. He had shown a knack for identifying cheap, effective relief pitchers and cobbling together a dominant pitching staff during the Dodgers' playoff runs at the end of the previous decade. In 2008 and 2009 the Dodgers led the National League in earned run average, thanks to the performances of afterthoughts and castoffs resurrected by his staff. Guys like Hong-Chih Kuo, Ramón Troncoso, and Ronald Belisario dazzled in their unsexy roles of holding a lead, and they did it while earning salaries that hovered near the major-league minimum.

Colletti had also shown respectable restraint when it came to trading top prospects. When he took over as GM, the Dodgers farm system was bursting with talent, highlighted by the gifted but raw young outfielder Matt Kemp. In 2006, when Kemp was called up to the big leagues, many Dodger veterans didn't appreciate his cocksure attitude and thought he needed at least a full season under his belt before he could strut around the clubhouse as if he'd already been elected to the Hall of Fame. Nevertheless, Kemp excelled in his first four years in the majors, flashing all five tools on his way to winning a Silver Slugger award as one of the best-hitting outfielders in the National League, and finishing tenth in the Most Valuable Player voting in 2009.

But his play collapsed the following year when his enjoyment of the Hollywood lifestyle caused him to show up to the field mentally if not physically hungover many days. In 2010 Kemp hit .249 and struck out 170 times—a franchise record. And on the rare occasion when he did make it to first, he often ran the bases as though he needed directions, and frequently stumbled into outs.

Unfortunately for Kemp, the Dodgers' coaching staff in 2010 was short on sympathy. At age seventy, the club's manager, Joe Torre, had little patience for theatrics from his moody center fielder during what was supposed to be the victory lap of his Hall of Fame coaching career. The club's third-base coach and Torre consigliere, Larry Bowa, enjoyed a hard-earned reputation for being merciless on temperamental young players, with the *Chicago Tribune* once describing his coaching demeanor as "more psychotic than a psychologist." That was back when he managed the Padres in 1988, and by many accounts he had only grown more intolerant of bullshit with each passing year. Bowa and Torre both saw Kemp as a player who could transcend the game if he wanted to. But they had no patience for a head case, regardless of his potential.

Much ink was spilled over whether the Dodgers should cut their losses and trade Kemp, with grizzled, old-school ball writers wailing about team chemistry while the new generation of numbers geeks reminded everyone that the only good reason for parting ways with a center fielder who has the potential to hit forty home runs and steal forty bases is if he moonlights as a serial killer in the off-season. Though no one would ever accuse Colletti of bending to the will of the sabermetric crowd, he took their side. In Kemp, Colletti saw a twenty-five-year-old kid with physical gifts that couldn't be taught. Kemp was immature, yes, but the last thing Colletti wanted to do was sell low on a guy who could wind up being one of the best players in the game.

Colletti had traded a few dozen young players in his six years as the Dodgers' GM and the only one who turned out to be a star was the Indians catcher Carlos Santana, a fact that he was quick to point out to the press. The Dodgers received veteran third baseman Casey Blake from Cleveland in that trade deadline deal, and Blake became a critical member of the club's NLCS runs in 2008 and 2009. That didn't change the fact that Santana—who went on to average twenty-two home runs with a .364 on-base percentage during his first three full seasons with the Indians—never should have been traded. But even that mistake wasn't just Colletti's fault. Santana was the price the Dodgers had to pay to get the Indians to pick up the remaining few million dollars left on Blake's tab; he became a victim to the notorious cheapskate tax of the McCourt era.

Colletti's instincts about Kemp proved right. In 2011, the Dodgers replaced Torre with his hitting coach, the Yankee legend Don Mattingly. Kemp flourished. He raised his batting average seventy-five points and his on-base percentage eighty-nine points, hit thirty-nine home runs, and stole forty bases. He finished second in the NL MVP award voting to Brewers left fielder Ryan Braun—who the world learned later had tested positive for performance-enhancing drugs during the season. Kemp became one of the few bright spots for the Dodgers during one of the bleakest years in franchise history. Colletti responded to Kemp's resurgence by locking him up that November with an eight-year deal worth $160 million. It was the largest contract the Dodgers had ever given a player.

While general managers are judged by the moves they make, their best deals are often the ones they don't make. Perhaps because McCourt was so keen on keeping the payroll down, Colletti didn't often sign free agents to long-term, exorbitant contracts that torpedoed so many other teams when those players underperformed. He did make one infamous mistake, though, when he inked thirty-three-year-old former San Francisco ace Jason Schmidt to a three-year, $47 million deal in 2007—despite an MRI revealing that Schmidt's throwing arm appeared to be fastened to the rest of his body at the shoulder with chicken wire. In 2003, while Colletti was San Francisco's assistant general manager, Schmidt led the National League with a 2.34 earned run average, an incredible number considering he posted it at the height of the steroid era. So, three years later in his new capacity as the GM of the Dodgers, Colletti took a flyer on Schmidt, hoping he would heal and recapture at least some of his old form. He didn't. Schmidt went on to appear in just ten games for the Dodgers, winning three. The signing was mocked as one of the worst of the decade, especially when it emerged later during the Dodgers' attempt to collect insurance money that the club was aware of Schmidt's partially torn rotator cuff when it signed him. Many Dodger fans were frustrated by Colletti's infatuation with former Giant players, and it was easy to wonder if his judgment was clouded by deep emotional ties to the archrival organization. When the Giants won their first title in fifty-six years in 2010, Colletti cried. Those around the game assumed that if he ever left the Dodgers, he would go back to work in San Francisco.

Ned Colletti's newfound fiduciary flexibility came with a catch. After Mark Walter took over the Dodgers he installed Stan Kasten as team president to run the club's day-to-day operations. Kasten had worked in that same capacity for the Braves from 1986 to 2003, before moving to Washington to help guide the Nationals after they relocated from Montreal. During his tenure in Atlanta the Braves became the class of the National League, winning fourteen division titles in fifteen years and five NL pennants with homegrown talent and the best starting rotation of the modern era. During that dynasty, future Hall of Famers Greg Maddux, Tom Glavine, and John Smoltz functioned like a three-headed monster that chewed through opposing lineups with devastating results. Kasten brought with him to Los Angeles an emphasis on pitching and developing a strong farm system. But on the surface, he was a counterintuitive choice to run the new cash-drunk Dodgers. "I just don't like giving a lot of money to players," said Kasten.

Nevertheless, the job was his. The Dodgers were setting themselves up as the new Yankees West, and they made no secret of the fact that they were hungry for superstars to showcase on their new television network. Kasten hadn't run the Braves that way. When he took over in Atlanta the team held the impressive distinction of having the highest payroll ($16 million) in the National League and finishing last in its division. Knowing the Braves' farm system was also in tatters, Kasten traded better-known players for prospects and slashed the club's payroll to $12 million. The press roasted him. But Kasten preached patience to his owner, Ted Turner, even advising the media mogul to avoid local sports talk radio for the next few years. After finishing in last place in the NL West the next three seasons, the Braves rebounded in 1991, winning their division and advancing all the way to the World Series. They captured the NL pennant the following year as well. Most impressive, the Braves didn't sign their first big free agent, Greg Maddux, until after they'd been to the World Series twice. "We kept everyone as they were growing and becoming all-stars," said Kasten. "My last year there our payroll got up to eight-five or ninety million dollars—which was maybe the highest payroll in the National League—but we had earned our way there because we had started from the bottom."

Kasten hated the idea of trading away blue-chip prospects for veteran rentals who could help his club win in the short term while wrecking its future. Instead, he believed that in order to win year in and year out, the first thing an organization had to do was stuff its farm system with young talent. Kasten's measured approach relied on self-control. But Mark Walter didn't want to wait. While Dodger fans welcomed Guggenheim with much excitement, Walter was smart enough to know that the honeymoon affection his new ownership group enjoyed from the city would evaporate if the club went into rebuilding mode. In order to bring back fans alienated by McCourt and compete with the Lakers, he knew his team had to win, and to win now. Walter couldn't be at Dodger Stadium every day to deal with the minutiae of overseeing a major-league baseball team because he still lived in Chicago, where he ran his multibillion-dollar investment firm. So he turned the keys to the club over to Kasten. The Dodgers were not Walter's team or Colletti's team or even Mattingly's team: the Dodgers were Kasten's. Everyone knew it.

Stan Kasten never stood still. On game days, he arrived at Dodger Stadium by eight in the morning and often stayed until midnight. During the sixteen hours or so he was at the ballpark each day he roamed the premises like a shark that feared it would die if it ever stopped moving. Kasten was not only the captain of the Dodgers' ship, he was also the club's hall monitor. His constant motion put everyone he came into contact with on edge. While baseball was a game to many, it was a high-stakes business to him. If something went wrong, Kasten had to answer to billionaires who did not like it when things went wrong. He could not rest when there was anything to be done, and there was always something that needed doing.

After the new ownership group came in, Kasten sat down with Colletti and made a wish list of players they would love to see in Dodger blue—whether they were available or not. At the top of that list was Boston's first baseman, Adrian Gonzalez. "He was offensively great, defensively great, bilingual, from Southern California, a pillar of the community," said Kasten, of Gonzalez. "He just checked all the boxes. So he was on the list of the most perfect guys we could ever get some day."

The Dodgers had employed James Loney at first base for the past seven seasons but were looking to upgrade the position. Loney was a lanky high school senior from Houston when the Dodgers selected him in the first round of the 2002 draft, and he'd spent his entire career in the organization. His slick fielding made him one of the best defensive first basemen in the game, but he'd never hit more than fifteen home runs in a year. That lack of sock in his swing wouldn't do for a burgeoning super team. Getting Gonzalez from Boston wouldn't be easy:

the Red Sox had just signed the left-handed slugger to a seven-year, $154 million contract extension before the previous season. But Gonzalez's tenure with the Sox had started on an awkward note. Though he had hit twenty-seven home runs in his first season with Boston and collected an MLB-leading 213 hits on his way to a .410 on-base percentage, Gonzalez drew the ire of Red Sox Nation when, after the team suffered a spectacular collapse in the season's final month and failed to make the playoffs, he shrugged and told the media that a championship just wasn't God's plan. The following year when he struggled to start the season, the boos rained down on him at Fenway. It stung.

Gonzalez had played most of his career in San Diego, a sleepy city whose fan base gives its players minimal grief when they sputter. He never got used to playing under a microscope. When Boston scuffled in the final months of his first season with the team, Gonzalez blamed the club's schedule. Because the Red Sox were one of the league's best teams, many of their Sunday day games were moved to the evening so they could be shown nationally. Late Sunday start times meant more overnight flights on getaway days—something Gonzalez rarely had to deal with as a Padre. But they also meant that he was playing on a winning team—and he was mad about that? Gonzalez had moved from one of the most relaxed cities in America to the one wound tightest. "You go to the grocery store and you're getting hitting advice," said teammate Nick Punto, of Boston. "You go to the barbershop and you're getting hitting advice." That kind of pressure bothered Gonzalez. "They didn't like that I was a calm person," he said later to the *Los Angeles Times*, of the Boston media. "I won't throw my helmet. I won't scream, I won't use bad words if I strike out. That's what they want over there."

That Kasten had finessed control of player transactions from Ned Colletti's grasp became evident on the night the Boston mega-trade was struck. Colletti had called the Red Sox general manager, Ben Cherington, in early May 2012 and asked what it would take to land the power-hitting first baseman in a trade. Cherington told him Gonzalez was not available. So the Dodgers got creative. Kasten knew the struggling Red Sox had a handful of albatross contracts they would love to be rid of, so he called Boston's president, Larry Lucchino, and told him his club was in the somewhat rare position of having an owner who was willing to take on a ton of extra money in player salary if Gonzalez was packaged with guys who were way overpaid. Lucchino was intrigued. That July, Colletti thought the Dodgers had struck a multiplayer deal for Gonzalez—but it fell apart on the day of the trading deadline, in part because the Red Sox still believed they had a shot to make the playoffs and they didn't want to trade away one of their best hitters. "It just didn't happen and we were all disappointed," said Kasten.

The bitterness of that failure had been lingering for two weeks when Kasten approached Walter and said he wasn't ready to give up. The two men brainstormed how far they would be willing to go to take one final crack at landing Gonzalez. Then, opportunity struck. Kasten and Walter were in the lobby of the Four Seasons hotel in Denver for Major League Baseball's quarterly owners meetings when they noticed Red Sox owner John Henry smoking a cigar on the hotel patio with a group of men that included White Sox emperor Jerry Reinsdorf. Kasten was about to make a beeline for Henry when he saw something out of the corner of his eye that could thwart his plans. Also in the lobby stood two veteran national baseball writers who were in Denver covering the conference. Had either of them seen Kasten lure Henry away for a private conversation, they would have poked around to find out what was up. Kasten knew each man had been in the business long enough to have the sources necessary to break the story of the trade before it happened, which could have wrecked it. Striking a deal with another team before the nonwaiver deadline was difficult enough. But trades after July 31 were always trickier to pull off because by rule a player must be placed on waivers before he is traded, and, for the sake of competitive balance, every other team with a worse record than the club that wants him has first dibs. What that meant was that if any of the Dodgers' or Red Sox' rivals got wind of the mammoth trade they were scheming, they could have claimed one of the players involved in the deal just to derail the whole thing.

Kasten had to think fast. He had an idea. Walter had owned the Dodgers for only three months, and he was still a mystery to the national media. Kasten approached the reporters. "How would you guys like an exclusive sit-down with our owner?" he asked. The men jumped at the chance. An interview with Walter, the man crazy enough to plunk down $2 billion for a sports franchise, would make for great copy. Kasten ushered the reporters to a table with Walter, making sure their backs were facing the patio. Then, after they were tucked away, he walked up to Henry. "John," he said. "Can we talk?" Henry extinguished his cigar and followed Kasten out of the lobby.

When Kasten pulled Henry off that patio on that August night in Denver, the Dodgers and Red Sox could not have been in more disparate positions. Kasten was looking for bold-faced names. Henry had them, and his team was flailing. In 2011, Boston had played well for five months before imploding down the stretch, becoming the first team in baseball history to blow a nine-game wild card lead in September. The Red Sox dropped eighteen of their final twenty-four games and were eliminated from the playoffs on the last day of the season after a furious ninth-inning comeback by the lowly Orioles. The club's manager, Terry Francona, and general manager, Theo Epstein, were both run out of town.

In an effort to reboot, before the 2012 season the Red Sox brass hired Bobby Valentine, a known authoritarian, to manage the team, and installed Cherington as general manager. The players hated Valentine. But the front office had every reason to believe its talented—and very expensive—team would bounce back and perform well that year. Their center fielder, Jacoby Ellsbury, had finished second in the AL MVP voting the year before, Gonzalez had finished seventh, and second baseman Dustin Pedroia had placed ninth. The Red Sox took the field on opening day in 2012 with a $161 million payroll, third highest in MLB behind the Yankees and the Phillies. That kind of money brought huge expectations, which is why Boston didn't want to give up Gonzalez on July 31 when they were just three and a half games out of earning a wild card berth to the playoffs.

But when the calendar flipped to August, the Sox lost eight of their first twelve games. And on the evening that Henry stubbed out his cigar and accompanied Kasten out of that hotel lobby, Boston had fallen to eleven games back of the Yankees in the AL East, and five and a half games out of the wild card race with just six weeks left to play.

Though Gonzalez was only a season and a half into his seven-year deal, it was becoming clear he might benefit from a change of scenery. His coaches and teammates compared him to a clubhouse lawyer who liked to argue for the sake of arguing. Some even began referring to him as the Professor behind his back, a dig at their perception that he thought he was smarter than everyone else.

It was true that Gonzalez didn't display his emotions on the field very often, which made it difficult for fans to tell how much he cared. The only time he seemed to react was when he disagreed with an umpire's call. Thanks to his exceptional plate discipline, Gonzalez led the major leagues in walks in 2009, with 119. But his walk total decreased in the years after that, and he walked only 42 times in 2012. The explanation was simple enough. He told teammates and coaches that he was tired of taking pitches in 3-2 counts, because it gave the umpire a chance to mistake a ball for a strike. If taking the power out of an ump's hands to call him out on strikes meant that he was going to walk only a third as often as before, well then so be it. It was also true that Adrian Gonzalez was more verbose than the average baseball player. And though he may have exhausted some teammates with his argumentative streak, his benign transgressions fell far short of the stage-four clubhouse cancer some in the Boston media made him out to be. Even those he annoyed couldn't help but respect his work ethic.

Gonzalez had been the first overall pick in the 2000 draft, and he had lived up to his potential. During his nine-year career he had kept his nose clean, never having been mentioned on a human growth hormone mailing list or in a police report. And above all else, the man could still rake. Even though the Red Sox had fallen out of contention in 2012, Gonzalez wanting out of Boston wouldn't have been enough to force the club's hand. The Dodgers made the Red Sox an offer they couldn't refuse, at precisely the right moment. That morning, Yahoo! Sports reported that a frustrated Gonzalez had texted Henry to complain about Valentine. Players had met with ownership to discuss their unhappiness, and details about that meeting leaked as well. When Kasten approached Henry in that Denver hotel, a frustrated Henry was ready to blow up everything and start over.

After months of failed negotiations, it took Kasten and Henry just fifteen minutes to agree to the most expensive trade in baseball history. When the deal was done, Kasten returned to the lobby and flashed a thumbs-up to Walter, who was in the middle of his interview and snuck a glance at his lieutenant over the reporters' shoulders. The two journalists had no idea what had just gone down.

Ned Colletti wasn't even in the state of Colorado.

Eleven days after the Denver summit, after medical records were reviewed and the Red Sox finalized the list of young prospects they wanted from the Dodgers, the two sides announced the trade. In the nine-player deal, the Dodgers got Gonzalez, Josh Beckett, Carl Crawford, and Nick Punto in exchange for James Loney and a package of minor leaguers that included pitcher Allen Webster, outfielder Jerry Sands, infielder Ivan DeJesus, and, the gem of the deal, the Dodgers' top right-handed pitching prospect, Rubby De La Rosa. To complete the trade, Los Angeles also took on a staggering $250 million in player salary. In Gonzalez, the Dodgers got the slugging first baseman they craved to anchor their lineup. In Beckett, they landed a veteran starting pitcher whose brilliant early career included being named the World Series MVP at age twenty-three after leading the Marlins to an improbable championship over the mighty Yankees. They also got an injury-prone player on the wrong side of thirty who had posted a 5.23 ERA in Boston that season. Beckett was owed a cool thirty-five million bucks over the next two years, and it was doubtful he'd be worth half that.

Crawford, a speedy left fielder, had also been miserable in Boston. After he had spent his entire career in Tampa Bay, the Red Sox had signed him to a massive contract following an intense round of free agent bidding before the 2011 season. And like Gonzalez, he never fit. A tremendous high school athlete in Houston in the late nineties, Crawford received a scholarship offer from the University of California, Los Angeles, to play point guard for its basketball team, and an offer from Nebraska to run the read option at quarterback. After mulling his options, Crawford chose to skip college when the Devil Rays took him in the second round of the 1999 draft and offered him a $1.2 million signing bonus to play baseball instead.

For the most part, life in Tampa was good for Crawford. The Rays had called him up at age twenty and made him their full-time left fielder and leadoff hitter when he was just twenty-one. By twenty-two he'd made his first All-Star team, and led the American League in stolen bases (55) and triples (19). He stole six bases in a game against the Red Sox in 2009, tying the modern major-league record. For someone so fast his bat had a noble amount of pop in it, too. During his last year in Tampa, Crawford hit a career-high nineteen home runs. That off-season he was considered to be one of the best players on the free agent market, and the Angels were among the teams that had courted him. Still, when the Red Sox signed him that December to a seven-year deal worth $142 million—the second-richest contract ever for an outfielder—it was a bit of a surprise. Boston's lineup was already full of expensive talent, and the club had traded for Gonzalez just two days earlier.

The Red Sox didn't part with that money freely. In an interview with a local radio affiliate during Crawford's first spring training with the team, Epstein divulged that the club had conducted a thorough background check on the left fielder before backing up the Brinks truck to his door. "We covered him as if we were privately investigating him," Epstein told listeners. "We had a scout on him literally the last three, four months of the season at the ballpark, away from the ballpark."

That revelation unnerved Crawford. "I'm from an area where if somebody's doing that to you they're not doing anything good," Crawford told Boston reporters. "I definitely look over my shoulder now a lot more than what I did before. The idea of him following me everywhere I go, was kind of—I wasn't comfortable with that at all."

Being watched by anyone was something Crawford wasn't used to in Tampa. In his first six seasons with the Rays, the club finished last in the American League in attendance. Those Tampa squads were terrible, but it's not as if the city embraced baseball as soon as the team started winning. In 2008 the Rays rode an incredible season all the way to the World Series. Their stellar play was rewarded with a third-to-last-place finish in attendance in the AL. For almost a decade, Carl Crawford was the human embodiment of a tree falling in the woods and making no sound: he was the best baseball player that no one saw.

Crawford liked to tell a story about an experience that summed up the anonymity afforded to a player who stars for the Tampa Bay Rays. One day he was hanging out with teammates in the home clubhouse at Tropicana Field when members of the Tampa police department turned up looking for him.

"Carl Crawford?" one asked.

"Yeah," Crawford said.

"We need to talk to you about the Navigator," said the officer.

"What Navigator?" asked Crawford.

"Well, earlier today a man walked into a dealership in town and said his name was Carl Crawford and asked to test-drive a Navigator and never came back," said the officer.

Crawford was confused. He told the cops he'd never driven a Navigator in his life. As it turned out, a crafty car burglar wearing Crawford's jersey had taken a gamble on a Tampa Lincoln dealer having no clue what the best player on the city's baseball team looked like. It worked.

That sort of caper would never fly in Boston. Even the thickest thief in the state of Massachusetts wouldn't be dumb enough to pose as a member of the vaunted Red Sox. When he signed with Boston, Crawford knew he was going to go from playing in an empty stadium to suiting up in front of a packed house of die-hard fans every night. Realizing how uneasy the revelations about Crawford's private life had made his new star player, Epstein backtracked and insisted he misspoke; that the team acquired information in the same way it did on every free agent in its sights. But the damage was done. Crawford's tenure in Boston began on a sour note, and in the season and a half he spent with the Sox he never grew comfortable.

In some ways, however, Crawford might have gotten too comfortable. He later told a teammate that he felt like the Rays strung him along for years toward a big payday that never came. His desire to earn the huge money that many of his peers enjoyed drove him to play hard every day. But as soon as he signed his fat contract with Boston he confided in friends that he found it difficult to keep his edge. Crawford still wanted to be great but his motivation was buried somewhere, deep under his millions. He didn't like that about himself, but it was the truth. "That guy used to terrorize us with his bat and his speed when he was in Tampa," said one player who faced Crawford when he was with the Rays and later became his teammate. "But after he went to Boston it was like, how is this the same player?"

A career .300 hitter, Crawford hit just .255 while he battled a wrist injury during his first year with the Red Sox. His on-base percentage plummeted from .356 in 2010 to an awful .289 the following season, and his slugging percentage also fell ninety points. While the number of times he struck out (104) remained identical to the season before, the number of walks he took halved from 46 to 23. More troubling: his stolen base total nosedived from 47 to 18. Every ballplayer's speed declines as he ages, but this drop-off was staggering. Crawford was just twenty-nine years old when he signed with the Red Sox. His legs were his livelihood.

The 2012 season brought even more injury trouble. And after appearing in only thirty-one games, Crawford was shut down for the rest of the year with a torn ligament in his throwing elbow. Of this time in Boston, Crawford said: "For two years I was afraid to smile. Everyone was so uptight."

"I started growing grey hairs on my face from the stress," he told *USA Today*. "Deep down, it's like I know I can still play baseball but after being told how much you suck for two years straight, it kind of messes with your mind."

But for as much as he wanted out of Boston, Crawford knew the odds of that happening were slim. Not only was his body battered, but he was also still owed $109 million on his current contract. Even if he were healthy and back to torturing other teams with his power and speed, there were only a few clubs in baseball that could afford to take on such a salary commitment, and everyone knew he was no longer worth the money he was due. The severity of his injury meant that in order to be liberated from Boston, Crawford would have to find a team that was both rich enough to pay his fee and crazy enough to want to. Had the Dodgers not been so hell-bent on getting Gonzalez, Crawford might not have gotten out. "I was completely shocked," Crawford said, of when he was told he was traded. "I thought I was gonna be stuck in Boston for seven years."

Forty-eight hours before the trade was announced, Crawford had Tommy John surgery to repair his elbow. The estimated recovery time was six to nine months.

After the Boston deal was finalized, a giddy Walter was so excited to bring the players he just bought to Los Angeles that he sent a private jet to Boston to retrieve them. The trade with the Red Sox had added a quarter of a billion dollars in salary to the team's payroll through the 2018 season. Walter didn't look at it that way. "I broke it down into years and just saw it as thirty-five million over seven years," he said. "Which really isn't that bad." Still, if he was going to pay that much to get Gonzalez, then by God his bat was going to be in the starting lineup that night.

Walter, Kasten, and Colletti were just as surprised as the players that the trade went through. Crawford and Beckett posed no real threat to wrecking the deal because their contracts were too enormous for teams to want to take on. But for the Dodgers to be able to successfully claim Gonzalez, every single American League team had to pass on the chance to pluck him off the waiver wire, and then so did all the NL clubs with a worse record than Los Angeles's. Though Kasten knew that only a handful of teams would be able to afford the money left on Gonzalez's deal, if one of those clubs did claim the first baseman then the entire trade would be blown. He told Walter he thought the Dodgers had a 50 percent chance. When Colletti sent an email to Walter with the final word on whether their waiver claim of Gonzalez had been successful, Walter was so nervous that he let it sit unread in his inbox for half an hour. The news was good.

Shortly after word of the trade broke, Gonzalez, Beckett, and Punto were already making their way west. In a nod to his new Southern California address, Gonzalez wore a soft blue T-shirt with a beaming Mickey Mouse emblazoned across his chest. The city's sports fans were ecstatic. Some Dodger fanatics even tracked the plane's flight path online. While Crawford remained in Florida to recover from his surgery, the three able-bodied players were ushered into Dodger Stadium ninety minutes before the game, after the team had already taken batting practice. Their late arrival caused some harried moments for the Dodgers's clubhouse attendants, but because the team had been working on the deal for weeks, the rush to prepare uniforms for the new players wasn't as frantic as when Los Angeles had traded with the Red Sox for Manny Ramirez four years earlier. On that day, the Dodgers' clubhouse manager, Mitch Poole, ran out of time and was forced to spray-paint Ramirez's navy blue glove a royal Dodger blue before he took the field. Poole had run the Dodgers' clubhouse for almost thirty years, and even tossed Kirk Gibson his warm-up pitches in the team's underground batting cage before Gibson hit his famous pinch-hit home run off Oakland's Dennis Eckersley to win Game 1 of the 1988 World Series. That these three Boston players were being shuttled across the country by private jet and chauffeured to the stadium in a fancy SUV made Poole chuckle. When the Dodgers traded Mike Piazza and Todd Zeile to the Florida Marlins for Gary Sheffield, Jim Eisenreich, Charles Johnson, and Bobby Bonilla in 1998, Poole was handed the keys to a beat-up van and told to retrieve the ex-Marlins from the airport. The van's tire treads were worn so thin he worried it wouldn't make the twenty-five-minute ride.

Gonzalez found his locker, said hello to his new teammates and coaches, threw on his uniform, located his equipment bag, which housed his gloves and cleats, snuck in a few quick swings in the team's underground batting cage, then ran out onto the field and introduced himself to the patch of dirt to the right of first base that would be his home for at least the next six seasons.

When he dug in to the batter's box for his first at-bat at Dodger Stadium the crowd roared. The score was knotted at one, and the home team had runners on first and third with no out. Marlins veteran right-hander Josh Johnson stepped off the rubber, turned his back to the plate, and sighed. Miami's pitching coach, Randy St. Claire, trotted from the dugout to the mound to try to settle Johnson down. Gonzalez wandered out of the box, snapping his bubble gum and tugging a handful of his crisp white jersey out from his belt. With nobody out, the runner on third was a lost cause. Johnson's best bet was to forget about him and focus on getting Gonzalez to ground into a double play. The Marlins' shortstop and second baseman moved back toward the cut of the grass to set up for the 6-4-3, or the 4-6-3, or any other type of twin killing.

Johnson guessed that Gonzalez, revved up by the crowd noise, was looking fastball. He was right. Johnson threw a first-pitch curveball and

Gonzalez swung way out in front of it and spun around on his heels, fouling it into the stands off first. Strike one. After greeting him with a hook, Johnson thought he could sneak the next pitch by him. Gonzalez was ready. With the count 0-1, Johnson reared back and fired a fastball down the center of the plate. Gonzalez crushed it through the shadows. It landed in sunlight, thirty feet behind the right-field fence, a million miles from Boston. Dodger fans, so demoralized by the depressing McCourt years, saw the promise of better days ahead in one sweet swing. Of course, Gonzalez wouldn't do that in every at-bat. Still, that home run may have meant more to the organization than any since Gibson's. The 2012 Dodgers squad wouldn't make the postseason. But Gonzalez's homer did something just as important: it closed the book on the McCourts forever.

3

THE ACE

On the morning of April 1, 2013, Clayton Kershaw was asleep in bed next to his wife when the alarm on his cell phone jolted him awake. He checked the time. Seven a.m. He stood up, walked to the bathroom, considered vomiting, thought better of it, trudged to the kitchen, poured himself a bowl of cereal, and flipped on the television. He didn't like to set an alarm on the days he pitched, preferring instead to sleep until 10:30, 11, or whenever his lanky body floated into consciousness on its own. But it was opening day, and he was scheduled to throw the first pitch at 1 p.m., which meant rolling out of bed at an hour unholy to him.

Kershaw was not a morning person, which made him like every other Major League Baseball player since the invention of stadium lights. Being a ballplayer was like working a second shift. Go to work around one, out by eleven. Lather, rinse, and repeat more than one hundred times per year. Any hope of surviving in the big leagues meant one must attune his body to achieve peak physical strength, mental acuity, and emotional equilibrium between the hours of 7 and 10:30 every night. Because the adrenaline rush of triumph or the uneasiness of personal failure stayed in the bloodstream for hours after the last out was recorded, the average player knocked out around two. The guys who were wired the tightest—or partied the hardest—often greeted dawn.

On days he did not pitch, which was 80 percent of the time, his wife, Ellen, would wake him by eleven so they could spend as many hours as possible together before he left for the ballpark. They were twenty-five years old. Married for three years, but together since they were freshman classmates at Highland Park High School in Dallas. Kershaw had taken another girl to the homecoming dance in ninth grade, but that was the only date he'd ever been on in his life with a girl who wasn't Ellen. They'd been sweethearts for ten years but somehow hadn't yet run out of things to do together. On the mornings of days he wasn't pitching, they'd hit up museums, television tapings, maybe drive a half hour to try a new breakfast joint before she sent him off. Ellen always had something planned. Four days out of five he was like any other young husband very much in love with his wife, finding bliss in otherwise mundane domesticity. But every fifth day he turned into something else.

At just twenty-five years old, Clayton Kershaw woke up on opening day 2013 with the weight of the Dodgers' franchise on his broad shoulders. Having already established himself as one of the best pitchers in the game at such a young age, it was not outside the realm of possibility that he could one day be crowned the greatest ever. He had won his first Cy Young Award at age twenty-three and finished as the runner-up at twenty-four. Of the 6,797 starting pitchers who had taken the mound since the live-ball era began in 1920, Kershaw had posted the lowest earned run average of any starter through his first thousand innings. By giving up just 2.70 runs per nine, he bested Hall of Famers Whitey Ford (second at 2.75) and Dodger legend Sandy Koufax (third, 2.76)—among everyone else.

Kershaw had been MLB's ERA champ at age twenty-three and

then turned around and did it again at twenty-four. In that same time frame he'd also struck out more batters than anyone else in the National League. Those statistics were nice, but they didn't impress him much. It was Kershaw's belief that while strikeouts and earned run average got the glory, the best way to measure a starting pitcher's greatness was in how many innings he gave his team. (He'd led the NL in that category over the past two seasons, too.) The Dodgers hadn't won a world championship since the year he was born. In the year they owned the team, the Guggenheim group had added hundreds of millions in player salary to the payroll to make that happen. But they weren't going anywhere without Kershaw.

When he was called up to the big leagues in 2008 at age twenty, he was the game's youngest player. To prove he belonged he took a typical tack. "I tried to strike everyone out," he said. The problem with going that route is strikeouts are tiring: each one takes at least three pitches if you're lucky, but more often cost five, six, or seven. Starters are given 100 to 110 or so pitches before they're removed from games. If they try to strike everyone out, they can burn through their bullets by the fifth inning, and leave the next four innings up to the bullpen. Kershaw learned that if he wanted to stick around deep into games to have more of a say in the outcome, he'd have to learn how to get as many cheap, one- or two-pitch outs as he could. In his first season he went seven innings just twice. In 2012 he did it twenty-two times.

But being great wasn't enough for Kershaw to sleep well at night: he pushed himself to be perfect. Kershaw had a gift for making hitters fail in spectacular fashion. He had done this, generally, by moving about the world as if he were a machine on the days he pitched. And he'd done it specifically by crafting two of the nastiest pitches opposing hitters had ever seen. In his five big-league seasons, Kershaw had used his left hand to spin 1,688 curveballs toward home plate—many of those right into the wheelhouses of men who were paid millions of dollars a year to identify mistakes and pulverize them. Just one of those pitches had been hit for a home run.

Kershaw's breaking ball, christened public enemy number one by Dodger broadcaster and high priest Vin Scully, moved like a symphony when he snapped it off right. Sometimes it started out high and huge, like a harvest moon heading toward the batter's eyes. Other times it looked like a strike forever. No matter where it began it would fall straight down like an anchor as it hurtled toward home plate. When hitters were looking fastball they often fell over the pitch on their front foot. And even when they guessed right, when they sat back and waited on it and swung as hard as they could, their wobbling knees made it damn near impossible to generate any power. When Kershaw's curve resulted in a called strike three, as it often did, the average batter shook his head in defeat and began the slow walk back to his team's dugout because there was nothing else to do. A good hitter collects a hit 30 percent of the time. Against Kershaw's breaking ball they stood a 10 percent chance.

Most pitchers are lucky to have one breaking pitch they can use to strike out hitters. Kershaw had two. Halfway through his second year in the big leagues, batters realized that swinging at his curveball was futile, so they stopped doing it and sat on his fastball. Kershaw began to struggle, often needing 100 pitches to get through five innings. There was even talk of sending him back down to the minors. Before a game at Wrigley Field, he was getting ready to throw a bullpen session with catcher A. J. Ellis. The Dodgers' bullpen catcher at the time, Mike Borzello, approached Kershaw with an idea. "He asked me if I could try throwing a slider," said Kershaw.

Ellis had caught Kershaw when he was working on a new pitch before, with mediocre results. At the beginning of the 2007 season, Kershaw skipped High-A ball and went from Low-A ball to Double-A Jacksonville. Because he didn't yet have an effective changeup, the Dodgers wanted him to throw fifteen of them a game, no matter what, to try to develop one. They didn't care if batters hammered it. Though Ellis and Kershaw would later become the best of friends, their first meeting was no lovefest. Ellis went to catch one of Kershaw's bullpens in Jacksonville when Kershaw was working on his changeup. Frustrated by the pitch's lack of deception, he kept throwing it high and away so the batter wouldn't swing at it. Ellis called out to him and said: "Hey! Get the ball down!" Annoyed, Kershaw looked back at Ellis and yelled: "Hey! Relax!"

"And that was when I realized it was better if I didn't try to talk to him when he pitched," said Ellis.

It was a fluke that Ellis wound up being present for the moment at Wrigley Field two years later that changed the course of Kershaw's career. It was May 2009 and Ellis had just been called up to the big leagues that morning to be the third catcher on the Dodgers' roster, to be used only in an emergency. Joe Torre told him he was going back down to the minors after the weekend. Borzello mentioned to Ellis that he had Kershaw toss him a few sliders the day before on flat ground, but he wanted the kid to try throwing the pitch from a mound. "So Clayton steps on the mound, and the very first one he throws is just, like, unbelievable, and my eyes are huge and Mike's eyes are huge and we're just looking at each other like did you see that?" said Ellis. "And Clayton walks over to us kind of shy and asks, 'So what do you think?' And I'm thinking, Well, no one's ever going to talk about you going to the minors again."

Kershaw's curveball may have gotten him into the show, but his slider made him a star. When he threw it where he wanted to it darted across the strike zone from ten o'clock to four o'clock, a perfect complement to his 12-to-6 curve. It approached the plate traveling anywhere from 82 to 86 miles per hour, which made it even trickier for hitters to pick up his mid-90s fastball or his mid-70s curve. Not that it mattered much. Even if batters knew what was coming, when he located the slider where he wanted it was damn near invisible.

"You just don't see that pitch," said Arizona Diamondbacks manager and former Dodger great Kirk Gibson. "He buries it down and in, and you wonder, Why are hitters swinging the bat? They don't see it."

Most hitters study the opposing pitcher's tendencies before his starts, looking for tics and tells to solve him. With Kershaw, however, the best use of a batter's time might be spent in a pregame prayer asking that his slider not be working that night.

"You watch tape, or you watch him on TV, and you come up with a game plan," said Arizona's left fielder Mark Trumbo. "But then when you get in the box it's totally different. You've gotta trust what your eyes see. But when he's on the mound nothing adds up. You think the ball's going to be in one area and it ends up being somewhere else and then you're just not quick enough to get to it."

Kershaw may have been better at spinning baseballs 60 feet and 6 inches than anyone else, but as he tucked into his cereal a few hours before opening day in 2013 there was something bigger on his mind than his start versus the San Francisco Giants. In a few hours he would embark on the most important year of his life. Kershaw had two more seasons under the Dodgers' control until he became a free agent, at which point he would be allowed to auction off his prized left arm to the highest bidder. He had only ever worn Dodger blue. The club's new owners had promised the city of Los Angeles multiple championships. Locking Kershaw into the top of their rotation for as long as they could was their number-one priority, and had been for months. The stakes were enormous, and both sides knew it. What no one knew was how much it would cost the Dodgers to extend his deal to take him off the market before they potentially lost him forever. Kershaw had played his contract negotiations so close to the vest that even his closest friends had no idea whether he would stay.

To help stack their rotation behind Kershaw, four months earlier the Dodgers had signed another brilliant starting pitcher and former Cy Young winner, Zack Greinke, to a six-year contract worth $147 million. It was the second-most lucrative deal for a pitcher in baseball history, behind only the seven-year, $161 million contract the Yankees gave to C.C. Sabathia. Greinke and Kershaw shared the same agent, Casey Close. J. D. Smart had represented Kershaw since the beginning of his career, but when Smart joined Excel Sports Management at the end of 2012, Close, the head of its baseball division, began assisting in Kershaw's contract negotiations. Six weeks earlier, Close approached the Dodgers with an idea for an offer he found suitable for Kershaw: seven years, $195 million with an opt-out after five, just in case the marriage wasn't working out. Close had negotiated the same escape clause in Greinke's deal, and Kershaw knew he wanted it, too. It wasn't that Kershaw didn't want to be a Dodger for the rest of his career. It was just that at twenty-five, when he tried to imagine his life beyond thirty, he couldn't do it.

There was something else, too. Kershaw didn't care about money. Well, of course he cared about money, but not in the way professional athletes who worship the Louis Vuitton quarterly catalog did. The team dress code required players to wear slacks on travel days. Aside from those occasions—and when he was in uniform—one of Kershaw's goals for 2013 was to make it through the season without having to put on long pants. (He made it a month before a forty-degree day in Baltimore forced him to change out of shorts and throw on a pair of jeans.) For special occasions, like Cy Young announcements and all-star press conferences, he might break out his favorite dress shirt: a red and blue checked long-sleeve button-down he liked to roll up to his elbows. But other than that he preferred plain T-shirts and basketball shorts.

It wasn't that Kershaw didn't think he deserved to be paid for his talent. His competitiveness inspired him to fight for every dollar. It was just that wearing money on his feet or around his neck embarrassed him. A devout Christian, Kershaw believed that his wealth could best be used to help others in need. His faith had taught him that he needed only enough money to ensure his family never had to worry. The rest was for giving away. Major League Baseball had recognized him for his work with orphans in Zambia months earlier by presenting him with the Roberto Clemente Award, the prestigious honor given annually to the player who best exemplifies the Pittsburgh Pirate legend's service to others. Besides, Kershaw believed that money didn't change who a person already was: it only amplified it. He had spent his entire life struggling to surrender to things he couldn't control. Promising five prime seasons to the Dodgers seemed long enough. The new owners said they wanted to win, sure, but before they bought the team the Dodgers had been run by a professional litigant who rode into town making the same glittery championship promises before driving the organization into bankruptcy. Kershaw had no reason to think it would happen again. Except: what if it did and he was stuck? No, he wanted to sign for five years. Any longer than that was terrifying. But the Dodgers had something else in mind.

Clayton Kershaw knew that every pitch he threw could be his last. Every pitcher did. But he didn't believe it, not really. He'd never been injured during his five-year career, at least not badly enough to warrant going on the disabled list. Not only did he have that curveball and slider going for him; he also went through the world with the same sense of invincibility that informs the thoughts and actions of every healthy twenty-five-year-old man yet to suffer the indignities of a body in decline. He stood six foot four and weighed 225 pounds, a perfect frame for a major-league pitcher. In perhaps the biggest blunder in franchise history, the Dodgers had traded a young Pedro Martinez away twenty years earlier because management thought his body was too scrawny to hold up. He went on to have a Hall of Fame career. Kershaw had about seventy-five pounds on Martinez. Still, a large frame didn't guarantee wellness. By signing his contract extension before the season began, Kershaw could have eliminated the risk of getting injured and losing a nine-figure deal. But when the Dodgers didn't meet his agent's terms, rather than settle he decided to roll the dice.

Every time Kershaw took the mound before signing that extension he staked his future livelihood to his ability to throw baseballs as hard as he could while keeping his elbow and shoulder from getting hurt. His meticulous routine was the only thing standing between him and insanity. Kershaw had used the same glove for three years. He also loved the comfort of numbers, and found it soothing to commit license plates in parking lots to memory. On days he pitched, he clung to his schedule with military precision.

The majority of Kershaw's home starts began at 7:10 p.m. The days he pitched went like this: After waking up and eating his cereal, he would sit and watch TV with Ellen. Around 2 p.m. he would arrive at the field and make himself a turkey sandwich with cheese, pickles, and mustard, and grab a side of potato chips. Between the hours of 2 and 4 p.m. he attempted to burn off his nervous energy by alternating between walking around the clubhouse, bouncing baseballs off the walls, and trying to guess the other team's lineup—which he wasn't often wrong about. Though Kershaw rarely watched himself pitch, between outings he liked to study the most recent starts that Giants pitcher Madison Bumgarner and Phillies pitcher Cole Hamels made against the opponent he was set to face. Because Bumgarner and Hamels were both excellent lefties, he found value in scouting a team's approach against them, figuring they'd try to attack him in a similar way. Then, at 4 p.m., Kershaw would grab a yogurt and a handful of fruit and head into the training room in the team's clubhouse to take a nap. On days he could not sleep, he consoled himself by watching East Coast ball games that had already started.

Between 5:15 and 5:30, Ellis and pitching coach Rick Honeycutt joined him to go over the other team's lineup and talk strategy. Most starting pitchers develop a game plan based on the weaknesses of the hitters they face that night, but it's subject to change. Greinke, for instance, pitched by feel: he corrected course after every pitch and bounced ideas off Ellis in between innings. Not Kershaw. Since his strengths typically bested a batter's strengths, once his game plan was set he didn't often deviate course. "We're like the pit crew," said Ellis. "He comes to us when he needs something, otherwise we don't interfere."

At 5:58 p.m. on the dot Kershaw placed heat packs on his shoulder, elbow, and sometimes his back. Then he covered the same areas with Icy Hot and finished getting dressed. At 6:20 p.m. he walked into the dugout wearing a blue Dodgers team jacket over his uniform and poured himself a cup of water. For the next three minutes, he sat on the bench and alternated between staring at the ground and staring into space. "Just zoning out," he says. At 6:23 on the dot he took the field and began warming up. Though Kershaw wore number 22 and is superstitious about numbers, he had good reason for not walking onto the field at 6:22. "I don't need the extra minute," he says.

After taking the field, Kershaw trotted down the line toward the outfield grass and put his hands on the ground to elevate his body into the yoga pose known as crow. Then after a couple of arm windmills, he jogged to the center-field wall and punched it once with his right (nonpitching) fist. After a few more laps from the foul line to the fence, some backward and some with high knees, he stretched with the help of a Dodgers strength coach, starting at 6:36.

At 6:40 p.m. he began playing catch with Ellis. "Sometimes I'll joke with him, 'Six thirty-eight today? Six forty-one?' " says Ellis. "I don't think he finds it very funny." Ellis loved Kershaw like a brother but sometimes worried the young pitcher's intensity would cause him to have a stroke. A few months earlier, a well-meaning man sat next to Kershaw in the dugout before he was about to take the field and pitch a meaningless spring training game and attempted to make small talk. Kershaw squirmed in his seat and offered a few polite one-word answers. But after a few minutes he couldn't take it anymore. He looked the man in the eye, apologized, and ran. That man was Mark Walter, the principal owner of the Dodgers. Walter had no idea about Kershaw's strict pregame regimen, and when he found out later, he felt terrible. Still, to be so focused that you blow off the man who has the power to make you the highest-paid pitcher in baseball history was pretty damn impressive.

From 6:40 to 6:48 Kershaw played long toss with Ellis, stepping back a few feet after each throw until he reared back and lobbed balls some two hundred feet to his catcher. At 6:50, he walked to the Dodgers' bullpen to begin throwing to Ellis off a mound. At 7:02, after the national anthem was sung, he began the long walk back to the dugout. At home, Dodger faithful screamed his name and begged for autographs. On the road, visiting fans shouted obscenities. He blotted out all of it. At the beginning of each season Kershaw showed up clean-shaven and wore his sandy blond hair cropped close to his head. But as the season wore on he let the hair on his head and on his jaw grow long and scraggly. Before he threw a pitch, Kershaw put his glove in front of his face so that only his eyes were visible to the batter. He tried to grow a beard to look older, but his hair was too fine and wispy to make him look menacing. And even if his facial hair could grow in thick on his cheeks, his eyes were too open and vulnerable for him ever to look mean. By Memorial Day the ends of his hair would poke out from behind his ears under a ball cap he never washed. Before 7:10 starts, he would walk to the rail of the Dodgers dugout and stand on the edge, nod to his teammates, then lead them onto the field. "It might sound stupid, but it's the little things that help me in baseball," Kershaw says. "Like if I didn't do one of those little things and then went out and pitched bad it'd probably be in the back of my head like, Why didn't I do that? And then in my head afterward I'd be like, You know what? I let the team down today because something was off by a minute."

Clayton Kershaw was born on March 19, 1988, in Dallas. His mother, Marianne, worked as a graphic designer crafting logos for companies like Bibbentuckers, a local dry cleaner. His father, Chris, wrote radio jingles that won awards. They both made decent money when he was a little boy—enough to be middle class—and his father coached his Little League teams. Life was good until it wasn't.

Kershaw's parents started having problems around the time he turned ten. He remembers noticing them sleeping in different bedrooms, but thought it was just a by-product of his dad working late.

"He was crazy talented," Kershaw says of his father. "He played every instrument. But you get in that lifestyle and it's like, Oh I'm not talented until three or four in the morning. And then you stay up all night."

Even though he was an only child, he was spared from being caught in the middle of their demise. "They did a good job protecting me from it," he said. "I didn't know a whole lot of it. I didn't know about any of that stuff going on when I was little, so that was huge."

After his parents divorced, Kershaw lived with his mother. Money was tight and private school was no longer an option. So his mom stretched herself thin renting a home in affluent Highland Park, just outside Dallas, so he could go to public school there. Kershaw had played youth soccer with two boys from his new school: future Detroit Lions quarterback Matthew Stafford, and another friend named Josh Meredith. When he switched schools, he was relieved to wind up in Meredith's class, so he at least had one friend. Years later, Meredith was the best man in his wedding.

Kershaw was an anxious child. "I was kind of a worrier," he said. "I wanted to control everything. I had friends, and Josh was always around but I was always worried about different things. Being late was the scariest thing. Like if I was late for baseball practice that was the end of the world for me. My dad was perpetually late. He'd pick me up sometimes to go to practice and I would just wait like a dog in the front window. Like, please show up, please show up, please show up." He cites his sixteenth birthday as one of the best days of his life, because he got his license. He could finally drive himself somewhere two hours early if he wanted.

The upside to Kershaw being a worrier was that his mother never bothered to remind him to do his homework or turn the TV off and go to bed at a reasonable hour on a school night. She knew he would do it on his own.

Because his mom worked late, Kershaw would usually head to a friend's house after school, and often camped out there for a few days. Sometimes he wouldn't check in for hours. That was no problem, because his mother knew he was so paranoid about following the rules that he would never do anything to get himself in trouble.

"She took a very hands-off approach because she knew I would take care of myself," Kershaw said. "That lack of authority was perfect for me. The responsibility I took on helped me grow up."

When Kershaw's parents split up his life became about controlling variables. He found Jesus as a teenager because the idea of turning over his worries to a higher power was a huge relief. He couldn't control everything, but he could build his own family, and once he let someone in, he remained fiercely loyal. He was a man who met his best friend in the second grade and his wife in the eighth.

In Dallas there are two high school sports seasons: football and off-season football. Kershaw played center on the freshman football team and Stafford lined up behind him. The coach put him on the offensive line because he was, as he describes it, "a pudgy little doughboy." But he got bored and quit after one year, because being a lineman wasn't the most fun job for a fifteen-year-old.

He grew six inches in the summer between his sophomore and junior years, and turned his focus to baseball full-time. His father went to his games and sat in the stands, but the two seldom spoke. "I'd say hi to him, maybe see him for a dinner every once in a while," he said. When he talks about his father now, which isn't very often, he doesn't let himself acknowledge the pain of having a complicated relationship with one of the principal people in his life. "The years that I needed a dad around, like age one through ten, he was there," said Kershaw. "And they had a great marriage and I had a great dad. I was raised by then, so that's good."

He also had the Melsons. Ellen Melson grew up in a close-knit family with two brothers and a sister. Kershaw became a fixture at their home, and reveled in its wholeness. Every Thanksgiving the Melsons would have Kershaw and his mother out to their ranch outside Dallas. Kershaw's father passed away a month into the 2013 season at age sixty-three, never having made it to Dodger Stadium to see his son play. The cause of death was diabetes and other health problems. "He deteriorated really fast," said Kershaw. He left the team to go back to Texas and attend his father's funeral.

Because he was raised by a single mother who struggled to make ends meet, Kershaw knows his life could have gone another way. But the early anxiety he endured propelled him to greatness. The fear of having no control became the fuel that remained. On the mound he was an unflinching warrior who had never been wounded. But off the field his shyness could still appear in fleeting moments. "Some people can go to a party where they don't really know anyone and be totally social and have a great time," he said. "I am not one of those people." Every year he had been in the big leagues he collected the autographs of his coaches and teammates on a baseball. During his first three seasons on the Dodgers he played under Joe Torre. But the 2008 ball from his rookie campaign is still missing Torre's signature. He'd been too timid to ask.

Scouts began noticing Kershaw in the eleventh grade. By the time his senior season rolled around he was a six-foot-four, 215-pound lefty who mixed a 95 mph fastball with a curveball teenage boys had no hope of hitting. He went 12–0 for the Highland Park Scots that season, with a 0.77 ERA. He struck out 139 batters in 64 innings. *USA Today* named him the 2006 national high school player of the year.

Teams with the highest picks in the Major League Baseball draft have one job and one job only: not to screw it up. And while Kershaw had been dominant, there was no greater draft risk than a high school pitcher. Throwing a baseball overhand at 95 miles per hour for a living is a horrendous thing to do to an arm. And teenagers who touched the mid-90s with their fastball flamed out quicker than most. High school coaches rarely consulted with travel ball coaches on the appropriate workload a young arm could handle. Fundamentally, a prep school coach's goal (to win) was at odds with what was best for a teenage pitcher (to advance to the next level with an intact elbow and shoulder).

After graduation, Kershaw planned to go to Texas A&M, where Ellen would enroll in the fall. If he played ball for the Aggies, he'd be eligible for the draft again after his junior season. Conventional wisdom says that drafting a twenty-one-year-old pitcher with three years of college experience is less terrifying than betting on an eighteen-year-old who has only ever faced other teenagers. The Dodgers held the seventh pick in the 2006 draft, a consolation prize for their 2005 season being their worst in thirteen years. The last time Los Angeles had picked in the top ten was in 1993, when they selected Wichita State pitcher Darren Dreifort second overall, right after the Mariners took Alex Rodriguez. Though he was billed as a future ace, Dreifort struggled to stay healthy during his nine-year career, and underwent at least twenty surgeries for a degenerative connective tissue disease before he was forced to retire. Dreifort posted a 4.36 career ERA. The Dodgers lost more games he started than they won.

While Kershaw was considered the top high school pitcher going into the draft, there was even more pressure on the Dodgers than usual to get their first-round pick right. The club had been burned the year before, when they drafted University of Tennessee pitcher Luke Hochevar in the first round. They reached an agreement with Hochevar's representative, but when he dumped that counsel and hired the super-agent Scott Boras, the deal fell apart and they failed to sign him. Hochevar opted to pitch a year in independent ball instead.

With that debacle fresh in their memories, the Dodgers' front office was wary of selecting another Boras client. So the club's director of amateur scouting, Logan White, put Kershaw and Long Beach State third baseman Evan Longoria at the top of the team's draft board. Six teams picked ahead of them. The Dodgers held their breath.

The Royals, Rockies, and Devil Rays picked 1-2-3. They selected Hochevar, Stanford pitcher Greg Reynolds, and Longoria, respectively. Hochevar posted an ERA over five in his first seven seasons. Reynolds blew out his shoulder right away. He won six games total over three seasons in the big leagues before moving to Japan to play for the Seibu Lions. Longoria became a superstar for the Rays, and the face of their franchise.

The Dodgers had hoped to draft the face of their franchise on that fateful day as well. But it was the day before the draft that altered the course of their history. That day, Kershaw pitched a high school game on a tiny field in Lubbock. The night before his start, University of Houston right-hander Brad Lincoln pitched across the state in a game versus Rice. Teams picking near the front of the draft sent their top scouts to Texas to take one final look at both pitchers. Lincoln dazzled. Kershaw stunk. In Kershaw's final audition before the draft, the first guy he faced hit a home run. He couldn't throw his breaking ball for a strike and walked four batters. His team still won the game, but he said later his performance made him want to puke.

The Pirates picked fourth and took Lincoln. The Mariners went next and selected Brandon Morrow, a pitcher from the University of California, Berkeley. Detroit was on the clock. "I totally thought I was going to the Tigers," said Kershaw. "I was sure of it."

But Detroit decided to go with University of North Carolina pitcher Andrew Miller instead. When Kershaw fell to the Dodgers at the seventh pick, White was ecstatic. "If he had pitched well that night we might have lost him," White told the *Los Angeles Times* years later. In his first six seasons with three different teams, Miller posted a 5.79 ERA, bouncing between starting jobs and the bullpen. He eventually became a dominant relief pitcher, but given the way Kershaw panned out, the Tigers would love to have that pick back.

After the Dodgers drafted Kershaw and offered him a $2.3 million signing bonus, he decided not to play ball at A&M after all. The first thing he did was write a half dozen checks to the people his mother had to borrow money from so they could afford to stay in the Highland Park school district. Kershaw says he never knew about those loans until after he signed. "She took on some pretty serious debt so I could play on the best sports teams," Kershaw said. "She did a great job making sure I never went without."

The next pitcher chosen in the draft was a skinny kid out of the University of Washington named Tim Lincecum. Though the five-foot-eleven righty had overwhelmed collegiate hitters for the Huskies, and won the Golden Spikes award as the nation's top collegiate baseball player, teams were terrified of his unorthodox, windmill-like delivery, and unimpressed by the fact that, like a young Pedro Martinez, he appeared to be 150 pounds soaking wet. Undaunted by his slight frame, San Francisco selected Lincecum tenth. He dazzled in his second year in the big leagues in 2008, winning the National League's Cy Young and earning the nickname "the Freak" for his ability to dominate the competition despite being so small. When he won the award again the following year, Dodger fans groaned. Many wondered why the club selected Kershaw while Lincecum was still on the board. Making matters worse, while the Dodgers were mired in the McCourt mess, Lincecum helped the Giants win World Series championships in 2010 and 2012. When Kershaw took the ball for the Dodgers on opening day in 2013, he was facing the reigning champs. Over time, Lincecum's size would catch up with him. And when Kershaw made his ascension to the top of the baseball universe, Lincecum began his fall back to earth. In 2012, Kershaw's earned run average was about half of Lincecum's. White was right to draft him ahead of the college righty after all.

With Lincecum deposed as ace, the Giants gave the opening day start to Matt Cain. Though Cain didn't have his best stuff, he labored through six innings to match Kershaw scoreless frame for scoreless frame. The 0–0 tie was nothing unusual for Kershaw. The Dodgers had a difficult time scoring runs when he pitched, a fact that had cost him wins, and without them the Cy Young the year before. But it wasn't as if Dodger hitters went into hibernation on purpose when he took the mound. It seemed as though every opposing pitcher Kershaw faced was inspired to pitch the game of his life, hoping he could one day tell his grandchildren he had beaten the best.

In the eighth inning, with the score still tied at 0–0, Kershaw had grown tired of the ineptitude of Dodger hitters. The Giants had replaced Cain with George Kontos, a right-handed reliever in his third year in the big leagues. Kontos knew the scouting report on Kershaw's hitting: awful. In his five big-league seasons he had hit .146, with one extra-base hit in 332 plate appearances. Just after Kershaw stepped into the batter's box, Kontos fired a 92 mph fastball right down the middle of the plate. It was exactly the wrong thing to do. Early in games, Kershaw might take a couple of pitches to do his part to help tire the opposing starter out. But as the game reached the seventh, eighth, and ninth innings, his typical strategy was to grab a helmet and run to the batter's box before Don Mattingly could lift him for a pinch hitter. Then, if he led off the inning, he'd swing at the first pitch to end the at-bat as fast as possible. His energy was precious in crunch time, and he needed to conserve every ounce of it for the mound. Plus, there was something else. Cain had struck him out in his first two at-bats that day, and he was embarrassed. "I went up there swinging at the first pitch because I really didn't want to strike out again," Kershaw said afterward.

He started his swing almost as soon as the baseball left Kontos's right hand. His bat whizzed through the strike zone and *whack*! The crowd knew it was gone before he did. Kershaw sprinted out of the box toward first base with his eyebrows raised in disbelief and his mouth hanging open. And when he rounded the bag and saw the ball clear the center-field fence to give the Dodgers the lead, he screamed and continued to race around the bases toward home, as if he had to cross the plate before they could take the home run away from him. He grinned the whole way round. It was the first time his teammates could remember seeing him smile during a game in which he was still pitching. It was his first career home run. The last time he homered was in a spring training game on his twenty-first birthday. On every birthday since, Ellis had wished him a happy anniversary of his last home run.

After he touched home and returned to the giddy mob of teammates waiting to pounce on him in the dugout, Kershaw did something else he was loath to do: he granted the crowd a curtain call. In the top half of the ninth inning, Kershaw returned to the mound and retired the defending champs in order on nine pitches. On the biggest day of his professional career to that point, Kershaw had tossed a four-hit shutout on ninety-four pitches and gave the Dodgers the lead with a late home run. He'd beaten the Giants in every way possible. After the game, before he went and found Ellen, talked to the media, or did anything else, Kershaw headed straight for the team's weight room to ride a stationary bike alone. Nothing would interrupt his routine.

When Kershaw hit the home run, Magic Johnson jumped to his feet in the owners' box next to the Dodgers dugout. After he rounded the bases and crossed home, Johnson turned and high-fived Mark Walter with both hands, then leaned toward him and yelled, "Wow!"

The next day, Kershaw was shagging balls on the warning track at Dodger Stadium during batting practice when the team's traveling secretary, Scott Akasaki, walked out onto the field from the dugout and waved at him. This was odd. Typically, the only time Akasaki ever flagged down a player during BP was when he was being traded or demoted. Neither scenario seemed possible. Curious, Kershaw jogged back toward the dugout and asked Akasaki what was up. Akasaki led Kershaw into a tunnel, saying that Ned Colletti wanted to see him. Colletti walked Kershaw back to a room under the stadium near the batting cages that he'd never seen before. The door swung open to reveal the secret owner's bunker. Inside sat Walter, Stan Kasten, Todd Boehly, and Kershaw's two agents, Casey Close and J. D. Smart. They wasted little time with small talk. On the table was an offer for $300 million.

4

IT'S TIME FOR DONNIE BASEBALL

The new owner's bunker had been open for two business days when it became the setting for the biggest contract offer in American sports history. After Colletti led Kershaw down the tunnel for his impromptu sit-down with ownership and his agents, Colletti learned that he wasn't needed for anything else. "That'll be all, Ned," he was told. The door closed. Despite being the team's general manager, Colletti was shut out of the conversation. His loss of power was an open secret in the clubhouse.

The pressure to win was enormous. On opening day in 2013, the Dodgers' payroll was $214 million, or about three times what Frank McCourt intended to pay players annually. When Kershaw took the mound to face the Giants, the southpaw ace led a team onto the field that was favored to win it all. Gonzalez jogged over to his position at first base and skipped the ball across the dirt to the club's sure-handed second baseman, Mark Ellis. At thirty-five years old, Ellis was starting his eleventh season in the big leagues, and his second with the Dodgers.

He'd spent most of his career in Oakland playing on excellent teams, and was a rookie on the famous Moneyball club. But he'd never won a championship. With his career winding down, this figured to be his best chance.

As the Dodgers' best fielder with the least amount of thwack in his bat, Ellis stood out on a team that prioritized offense. He was different from many of his teammates in another fundamental way, too. Baseball was serious business for him. Though teammates agreed he was one of the nicest human beings ever to swing a bat, he played the game with a silent, gnawing intensity that made it seem like it was no fun for him at all. He didn't like to make small talk with opposing catchers as he stepped into the batter's box and tortured himself without mercy whenever he slumped. While many of his teammates enjoyed the never-ending spoils of being young and rich in Los Angeles, Ellis's idea of a good time was hitting the ball to the right side to advance a runner. He batted second in a lineup crowded with superstars, and in many ways functioned as the club's captain. He was as steady as he was respected, and his teammates wished he could be as kind to himself as he was to others.

To Ellis's right was a plucky young man doused in tattoos and hair gel named Justin Sellers. At 160 pounds, Sellers skipped onto the field that day with a noticeable spring in his step, as a scrub occupying one of the glory positions on baseball's most glamorous team while the Dodgers' starting shortstop, the superlatively talented Hanley Ramirez, was off nursing a torn thumb ligament. (Sellers was sent to the minors weeks later and cut after the season.)

At third base stood Luis Cruz, a journeyman infielder who spent the better part of twelve seasons in the minor leagues with six different organizations, even taking a whirl through the Mexican leagues before earning a shot to make the Dodgers' opening day roster. With the team's regular third baseman, Juan Uribe, slumping in 2012, the unknown Cruz emerged from bush-league obscurity in the final three months of the season and hit .300. That he hailed from nearby Mexico endeared him to hometown fans even more.

Cruz had the inglorious distinction of taking the job of the most popular man in the Dodgers' clubhouse. Like Jeff Kent, Uribe was another former Giant nearing the last licks of his career when Colletti rewarded him with a three-year contract before the 2011 season. His first two years in Los Angeles had been a disaster. Entering the 2013 season, his career batting average for the Dodgers sat at an abysmal .199; he'd hit just six total home runs. So feckless was Uribe at the plate that he was given just one at-bat in the last month of the 2012 season. But in the final team meeting of that tumultuous year, Mattingly singled him out for his leadership and his unselfishness. Addressing the group, he thanked Uribe for maintaining a positive attitude, and for showing up to work every day with a smile on his face despite all else. "He thanked him for being a professional," Colletti said. "Even though his year hadn't gone as he planned—or we planned—and even though September didn't provide him many opportunities, he singled him out because of who he is."

Uribe's teammates loved him just as much as Mattingly and Colletti did. Because of significant language and culture barriers, baseball locker rooms are almost always segregated by race, with white players hanging with white players, Latinos with Latinos, African-American players with other black players, and Asians with their translators. Not Uribe. He had an easy way of mingling with everybody and making outsiders feel included. When the Dodgers signed starting pitcher Hyun-Jin Ryu out of South Korea the previous off-season, Ryu showed up to spring training not speaking a word of English. "Coming over here I was worried about making friends," Ryu said later, through a translator. "Like would my new teammates like me?" Uribe took care of that. He noticed Ryu sitting alone one day, and, not having any idea how to say "Come hang out with us" in Korean, he walked up to Ryu and slugged him on the shoulder. Ryu looked up at him, confused. Uribe smiled, and wrapped his arms around him. Then it was on. The two men began wrestling until Ryu pinned Uribe, to the delight of cheering teammates. "He understood that I wasn't able to blend in and speak the language here, so he really reached out and accepted me for who I was," said Ryu. "He's got a great sense of humor and he's just a great person to be around." From that day forward the two men were inseparable, even though neither had any clue what the other was saying, ever.

A bear of a man, Uribe became the Dodgers' unofficial mascot. Bored by talk of hitting mechanics, he summed up his approach in the batter's box like this: "I see the ball, I hit the ball." He could make anybody in the room laugh with his penchant for self-deprecating jokes, and he had a black belt in teasing teammates, knowing exactly how far he could push a joke before he ran the risk of hurting feelings. "He's the best teammate I ever played with," said Matt Kemp, a frequent target of Uribe's ribbing. But as beloved as Uribe was, he still wasn't hitting. And so on opening day he took his spot on the pine.

Rounding out the bench were veteran utility infielders Jerry Hairston Jr., Nick Punto, and Skip Schumaker. Along with Uribe, those four owned a combined five World Series rings, which gave the club a lift if championship experience meant anything, because no one in the Dodgers' starting lineup had any. They weren't the stars of the team, but they were the glue. Hairston was months away from retiring and taking a position as a broadcaster with the team's new television network. Schumaker and Punto became close friends while playing together for the Cardinals and carpooled to Dodger Stadium together an hour up Interstate 5 from Orange County every day.

While Carl Crawford, Matt Kemp, and Andre Ethier took their places in left, center, and right, respectively, A. J. Ellis fastened his catcher's mask to his face and squatted into a crouch behind home plate. Like Luis Cruz, Ellis had toiled in the minors for the better part of a decade before the Dodgers gave him a real shot at starting in the majors. The front office had teased him by calling him for various cups of coffee during the 2008, '09, '10, and '11 seasons, but each time he felt like he was on the verge of winning the starting job, the team would sign a veteran or trade for someone else's backup and he was blocked again. Because minor leaguers are paid in pounds of peanut shells, his wife, Cindy, had supported their family during the early years of their marriage by working as a pastry chef at a resort during the season and as a caterer in the off-season. When their second child, Luke, was born in May 2010, Ellis was in the midst of his first extended stint as a backup on the major-league roster. Big-league players are allowed to take a few days' paternity leave after their children are born, and most do. But Cindy encouraged Ellis to stay with the team because she thought it was best for their family.

The next catcher on the Dodgers' depth chart in the minors was twenty-five-year-old Lucas May, who the Ellises kept hearing was the next big thing. If Ellis took even a day away from the club to be with his family, May would be called up to replace him, and then who knows what could have happened. So, Ellis stayed, and didn't meet his son until two weeks later. It was worth it. Two months after Luke Ellis was born the Dodgers traded May to the Royals. He appeared in twelve games for Kansas City at the end of the season and never played in the big leagues again. Ellis wouldn't miss the birth of his third child, however. A few weeks after the 2012 season ended, Ellis was with Cindy in their home outside Milwaukee when her water broke. The two set off for the hospital within minutes but didn't make it. Audrey Elizabeth Ellis was born in the front seat of the car they had borrowed from Cindy's father while Ellis was doing 75 mph down the interstate. He didn't even have a chance to pull over.

During his last few seasons in the minors, when a permanent promotion to the big leagues began to seem less and less likely, Ellis decided he would keep playing in the club's minor-league system for as long as they'd have him, with the idea that he would transition into coaching when his knees gave out. What Ellis lacked in athleticism he made up for in instinct and intelligence. Knowing full well he couldn't hit the ball as hard or as far as many of his teammates, he resolved to turn himself into a tough out. He began memorizing every opposing pitcher's fastball release point, and studied the window and the trajectory the ball took toward the batter's box. Then, based on where that fastball landed in the catcher's mitt, he would look for the spin of the ball out of the pitcher's hand to try to determine if it was a curveball, changeup, or slider, and calculate the likelihood that it would be a strike.

A standard home plate is seventeen inches wide. To be called a strike, the ball must pass over it somewhere between the bottom of the batter's knees and the letters across the chest of his uniform (or wherever the home-plate umpire determines the strike zone to be). To save his career, Ellis decided that if a pitch was not a strike then he would not swing at it. It started when his Single-A manager told him to stop swinging at pitches when the count was 3-1, believing that Ellis had a better chance of walking than getting a hit. He got so good at separating balls from strikes that in his last season in the minors he reached base 47 percent of the time he stepped up to bat, walking fifty times in fifty-nine games. Even if he had to take strikes to achieve his objective he didn't care. He became determined to see as many pitches as possible to make the opposing pitcher work hard. In 2012, he had led all of Major League Baseball in pitches seen per plate appearance, with an average of 4.44, because, he says: "There's no worse feeling than taking a bad swing at a first pitch and making an out and wondering what could have been." When opposing hitters faced Kershaw, Ellis marveled at how they seemed happier with a broken-bat first-pitch groundout to third base than striking out in an eight-pitch at-bat. He finally won the team's starting catching job in 2012, at age thirty-one. While still a young man by any other standard, it was ancient for a guy getting his first crack at a starting job—especially at a position so physically demanding.

With Kershaw as his best friend, Ellis's life's work had in many ways become more about ushering along the Hall of Fame dreams of others than chasing his own personal accolades, which was fine with him. But he didn't win the starting job on the super team because he was a nice guy. In 2012 he broke out and posted one of the best seasons of any catcher in the National League, hitting thirteen home runs to go along with a .373 on-base percentage—the best of any Dodgers regular. Still, entering the 2013 season Ellis knew that nothing was guaranteed. Should he falter, his backup, a twenty-five-year-old rookie named Tim Federowicz, felt more than ready to take his spot.

The Dodgers had a starting rotation problem. Following Kershaw, Zack Greinke, and Hyun-Jin Ryu they employed five guys jockeying for the remaining two spots, each with his own set of problems. Josh Beckett was healthy and penciled in as the fourth starter when the Dodgers began the season, but everyone knew it was only a matter of time before his body fell apart. Veterans Chris Capuano and Aaron Harang were interchangeable back-end-rotation types to whom teams gave $5 million a year in hopes that they'd give up fewer than five runs a game. Chad Billingsley, a talented young right-hander who came up through the Dodgers system, had spent the off-season nursing his injured pitching elbow, hoping to avoid the dreaded Tommy John surgery that would knock him out of the game for a year or longer. And at thirty-seven and already gray-haired, Ted Lilly was often mistaken for a coach by visiting reporters. Hitters had no trouble identifying his pitches and crushing them for home runs, however. He was injured, too. So while Billingsley and Lilly began the season on the disabled list, Harang became the club's fifth starter after a figurative coin flip, and an annoyed Capuano was sent to the bullpen.

Joining Capuano in the pen was a motley tribe of elder statesmen, a converted catcher, and one kid just old enough to drink. At twenty-one years old, Paco Rodriguez was four years younger than everyone else on the roster. The Dodgers had selected the lefty out of the University of Florida with their second-round pick in the 2012 draft and called him up just three months later, making him the first player from his class to get promoted to the big leagues. The club had good reason for doing that: in addition to his stuff being deceptive because his unorthodox delivery hid the ball longer than usual, the time bomb in his arm ticked louder than most. The front office felt it was smarter to use the innings he had left in the majors rather than the minors.

Rounding out the staff was Brandon League, a closer about to post the worst season of his life; Ronald Belisario, a Venezuelan whose sinker ball was almost as unpredictable as his visa issues; J. P. Howell, a jolly redhead who never had an unkind word for anyone until a memorable altercation three months later; veteran Matt Guerrier; and Kenley Jansen, a Caribbean Dutchman who switched positions from catcher to pitcher just four years earlier and was better than all of them.

The men on the Dodgers' roster owned twenty-six All-Star Game appearances—but more Bentleys and Rolls-Royces than World Series rings. Only four of them were drafted by the Dodgers, while two additional players were signed as international prospects. The rest were hired guns, leading one executive to quip that those men looked more like a collection of fancy baseball cards than an actual team. They were also, to paraphrase Dodger legend Don Drysdale, twenty-five guys who took twenty-four different cabs to the ballpark. The man in charge of player personnel knew they weren't all going to be friends and he was okay with that. But did they have to figure out a way to get along to win?

" 'Getting along' is probably not the right way to say it, but there needs to be a climate that provides acceptance," Kasten said of his roster. "You're not my kind of guy, I'm not your kind of guy, but we can coexist. We have a lot of different guys. We don't have twenty-five guys going to dinner."

But it wasn't Kasten's job to make this new Dodger team get along. That task fell on Don Mattingly.

For Don Mattingly it had all been a fever dream.

One minute, he was managing a punch-drunk team that was forced to file for bankruptcy because its debt-riddled owner didn't have the cash to write players checks that wouldn't bounce. The next, he was penciling in a lineup card full of multimillionaires bought and paid for by multibillionaires who seemed to be handing out gold bars to everyone.

Everyone except him, that is.

Capitalizing on the merriment of McCourt's departure, the Guggenheim group sold 31,000 season tickets before the 2013 season—an all-time franchise record. Over the course of the next six months the Dodgers would average 46,000 fans every home game, five thousand more than the St. Louis Cardinals, who hosted the second-most spectators. The Dodgers were Major League Baseball's biggest draw on the road, too, besting the popular Yankees, Red Sox, and Cubs. In 2013, MLB averaged 30,514 fans per game across the board. The Dodgers played in front of an average of 40,782 a night.

It wasn't just McCourt's exodus that had the viewing public excited, though. The Boston mega-trade for Gonzalez, Crawford, and Beckett followed the team's July 2012 acquisition of all-star shortstop Hanley Ramirez, which preceded the signing of superstar starting pitcher Zack Greinke. All this caused Dodger fans to lose their minds.

Mattingly knew what Kershaw would give the Dodgers, so his opening day shutout wasn't surprising. The southpaw continued his dominance in his second start against the Pirates, tossing seven innings of shutout ball, striking out nine, and giving up two singles. But Kershaw could pitch only every five days. For Los Angeles to make it deep into the playoffs, they would need at least one more starting pitcher who had the stuff to fluster elite teams. That's why Greinke was so important. His six-year, $147 million contract gave him the highest average annual salary for a pitcher in the game's history. That figure was made even more remarkable by the fact that the Dodgers intended him to be their number-two starter.

Going into 2013, Kershaw and Greinke made up the most formidable one-two punch of any rotation in the game. But there was a problem. During spring training, Greinke's throwing elbow started to bark. After tests revealed the damage wasn't significant enough to warrant surgery, the Dodgers' front office opted to rest him for a few weeks and cross its fingers. This hiccup meant that Mattingly couldn't send Greinke out behind Kershaw to face San Francisco for the second game of the season as he had wanted. He pitched Hyun-Jin Ryu instead, and the Giants shut out the Dodgers 3–0 behind their fantastic young starter, Madison Bumgarner. San Francisco roughed up Josh Beckett to take the rubber game of the series, and the new-look Dodgers ended their first week right where they had finished the previous year, looking up at their rivals. Greinke was activated right after San Francisco left town, and Mattingly handed him the ball to make his Dodger debut at home against the Pirates. The twenty-nine-year-old rightie was terrific in his first game in blue, pitching six and one-third innings of shutout ball, striking out six and walking none. While Mattingly was excited about Greinke's performance, he knew enough about arm injuries to temper his expectations. The real test would come in Greinke's second start. After throwing ninety-two pitches at max effort, would his elbow recover enough to do it again five days later?

In many ways Mattingly's composed temperament was the perfect antidote to Ned Colletti's mood swings. As good cop to Colletti's bad cop, the preternaturally patient Mattingly didn't believe he had to scream to get his point across. When Colletti walked through the locker room the players stiffened, as if they were young boys caught misbehaving by the teacher. "It's not the greatest working environment when Ned's around," one player said, after the second loss to San Francisco. "The stress is definitely felt from the top down." But the guys relaxed around Donnie, who felt like one of their own.

That was the other thing: no one called Mattingly "Don," except for his son Preston, who did so as a joke. To friends, opponents, and his players he was always Donnie. Mattingly had earned the nickname Donnie Baseball during his legendary fourteen-year career with the Yankees, which included a batting title, an MVP, nine Gold Gloves, an impeccable mustache, and his coronation as the most famous player of a generation. But none of those accomplishments mattered as much as what he didn't have. Like most of the Dodger players he managed, Mattingly had never won a ring. Though the Yankees have won twenty-seven championships—the most in the four major U.S.

sports—Mattingly's career in pinstripes had wedged cruelly into the club's longest title drought. In 1981, the year before Mattingly arrived in New York, the Yankees had made it all the way to the World Series before losing to the Dodgers in six games. They would not make the playoffs again until 1995, his last season. They lost to the Mariners in five games in the first round that year, but it wasn't Mattingly's fault. In the divisional series he hit .417 with a home run and six runs batted in. Perhaps his best shot at a championship had been the year before. The Yankees led the American League with seventy wins and just forty-three losses when the players went on strike in August, ending the season. It was the first time in ninety years no World Series was played. For Mattingly it was rotten luck. Despite hitting .288 in 1995 and walking more than he struck out, Mattingly retired after the season ended. The Yankees hired Joe Torre as manager the following year and kicked off a run that saw them capture four titles in the next five seasons. Mattingly missed it all.

In a strange twist, he succeeded Torre as manager in Los Angeles, after coming over with him from New York and serving as the Dodgers' hitting coach. By the time Torre landed in Hollywood, he'd won four World Series rings and was in the gloaming of his storied career. In that respect, though Mattingly was bitten by inexperience, some felt his hunger made him a better fit to run a team that was so desperate for a championship. There was no question Mattingly wanted a ring as much as his players did, maybe even more. His pedigree had earned him the skipper's cap, but he knew the goodwill he enjoyed as a bygone icon would wear thin if he didn't win. On the day that he sent Greinke out to face San Diego to find out if his arm was all right, he was not Donnie Baseball. In his mind, he was Donnie Lameduck.

In 1990, Mattingly had been the highest-paid player in the game, earning $3.8 million. In 2013, the Dodgers would pay twenty-one players more than that. Only twenty guys across both leagues would earn more than $20 million that season. Los Angeles employed four of them. Though Mattingly was entering his third season as the Dodgers' manager, he was not guaranteed a contract beyond 2013. The Guggenheim group hadn't hired him, and no one knew how long they intended to keep him around. That gnawing uncertainty bugged Mattingly. To keep his job, he knew he had to win the NL West, and probably go deep into the postseason. To do that, he had to inspire players who would be paid ungodly amounts of money even if they lost—and who perhaps would be there long after he was gone—to care about winning as much as he did. Some never would, no matter how hard he tried to convince them otherwise. He knew that.

It wasn't as if any of these Dodgers *wanted* to lose. Evolution dictates that, on a primal level, human beings are hardwired to want to beat nearby competition as a matter of life and death. (And being rich didn't make striking out any less embarrassing.) But most of these players had never won anything, and trying to describe the magnificence of something they'd never experienced was like trying to sell chocolate to someone with no taste buds. While baseball can be fraught with deep, tortured attachment for lifelong fans, some of these players had been Dodgers for a matter of weeks and had no emotional investment in the team or the city of Los Angeles. They weren't all like that, but to the mercenaries baseball would always be just a job.

Before Greinke's April 11 start in San Diego, Mattingly arrived at his office in the visiting clubhouse at Petco Park and fiddled around with his lineup card before posting it on a wall in the locker room:

Crawford	LF
M Ellis	2B
Kemp	CF
Gonzalez	1B
Ethier	RF
AJ Ellis	C
Cruz	3B
Sellers	SS
Greinke	P

Matt Kemp was struggling in his return from shoulder surgery and had collected just five hits in thirty at-bats in the first week of the season, with eight strikeouts. But it was way too early to consider dropping him from third in the batting order. Gonzalez was entrenched behind Kemp in the cleanup spot. But other than those two slots, Mattingly was juggling: every other spot in the batting order had already seen more than one name.

In some ways, managing less talented, younger players under the dysfunctional pall of bankruptcy was easier for Mattingly than culling through his new roster of high-profile veterans. "We had a lot of guys making less money that were fighting as they were reaching free agency," Mattingly said of his years managing under McCourt. "We didn't have quite the resumes in our clubhouse, so we had to do the little things better than everyone else. Play to the top of our capabilities, basically, and get some breaks along the way to be able to compete."

The new Dodgers would not be out-talented by anyone. But Mattingly worried they could be outplayed every night. Motivation was something that couldn't be taught. Mattingly knew Kershaw was in talks to sign a contract extension for hundreds of millions of dollars, but he also understood that Kershaw's payday wouldn't change his work ethic or how badly he wanted to win. If anything, the kid would only push himself harder so he could feel like he was earning his keep. That edge was something Mattingly couldn't will upon his men, especially the ones who had already been paid. It either came from within or it didn't exist. "They need to be self-motivated, number one," Mattingly said. "And they have to want to win. Some of these guys have already reached that carrot financially but now what else is there? There's gotta be more than that. Because there's a lot of people out there who are rich who aren't necessarily happy or fulfilled, and there's a lot of people out there who don't have money that are."

What kept Mattingly up nights was the minutiae he feared would saddle the Dodgers with dumb losses, the nebulous stuff that cost good people their jobs when added up but was rarely considered in contract negotiations. Things like remembering to throw a ball low enough so a teammate could cut it off on its way to home plate if necessary; taking a walk and passing the baton to the next guy; showing up early without being asked to field more grounders after a defensive clunker—basic fundamentals talented players didn't need to bother themselves with to be handed a check with a lot of zeroes on the end of it. The Padres entered the 2013 season with a payroll hovering around $70 million, or less than a third of the Dodgers' dole. To compete, they had no choice but to bust their asses. Mattingly worried about the Dodgers' want. As he looked around the clubhouse, it was starting to become clear that the guys he needed the most were the ones who needed him the least.

Don Mattingly had loved baseball his whole life, and baseball had loved him right back. It wasn't just that he was so good at it from the time he was a young child, though that had helped. He got hooked on the subtle parts of the game: the challenge of having to face a different pitcher every night, the focus and concentration it took to stand in the batter's box and hit a 95 mph fastball. He clung to the idea that if he got good enough at hitting these tiny dancing spheres that were in the air for only one second, he could make a life out of it, and get paid to play a children's game every day for almost nine months out of the year for decades.

Mattingly grew up in Evansville, Indiana, the youngest of five children. His father, Bill, delivered mail to support the family. He attended all of his son's ball games and never raised his voice. His mother, Mary, stayed home to raise the family. As the star first baseman in a proud midwestern town, Mattingly lived the dream adolescence as a high school jock hero, leading Reitz Memorial to fifty-nine straight wins and a state championship. The left-hander hit .463 as a prep, and still holds the Indiana state record for career triples, with twenty-five. Indiana State signed him to a scholarship, but when the Yankees took him in the nineteenth round of the 1979 draft, he begged off college and set out for A-ball.

Mattingly hit right away in the minors, but the Yankees thought he might be too scrawny to play first base in the big leagues. At six feet tall, 175 pounds, Mattingly was on the small side for a first baseman, and coaches considered shifting him over to play second. But like shortstops and third basemen, second basemen are almost never left-handed, because it's so difficult to turn double plays goofy-footed. Mattingly was ambidextrous, though, a talent he put on display later as manager of the Dodgers when he fielded throws at first base during batting practice with a righty's glove. In a testament to his physicality, had the Yankees moved him over to play second he would have covered the position with his off hand.

In the end, though, they thought better of making that change. And it was a good decision, too, because Mattingly was just as good at picking throws out of the dirt at first as he was at whacking line drives. The Yankees called up Mattingly for some quick licks at the end of the 1982 season, when he was just twenty-one years old. In his first full year in the majors two years later, he hit twenty-three home runs and won the American League batting title. He earned the MVP award the following year as an encore. In 1987, he homered in eight straight games and hit an incredible six grand slams, still a major-league record. (By comparison, the entire Dodgers team would hit one grand slam in 2013.)

During his time with the Yankees, Mattingly showed up to work each day and went about his business with a quiet dignity that endeared him to millions. Although the team included more exciting players like Dave Winfield and Rickey Henderson, television and radio commercials implored fans to come to Yankee Stadium to watch Donnie Baseball. He played hurt and he played sick. And no matter how high his star ascended, he never quite shook his underdog status, as the slightly undersized son of a mailman. Perhaps it was his noted ability to keep an even keel in the Bronx Zoo that had qualified him to run the Dodgers despite having no managerial experience whatsoever when he was hired. After playing under Yankees owner George Steinbrenner and managers Billy Martin and Lou Piniella for the Bombers, Mattingly seemed to have reached the point where it would take an actual bomb to faze him. That's not to say he was a robot. Toward the end of his tenth season with the Yankees he decided to grow a mullet to match his famous mustache. When the club's management asked him to cut his hair to adhere to the organization's famously strict grooming policy, Mattingly refused. He was pulled from the lineup, benched, and fined. Lest anyone confuse his levelheadedness with resigned acquiescence to bullshit, following the game he complained to reporters that the club's general manager, Gene Michael, only wanted players who were puppets, and suggested he might not belong in the organization anymore. "He hardly ever gets mad," said his son Preston. "But when he does, man, look out." (Mattingly cut his hair and stayed.)

As a late-round draft pick who became an idol in America's biggest city, Mattingly had all the requirements of a folk hero. But he did not want to be defined by the one thing he wasn't. In his mind, the truest measure of a man was how his children felt about him. During his playing days, a generation of young baseball fans grew up wanting to be just like him. He worried that if he kept on playing for them, his own sons wouldn't know him. While he was a Yankee, he and his first wife, Kim, made a home for their three young sons across the Hudson River in Tenafly, New Jersey. But the brutal nature of his baseball schedule meant that half his nights were spent in hotel rooms scattered across the country. Mattingly hated missing months of his kids' lives every year. So he made a decision. "Everybody always thinks it was my back," Mattingly told ESPN later, about why he retired. "But it was really about my kids. I had kind of figured how to play with the back. I went a couple of years where I couldn't find my swing, I was messing with different stances, and a couple years were lean for me. But the last year, I was rolling. I was really crushing." After the 1995 season, the Yankees offered him a multiyear contract. He turned it down. His eldest son, Taylor, was ten. Preston was eight, and the youngest, Jordon, was four. "If I re-signed, Taylor was going to be in high school, Preston was going to be right there," he said. "And I knew they weren't going to know me. I couldn't do it. I couldn't live my life with them not knowing me."

So at age thirty-four, Mattingly retired and moved back to Evansville. And because he was still a young man and he didn't know what else to do, he bought an RV so he could drive his boys all over the country so they could see all the things he'd seen—and many things he hadn't. He stayed away from the big leagues for nine years, but it wasn't because he wasn't wanted. Steinbrenner had tried to lure him into joining the Yankees coaching staff, to no avail. Mattingly wanted to be with his boys. From 1997 to 2003 the Yankees' boss was able to coax him into working as a special hitting instructor during spring training with the idea that if he just got Mattingly back into those pinstripes, even for a couple of weeks a year, Donnie would someday crave an even bigger role. The Boss was right. The year Taylor turned nineteen and Preston hit seventeen, Mattingly accepted a position as the Yankees' hitting coach under Torre. "Before he took the job he asked us if it was okay if he went back," said Preston. "We wanted him to. We pushed him to do it." Mattingly coached the Yankees for four years, until Torre wore out his welcome with management and went to Los Angeles. Mattingly interviewed for Torre's old job, but when the position went to another former Yankee, Joe Girardi, Mattingly followed Torre out west and became the Dodgers' hitting coach. Mattingly's hard luck continued. The year after he and Torre left for L.A., Girardi's Yankees won another title.

There was a silver lining attached to Mattingly's pilgrimage west, however. What no one knew then was that part of the reason Mattingly was talked into moving three thousand miles away was that he was promised he would succeed Torre when Torre retired, despite never having managed before. Mattingly had already accomplished enough in his career and didn't need to prove anything. With his children mostly grown, his reason for becoming a coach was simple. "I liked helping guys," said Mattingly. "I think at the end of my career

I had a good feel for hitting. I had a good vision of—I could tell good swings from guys that didn't have good swings. [Lou] Piniella taught me how the swing worked. And how one thing creates another. I knew mechanically how to break it down, how it pieced together."

During those three years in Los Angeles under Torre, Mattingly earned the affection of players with his relaxed attitude and approachability. Compared to Torre, third-base coach Larry Bowa, and the Dodgers then bench coach, Bob Schaefer, Mattingly was the laid-back stepdad who didn't have to discipline the kids because it wasn't his job. When Torre walked away after the 2010 season, in part because he was tired of trying to get through to young players he just couldn't reach, Mattingly would step into a role that was quite different from anything he'd done before. So the Dodgers' front office made sure his coaching staff was full of former ballplayers who were more than capable of helping him out.

Chief among them was pitching coach Rick Honeycutt, a former Dodger pitcher in his eighth season as a coach with the club. Honeycutt was so important to the success of the Dodgers rotation that A. J. Ellis said: "He's the most indispensable member of the organization." Zack Greinke believed that most pitching coaches were either strong at breaking down a hurler's mechanics or at concocting a game plan. When he joined the Dodgers he was surprised to discover that Honeycutt excelled at both. While watching video, Honeycutt had an uncanny knack for noticing when something was off for one of his guys, be it a slight hitch in his hip rotation or a degree drop in his arm slot imperceptible at first blush. By getting the most out of every arm given to him, he had a gift for resurrecting careers, which might have been one reason Ned Colletti signed so many broken former closers to fill out the club's bullpen.

In 2011 the Dodgers lured one of the best base stealers and base-running coaches of all time, Davey Lopes, away from the Phillies, and his impact was felt right away. Though every first-base coach uses a stopwatch to clock the time it takes between when the pitcher makes his first move toward home plate and when the ball reaches the catcher's mitt, Lopes was deft at reading pickoff moves and peppered his base runners with intel to keep them out of danger. But there was another reason the Dodgers were so keen on Lopes. The baserunning guru's best friend was Matt Kemp's agent, the former pitcher Dave Stewart. When Lopes came to L.A., Kemp was coming off the worst season of his career, during which he hit .249 and stole 19 bases while being caught 15 times. Stewart was optimistic that Lopes could help Kemp regain his form, and he was right. During Lopes's first season with the Dodgers, Kemp stole 40 bases in 51 attempts.

Over at third base was Tim Wallach, a man who many thought would be a better choice to manage the Dodgers when Mattingly got the job. Two years before Mattingly took over as skipper, Wallach led the club's Triple-A Albuquerque Isotopes to a franchise-record eighty wins and was named Pacific Coast League manager of the year. Respected for his sharp baseball intellect, Wallach was unaware of the unspoken agreement that Mattingly would succeed Torre and thought he had a shot at becoming the Dodgers' manager when Torre stepped down. Being overlooked had been a disappointment. Nevertheless, Wallach and Mattingly got along well. Should Mattingly get fired during the season, many thought Wallach would take over as interim manager. As much as Wallach wanted a chance to manage, he didn't want to be given that opportunity at Mattingly's expense.

The team got a gift when another ex-player who wanted to be closer to his children fell into its lap. Former superstar slugger Mark McGwire, he of the 583 career home runs, had worked with Cardinal hitters for the previous three seasons to rave reviews. Many exceptional athletes are so naturally gifted that when they try to teach what they do to others they just can't. McGwire was a rare exception. And because he hit most of his home runs while they were kids, players lined up to receive his secrets. McGwire had starred for St. Louis, and the Cardinals had even named the third deck in left field at Busch Stadium "Big Mac Land" in his honor. But McGwire's wife and five young children were living back in Orange County, California, and he missed them. So when the Dodgers offered him their hitting coach position, he jumped at the chance to go home. While minor on the surface, this move wound up having major implications six months later.

But of all the men surrounding Mattingly, perhaps the most important was his bench coach, Trey Hillman. Since a manager's typical day is filled with the exhausting balancing act of tap-dancing for media, keeping the front office happy, and massaging player egos, he isn't able to devote full use of his brain to setting a lineup and studying potential late-game matchups. That's where bench coaches come in. Hillman had managed in the Yankees' farm system from 1990 to 2001, and he got to know Mattingly when he came back to the organization as a part-time instructor. After the 2002 season, Hillman moved to Japan to manage the Nippon-Ham Fighters for five years, before the Kansas City Royals hired him as their skipper in the winter of 2007. While the Royals were stuck in a never-ending rebuilding slump thanks to a series of bad drafts and uninspired free agent signings, Hillman was fired six weeks into his third season.

During his brief tenure in Kansas City, Hillman noticed something that began to drive him nuts. The small market Royals hadn't made the playoffs since 1985 and had pinned their hopes to the influx of prospects rising up through their system, because they couldn't afford to outspend other teams in free agency. But when Kansas City promoted these youngsters to the big leagues, Hillman realized the kids weren't as prepared as they could have been had the organization's farm system been, well, organized. In a perfect world, each team in a club's minor-league system would use all the same signs and preach identical philosophies on things like advancing runners and defensive positioning, so that when players were called up to the majors they wouldn't be so overwhelmed with new information. In reality, communication was a mess. Nothing was streamlined. Hillman was certain that every team could benefit from an emphasis on this kind of organizational synthesis. So, jobless and looking to continue his baseball career in a new capacity, he mailed a folder with his ideas to all thirty teams after the 2010 season ended. The Dodgers had just hired Mattingly as their manager, but they had yet to name a bench coach. When Ned Colletti called Hillman and expressed interest in interviewing him, Hillman assumed it was for the position of minor-league instructional czar, a post he hoped to create. Hillman met with Colletti and told him his ideas. At the end of the meeting, Colletti surprised him by offering him the job as the Dodgers' bench coach.

It was a curious hire. A bench coach functions like a first mate, often serving as the manager's eyes and ears from the dugout, running through strategy and substitution ideas and acting as a sounding board during the tense late-inning decisions that come to define that manager's competence. Hillman had managerial experience, and he could craft a mean Excel sheet, but he had never coached in the National League before. To baseball purists, managing in the American League versus the National League was akin to the difference between playing checkers and chess. Because pitchers don't hit in the AL, there are far fewer in-game substitutions that need to be choreographed to outmaneuver the opposing skipper; and there are seldom any double switches. Mattingly had only ever played in the American League. Hillman had only ever coached in it. Some worried they would be overmatched. Mattingly was well aware of his limitations. So to help himself prepare to be a skipper someday, while he was still just a hitting coach he would sit in front of his television during the playoffs with a stack of note cards and write down what he would do in each scenario that unfolded in front of him.

But while his coaching staff focused on micro, Mattingly's most important objective was keeping twenty-five grown men who lived in uncomfortably close proximity to one another for nine months out of the year from killing each other. Hillman believed Mattingly was up for the task. In the three years they worked together, the two men became close friends. And, because they were both living away from their families, they bunked together in a rented home in Hermosa Beach and rode to and from the ballpark together every day. Of Mattingly, Hillman said: "I've never been around someone who always unwaveringly has seen the best in everyone."

Goodness came naturally to Don Mattingly. Heading into the 2013 season, his unbridled optimism was his greatest attribute. It took him ten days to fly into a rage.

Zack Greinke wasn't trying to hit Carlos Quentin. His teammates knew this for certain, because he told them so, and he wasn't any good at lying. And even if Greinke were capable of massaging the truth—if when he was asked a question he did not want to answer, his dimples didn't betray him by widening across his face and his dark blue eyes didn't fixate on the ground like a young child caught in a fib—he would not have wanted to, because he viewed anything other than the truth as a grand waste of time. Greinke had no energy for suffering fools, either, and, as if channeling Holden Caulfield, he referred to journalists who attempted to butter him up with small talk as phonies and ball washers. When the Dodgers signed Greinke in the winter of 2012, they became World Series favorites that afternoon. A team needs to win three games to advance past the first round of the playoffs, then four victories to make the World Series, then another four to win it all. With Kershaw and Greinke taking the mound twice in each round as the team's number-one and number-two starters, they could, in theory, do that on their own. The club finally had a Don Drysdale to Kershaw's Koufax.

After Greinke signed, he exchanged a few polite text messages with his new catcher, A. J. Ellis, about where he and his wife, Emily, should look to buy a home in L.A. On the morning Greinke threw his first bullpen session for the Dodgers the following spring, Ellis approached him and asked how he liked to warm up. Some pitchers liked to throw nothing but fastballs and curveballs for the first few weeks of training camp and wait until mid-March to mix in their slider because it's harder on the elbow. When Ellis asked him about how he preferred to get loose, Greinke smirked and stared at his feet. "I'm pretty easy," he said. "You go stand over there and I'll stand over here. I'll throw the ball and you catch it. Then you throw it back to me." Ellis couldn't contain his laughter. He laughed again when, weeks into the season when the Dodgers were stuck in a painful slump, he asked Greinke what roster moves he might make to improve the team. Greinke considered the question carefully, as he always did, then came back to Ellis later with his answer. "Well, the first thing I'd do is trade you because your value will never be higher," Greinke said. "And then I'd sign Brian McCann in the off-season to play catcher so we can upgrade the position offensively." He was serious. Unsure of how to respond, Ellis told him: "Oh yeah? Well, I'd trade you, too."

Greinke wasn't trying to be rude. He just lacked the ability to sugarcoat words as they stumbled off his tongue. Once, after Greinke had been riding Ellis hard for being so slow on the base paths that Greinke's bunts had to be perfect to sacrifice Ellis over, a teammate told Greinke that for every five mean things he said to someone he had to pay one compliment. He was half joking, but Greinke took it to heart. The next day, Greinke approached Ellis between innings and told him he'd done a nice job framing a low pitch. Ellis wondered what the hell he was talking about. Then he remembered Greinke's new orders to be nice. He laughed again.

Zack Greinke knew he was different, but he didn't want to be seen as a jerk. When he threw a pitch that missed too far inside he would often shout, "Look out!" to the batter from the mound. And when a hitter laid off a tough pitch, Greinke would yell, "Good take!"—not to patronize, but because he loved the game so much he couldn't hide his respect for those who were good at it. (Kershaw followed suit in his own way, sometimes tipping his cap to a hitter who resisted swinging at a nasty borderline strike, too.) When the Dodgers played the Tigers at Comerica Field in Detroit, Greinke, who had spent most of his career in the American League, knew he would face some batters he'd seen many times before, so he tried to mix things up. After he threw a first-pitch changeup for a called strike to Ian Kinsler, the second base-man stepped out of the box, impressed. Batters tend to look up at the scoreboard after each pitch to check the radar gun reading to help them figure out what type of pitch they just saw. A number in the 90s meant fastball. Eighties could mean changeup or slider; 70s a curveball. But the gun on the scoreboard wasn't working that day. So when Greinke noticed Kinsler looking around the stadium for help, he began wav-ing his arms at him. "Hey!" he shouted. "It was a changeup!" Kinsler shook his head and chuckled. "That's beautiful," he said, and nodded at Greinke in appreciation.

Some people looked at Greinke and saw a brilliant eccentric with a wicked sense of humor. Others saw something else. When Carlos Quentin stepped into the box against Greinke on that fateful April night, he'd already been plunked by 115 pitches in his short major-league career, including the night before by Dodger reliever Ronald Belisario. Despite playing in only eighty-six games in 2011, he'd led the league in hit-by-pitches with twenty-three. He was hit more times than anyone else in 2012, too, even though he played in only eighty-six games. It was no secret that hitters and pitchers fought for control of the plate, with some batters crowding it to have a better shot at making contact with pitches that were thrown outside. But Quentin's stance was extreme. He was twenty times more likely to get hit by a pitch than the average batter; he leaned so far over the plate that at least four of the balls that struck him could have been called strikes. Greinke had hit him twice before, but then so had seventeen other pitchers. One had plunked him four times. In fact, Quentin had been hit once in every twenty-four plate appearances, the highest rate of anyone in the history of the game.

It was the bottom of the sixth inning in San Diego, during that glo-rious time of the year when every team, even the bumbling Padres and their modest payroll, believed they had a chance. With their roster they did not, of course—but perhaps they could hang in for another month. San Diego had beaten its rich rivals two nights before, and could win the series if it pulled out another victory. So when the club's big left fielder stepped up to the plate to lead off the inning with his team trailing by a run, he was in position to tie the game with one swing.

Though Greinke had limited the Padres to just one run through the first five innings, he had been frustrated by his lack of command that day. When Greinke was on, which was most of the time, he threw seeds that hit their target some sixty feet away over and over again, like a world champion dart maestro. In his two seasons before coming to L.A., he used a heavy sinker and a tight slider to go 31-11 for contending teams in Milwaukee and Anaheim, with 401 strikeouts in 384 innings. And in 2009, when that slider was so good that he could throw it in any count, to any batter, and know it would not be touched, he posted one of the best seasons for a pitcher this century and won the American League's Cy Young Award. But what was most remarkable about Zack Greinke was that he was even playing baseball at all.

A superb athlete growing up in the suburbs of Orlando, Greinke excelled at just about any sport he tried. As an eight-year-old, he was one of the best tennis players in the country, compiling a 50-0 record before deciding it wasn't fun anymore and quitting the sport altogether. The pressure he put on himself to be perfect outweighed the sweetness of victory. And so he walked away, and turned his attention to baseball. He thought maybe a team sport, where a loss could not be pinned just on him, might be easier on his psyche. And it was, for a while. He struck out 118 batters in 63 innings his senior year of prep school, and like Kershaw, was named Gatorade's National High School Baseball Player of the Year. But unlike Kershaw, Greinke didn't become a starter until the twelfth grade. Before that, he was a slugging shortstop who fell into pitching by accident when coaches noticed how hard he threw the ball one day and put him on a mound. The Royals took him with the sixth overall pick in the 2002 draft, certain he'd be a star. And even though he had converted into a full-time pitcher, his athleticism on the diamond stood out. His excellent fielding reminded Colletti of Greg Maddux, who won eighteen Gold Gloves. After he stole second base in a tie game in September, a reporter asked him if the coaches told him to do it. "They didn't tell me not to," he said.

Greinke's adjustment to life as a professional baseball player wasn't easy, however. He had dealt with anxiety since childhood, since those tennis days as an eight-year-old when he'd make himself so nervous before matches he'd remind himself, "Just breathe, Zack," while choking down the vomit as it rose into his throat. The further he advanced in his career, the worse his anxiety got. His agile mind betrayed him by imagining everything that could go wrong in any given situation. Though he had some of the best pure stuff of any pitcher in baseball, he analyzed and reanalyzed every hitter's tendencies as if the key to his success lay not in his strengths but in their weaknesses. Greinke's intellect was his greatest asset and his biggest obstacle. "Sometimes," he said, "I try too hard and it backfires."

Greinke envied teammates who didn't think at all. In his second season with the Royals, he lost seventeen games, the most of any pitcher in the American League. By the time the 2006 season rolled around, his anxiety became so debilitating that he considered retiring at twenty-two years old. Two weeks after reporting to spring training that year, he told the Royals' brass he could no longer continue. On the mound, he was fine. Always. But he hated all the downtime that being a ballplayer entailed. Showing up to the ballpark five hours before each game and having to deal with writers and other people he didn't know or trust was as agonizing as waiting four days between each start. There was too much time to think. Unhappy with his routine, how antsy it made him to just sit and stew for a living, day after day, he thought about asking the Royals to convert him back to a position player so he could play every day. But there was no shot of that happening, not with his talent on the mound.

So, he told his bosses he needed a break. And he walked away from baseball, maybe forever if that's how long it took, to get his head right. He devoured self-help books with little results. Depression had run in his family, but he didn't think that was what was wrong with him. He had never thought of taking his own life, not even once. But then he saw a doctor who put a name on the cause of his suffering. *Social anxiety disorder.* The label didn't matter much, except that a diagnosis of a genuine illness meant that perhaps there was medicine out there that could fix it. By the time that doctor handed him a piece of paper with the word "Zoloft" scribbled on it, Greinke was ready to try anything. Two months later he picked up a baseball again, only this time the noise that pushed him out of the game was just a whisper. He could deal with whispers. And far from feeling embarrassed that he needed an antidepressant, his only regret was that he hadn't gone on the drug sooner. Three years after his diagnosis he won the American League's Cy Young Award.

As Greinke inched toward free agency, he knew the Royals didn't have the money to keep him. Kansas City wasn't going to let him walk with no consolation prize, however, and Greinke hoped they would trade him for prospects before the final year of his contract came up. The Royals had finished last or second to last in the AL Central in each of his first six seasons with the team, and he was sick of losing. So Greinke, ever the patron saint of honesty, stood in front of his locker, faced the cameras, cleared his throat, and said he wanted out. He was traded to Milwaukee. Years later, Greinke addressed the situation with his usual candor. "I was pretty rude on my way out," Greinke said. "But I wanted to be traded, so I had to be rude."

Greinke didn't like to talk about his anxiety disorder. He hated how it was mentioned in every lengthy story written about him, as if it were just another fact to rattle off, like his height or his hometown or his ERA. When Greinke showed up to his first spring training with the Dodgers in 2013, he addressed the media about his past struggles in hopes that he would never have to talk about them again. "In life you have to do things you don't want to do, but I was raised to do what you enjoy doing, whether you are making several hundreds of thousands of dollars per year, or thirty thousand per year," Greinke said. "That was my thought: Why am I putting myself through torture when I didn't really want to do it? I mean, I enjoyed playing but everything else that went with it, I didn't."

But it wasn't just the playing he enjoyed. Zack Greinke loved baseball more than perhaps anyone else in the sport. No major-league games to watch on television? No problem. He'd flip on a college contest and scout the players—thinking, thinking, always thinking—and anticipate who he might face one day. Hell, he even went to watch high school games, too, if his schedule allowed it. As the most talented pitcher on the free agent market in November 2012, Greinke had many suitors. He chose the Dodgers not just because they offered him a lot of money and had a good chance of winning, but also because he wanted to play for a National League team because he loved hitting so much. When he sat down with Stan Kasten to discuss signing with Los Angeles, he praised the club's most recent first-round draft pick, a high school shortstop named Corey Seager. (Greinke was right. The Dodgers stole Seager with the eighteenth pick overall, and the lanky kid tore his way through the minors and entered the 2015 season as one of baseball's top-five prospects.) A team's intelligence in the draft room mattered to Greinke when he set out to choose whom he would play for. Only a few clubs could afford his salary, of course, but he wanted to win. And if two teams offered him the same amount of money, Greinke would choose the club with the more competent front office—which he didn't mind saying out loud to members of those front offices. Kasten later called his meeting with Greinke the best, most interesting sit-down he'd ever had with a player in his thirty-plus years working in sports.

After Greinke signed with the Dodgers, baseball experts questioned whether he would wilt under the bright lights of a big city. Those who knew him and were well acquainted with his fierce competitiveness chuckled at the predictions of armchair psychologists and their weak grasp of the nuances of anxiety. His past afflictions had nothing to do with sold-out stadiums. After all, he'd quit the Royals, who in 2005 had played in front of an average home crowd of 17,000 people every night, second lowest in MLB. And anyway, that was eight seasons ago.

Greinke thought he might be a general manager someday, which was another thing about him that didn't jibe with the perception that he was an oddball who lived alone in a forest and came out of isolation to pitch every fifth day. He loved the strategy of the game, the cost-benefit analysis of signing certain players, and the way a twenty-five-man roster had to be solved like a puzzle. But a GM would have to socialize and schmooze with people for a living like Colletti, himself a former PR man. So Greinke resolved that one day he would run a team without anyone knowing it, and hire a good talker to deal with the media for him. And if he decided against taking a front-office job, because the hours were so long, he had a backup plan when he retired. "I could be in the lawn business, mowing grass," he said. "I could probably do whatever I want, not needing to get a salary involved. It could be fun. You could be outside a bunch and if you're running your own business you could make your own hours. Like if you needed a day off sometimes you could take a day off pretty easily."

As fun as lawn care sounded to Greinke, it was difficult to imagine him ever staying away from baseball for any length of time. He was so obsessed with it, so consumed with uncovering the game's mysteries, that the first thing he did after every start was pull up pitch-charting websites on a clubhouse computer and review the exact location of every ball and strike he had thrown that day, his velocity, the umpire's strike zone, and what he threw that batters swung at and missed.

With Quentin in a full count and the Dodgers leading the Padres 2–1, Greinke wound up to deliver the at-bat's deciding pitch, knowing his control was off that day. The lone Padres run had scored when he threw a fastball in the dirt that skipped to the backstop, and he'd cursed himself over it. Now Ellis put down the sign for another fastball, and Greinke rocked and fired. But instead of finding Ellis's mitt, it tailed away from him and popped Quentin between his left shoulder and elbow, right in the meat of his bicep. At first Quentin just stared at Greinke. And then something in him burst. Perhaps he didn't like that Greinke had rolled his eyes, frustrated with himself and annoyed that Quentin had taken three steps toward him. Or maybe Quentin was chafed that Greinke's body language didn't display concern for his throbbing arm. Whatever it was, Quentin charged at Greinke, all 240 pounds of him, all blood and guts and rage. Ellis was so stunned he didn't have time to react to stop him; he chased after him in full catcher's gear minus his mask, white as a sheet. Hitting a batter on purpose in the middle innings of a one-run game is as unusual as it is stupid. But Quentin was certain it was no accident. So the brawl was on.

When Greinke saw Quentin sprinting at him, he chucked his glove to the ground, in equal parts defiance and resignation, and turned his left side toward home plate so that if there were a collision, his non-throwing arm would absorb the blow. Though he was fifty pounds lighter than Quentin, he did not flinch. Quentin tackled Greinke and crushed him under his weight. Both benches cleared.

Matt Kemp watched the pitch leave Greinke's hand from center field, and saw it tail to the right of its intended target and smack Quentin on the arm. He thought it might have been retaliation for his almost getting hit in the face by a pitch in the first inning, but he couldn't be sure. He and Greinke had been teammates for only six weeks of spring training and nine regular-season games and hadn't yet said more than two words to each other. As Quentin charged toward Greinke, Kemp sprinted in from the outfield, screaming, looking for payback. Though he arrived too late to stop Greinke from getting squashed, he continued to yell and looked as though he might try to fight the entire San Diego bench. "Don't fucking touch me!" he yelled at Padres manager Bud Black, who tried to calm him down. "Don't you fucking touch me!"

After the heap of bodies on the ground was untangled, Greinke emerged with his shirt untucked and approached the Dodgers head athletic trainer, Sue Falsone, holding his collarbone. "It's broken," he said, expressionless. And because Greinke was not prone to hyperbole, his teammates knew it was true. By the time word of the injury reached Kemp, he became unhinged again. He pushed his way back toward the

Padres dugout, which caused both teams to erupt again. Kemp was looking for Quentin, but he was long gone, having been tossed right after he hit Greinke. Even after it was announced that Greinke had indeed suffered a broken collarbone, Quentin held firm in his conviction that the pitcher had it coming. "Myself and Greinke have a history. It dates back a few years. It's documented," he said. "There's a reason I reacted the way I did. It was the final straw."

Kemp, Greinke, and Hairston were also ejected. Alexi Amarista entered the game to pinch-run for Quentin. A shell-shocked Chris Capuano replaced Greinke, and threw a wild pitch that allowed Amarista to take second. Then, in a 3-2 count, Capuano lobbed a sinker that didn't sink, and Yonder Alonso singled to center, scoring Amarista to tie the game. With the game still knotted at two in the eighth inning and the pitcher's spot due up, Mattingly looked down his bench and told Juan Uribe to grab a bat. Dodger fans in attendance groaned. One writer in the press box quipped that perhaps the club would be better off letting relief pitcher Matt Guerrier, who had two at-bats total in his ten-year career, hit for himself. With Luke Gregerson, one of the Padres' best pitchers, on the mound, the slumping Uribe didn't appear to have a chance. He worked the count full. And on the sixth pitch of the at-bat, Gregerson hung a slider Uribe did not miss. The ball cleared the left-field fence, untying the game. Uribe sprinted around the bases with his jaw clenched tight, trying to keep the chewing tobacco from falling out of his right cheek. Vin Scully remarked that it looked as if Uribe was trying to hold back tears. His teammates mobbed him. Who better to save this awful game than the best-loved player in the clubhouse, who was coming off two abysmal seasons? The Dodgers held on to win, 3–2, and remained a half game behind the first-place Giants.

Moments after the game, the reality of what was lost in victory sank in. The usually stoic Mattingly let his emotions get the better of him, and snapped at a local reporter who asked about Greinke's role in the brawl. Kemp was still so incensed hours after the incident that he confronted Quentin in the tunnel under the stadium that led to the

Dodgers' team bus, shouting obscenities at him in front of teammates' family members. Further drama was prevented when Padres pitcher Clayton Richard, one of the largest men in baseball, grabbed Kemp by the wrists and restrained him.

Greinke insisted that hitting Quentin was an accident, but seemed annoyed he even had to dignify the accusation with a response, given that hitting a guy on purpose in that situation would have been pretty dumb. The Padres doubled down on blaming Greinke days later when their CEO, Tom Garfinkel, discussed the brawl during a meeting with season ticket holders, not knowing one of them was recording the session. "He threw at him on purpose, okay? That's what happened," said Garfinkfel, on the audiotape leaked to a reporter. "They can say three-and-two count, 2–1 game, no one does that. Zack Greinke is a different kind of guy. Anyone seen *Rain Man*? He's a very smart guy. He has social anxiety disorder. He doesn't interact well with his teammates. He doesn't really eat meals with his teammates. He spends his life studying how to get hitters out."

Garfinkel was right about Greinke's preparation, but he could not have been more wrong about the way Greinke's teammates felt about him. While it was true he hated talking with strangers and it took a while for him to warm to a new face, when it came to people he knew and liked, Greinke was an impish chatterbox; his friends on the team had a hard time shutting him up. And in a game that often chokes on its own clichés, they found his candor hilarious and refreshing. While Kershaw would rather swan-dive into a vat of acid than shoot the bull on the days he starts, Greinke earned the nickname "Trader Zack" for his propensity to offer fantasy football trades to his teammates right up to the minute he took the mound.

Greinke was vindicated weeks later when Quentin called to apologize for injuring him. "That's cool, man," Greinke said. "But just so you know, if you stand on the plate I'll hit you again." Quentin said he understood.

Major League Baseball suspended Quentin for eight games. The

Dodgers would lose Greinke for much longer than that. But it was more than the loss of a great player. Because it happened just a week into the season it felt like a terrible omen, as if their title dreams had been snapped right along with Greinke's clavicle. It was so badly broken that doctors would have to cut the right-hander open and affix a metal plate to his collarbone to stabilize it. His estimated recovery was six to eight weeks, but that was if everything healed right. In the eyes of many, the brawl was just what the Dodgers needed to bring them together, to turn this wayward band of rich misfits into a team rallying around a shared goal.

Instead, it sent them into free fall.

5

THE COLLAPSE

All winning teams are alike. Each losing team loses in its own way.

Throwing a round object overhand at 90-plus mph, over and over again, is not something a human limb was ever intended to do. Calling baseball America's pastime hides the violence of it. At its core the game is, quite literally, an arms race. The teams left standing in October are usually the ones who suffered the fewest elbow and shoulder injuries to their pitching staffs. The Dodgers' trainers knew this. But they did not account for one of their star pitchers having his collarbone snapped in a brawl.

The San Francisco Giants had won the 2012 World Series because their five starting pitchers missed only two starts combined during the entire 162-game season. Both Colletti and Kasten were disciples of the church of You Can Never Have Too Much Pitching, Never Ever. So, they loaded up on starters.

The Dodgers entered spring training in 2013 with eight healthy starting pitchers, which was three too many in theory, but three too few in practice. After a slew of injuries, on April 27 Los Angeles was forced to use its ninth different starter, the most the club had employed through twenty-three games in more than seventy years. Its revolving-door rotation could have been described as eclectic, which was a polite term for Frankenstein. By May 14, its disabled list resembled a triage unit in an emergency room: Greinke (collarbone), Billingsley (elbow), Lilly (rib cage), Beckett (groin), and Capuano (calf) were all too injured to pitch. And because the club took the field on opening day with such an embarrassment of riches at the starting-pitcher position, Colletti had traded Aaron Harang to the Rockies for Ramon Hernandez, a thirty-six-year-old backup catcher who would appear in seventeen games for Los Angeles, hit .208, get released, and never play in the big leagues again. The only starting pitchers to survive the first six weeks of the season intact were Kershaw and Hyun-Jin Ryu, and the twenty-six-year-old Korean was struggling to adjust to the schedule of American pitching.

Going into the season, Ryu was the team's biggest question mark. The big lefty had pitched well for the Hanwha Eagles in South Korea over the past seven seasons, giving up an average of 2.8 runs per nine, and striking out a batter an inning. At six foot two and 255 pounds, Ryu looked a bit like a Korean David Wells. He raised eyebrows by showing up to his first spring training in the United States even heavier, and by throwing fastballs that topped out in the mid-80s. With the idea that he would become their third starter after Kershaw and Greinke, the Dodgers had paid the Eagles $25 million to buy Ryu out of his contract, then gave the pitcher another $36 million to play in Los Angeles for six years. Some baseball analysts who saw him pitch that spring chalked him up to another instance of the Guggenheim group's lighting money on fire to watch it burn. The criticism caught Ryu off guard. Back home, players used spring training to get into game shape: that was the purpose of it. No one told him that he was supposed to show up to Dodgers camp already at his fighting weight. But there was something else he wasn't used to that was far more challenging than carb-cutting his belly away. In Korea, Ryu had pitched every six days. He would be expected to throw every five for the Dodgers, which meant one fewer day for his arm to recover from throwing one hundred pitches as hard as he could. Barring injury, the average MLB pitcher makes between 32 and 34 starts a year. Ryu hadn't started more than 27 games in a season in six years.

As if losing five starting pitchers to injury and a sixth in a trade over the course of six weeks wasn't devastating enough, two of them were wiped out by a single pitch. After Greinke broke his collarbone in the melee with San Diego, Capuano replaced him in the rotation. But in his first start, the veteran lefty gave up four runs in the first inning, and was pulled after two. After the game, Mattingly revealed that Capuano was removed because of a sore left calf muscle. Later, the lefty admitted he had injured it sprinting in from the bullpen in a futile attempt to stop Greinke from getting maimed by Quentin.

Chad Billingsley, a promising young righty the Dodgers drafted and developed out of high school, finished the previous year with a tightness radiating from the elbow of his throwing arm that almost always required Tommy John surgery, and its frustrating year-plus recovery time. Ever the optimist, Billingsley instead opted to undergo a relatively new procedure called PRP treatment, in which a patient's own blood is drawn from his body, whipped and separated into its different components, enriched with an infusion of its own platelets, and reinjected into the problem area like some kind of super healing potion. It didn't work. Billingsley made two starts, in pain, and then went under the knife, ending his season and his Dodger career.

After he was traded to Los Angeles in that Boston megadeal in 2012, the oft-injured Josh Beckett told Mattingly that he did not appreciate being removed during the middle of an inning. If the skipper was going to pull him from the game, that was fine, but he didn't like being yanked off the mound; he'd rather just not start the inning at all. During a game in Baltimore in late April, with the wheels already rattling off the Dodgers' applecart and their starting rotation in shambles,

Mattingly left Beckett in the game to face Orioles wunderkind Manny Machado with two on and two out in the sixth, trailing 3–1. Machado homered, sealing the Dodgers' sixth loss in a row.

Because he hadn't pitched well in spring training, the Dodgers placed thirty-seven-year-old Ted Lilly on the disabled list so that he could toss a few tune-up games in the minors before joining the big club. An angry Lilly told teammates he was healthy, and that the Dodgers were just phantom DL'ing him to buy time to figure out what to do with their poorly constructed roster. But his body wasn't right. And despite the aches in his back and the tightness in his side, he took the ball anyway—after Greinke, Capuano, and Billingsley went down—to prove a point. His first start, versus the Mets, went well enough. In his second start, the Rockies shelled him. Afterward, Lilly admitted to reporters that he had struggled because he was injured. Mattingly was livid. "It's fine that he felt it, but he's gotta say something," said Mattingly, in one of the first times anyone could remember him blowing up one of his veteran players in the press.

But it wasn't just the pitching staff that had a hard time staying healthy. One of the Dodgers' best hitters, Hanley Ramirez, missed all but two games in April after injuring his thumb while playing for the Dominican Republic team in the World Baseball Classic before the season, then missed most of May with a hamstring strain. The club's starting second baseman, Mark Ellis, sat out for three weeks with a bum quadriceps muscle. On May 8, the Diamondbacks completed a three-game sweep of the Dodgers, which sent Los Angeles to its seventh loss in a row, and a season-low .394 winning percentage (13-20).

The pressure was getting to everyone. Adrian Gonzalez was forced to leave one of those games against the Diamondbacks because his neck hurt. A few of his teammates questioned his toughness behind his back, and one even put on Gonzalez's neck brace and wore it around the locker room as a joke when the slugger wasn't in the room. The criticism that Gonzalez was soft was unfair, as tests on his neck showed a legitimate injury. But since many players looked to take out their frustrations on a new candidate every day, they ignored the facts.

Each defeat brought with it a new set of questions. The Dodgers had lost a flurry of men to the infirmary, sure, but were the uninjured playing their hardest? The farm system was bereft of international talent thanks to McCourt's tightfistedness, yes, but where the hell were the young American-born reinforcements? It had been seven years since the Dodgers called up a position player they drafted who became a star (Kemp), and five years since they promoted a homegrown starting pitcher (Kershaw) who stuck in the rotation. In fact, only three pitchers called up to the big leagues post-Kershaw had made more than ten starts for the Dodgers over the previous four seasons combined: Nate Eovaldi, who was then traded for Hanley Ramirez, and Rubby De La Rosa, who was dealt to Boston in the megadeal for Gonzalez, Crawford, and Beckett, were two of them. (The other, John Ely, started nineteen games for the team from 2010 to 2012, and posted a dismal 5.70 ERA.) While McCourt could be blamed for many of the Dodgers' deficiencies, the failure to draft and develop amateur players wasn't all his fault. The club's weak farm system left a void that could be filled only by aging, expensive free agents, many of them malcontents cast aside by their previous teams. And if those veterans got injured—which was one of the things players in their thirties did best—the Dodgers were toast.

By May 7, the most expensive team in baseball history sat in last place. A *Los Angeles Times* writer marked the occasion by noting that when the *Titanic* sank there was a Guggenheim on board. When the new ownership group took over, Stan Kasten had called the Dodgers a franchise worthy of being written about in all capital letters. Shipwreck headlines weren't what he had in mind.

The Dodgers' starting pitching woes wouldn't have been as devastating if Matt Kemp had been playing like, well, Matt Kemp. But after the brawl with the Padres, Kemp kept on scuffling, and hit just .182 through the club's first fifteen games. It wasn't just his batting average that was so alarming: his power appeared to be gone. "I don't think he's hurt," Mattingly said to a group of reporters before an April game, but everyone knew that wasn't true. Kemp used to stand upright in the box, tall and intimidating, and calmly wait for a pitch he could drive. Now his aching shoulder forced him to lean out over the plate so he could reach pitches on the outer half, with his bum sticking out behind him as if he were preparing to sit down. The hole in his swing became so pronounced that he even swung and missed at pitches lobbed at him by a machine during batting practice. When Mattingly removed him from the starting lineup to give him a mental day off on April 17, a frustrated Kemp told reporters, "I don't ever want to sit out." Mattingly inserted him into the game to pinch-hit with the bases loaded in the bottom of the seventh. Kemp struck out.

In Joe Torre's last season as manager of the Dodgers in 2010, Kemp had gone from future of the franchise to chief resident of its doghouse. Colletti criticized his effort on local radio. Matt Kemp was, without question, the most talented offensive player in the organization. Yet many wanted him gone.

After that disastrous season ended, Kemp knew he had to get out of Los Angeles to clear his head. When he packed up his locker and headed to his off-season home in Phoenix to decompress, he wondered if he would ever come back. Though he had two years remaining on his contract with the Dodgers, his agent did not shy away from suggesting to reporters that his client might be better off in another city surrounded by a supportive organization that could help him reach his full potential. *Potential.* Kemp couldn't escape that word, which to whoever said it must have felt like a compliment, but to him felt like a euphemism for failure. And here he was, a young black man who could hit the stuffing out of the ball and run like hell, in a sport that was hemorrhaging talented young black men to football and basketball, and nobody seemed to know what to do with him.

Kemp had only ever played for the Dodgers, specifically for old white men, which made him particularly aware of his blackness, as if it were something he ever forgot when he was out on a baseball diamond anyway. Baseball had served as a daily reminder of his race ever since he was a child. Growing up just outside Oklahoma City, he was always the token black kid on whatever Little League team he played for, unless he convinced his cousin to join the squad to hang out with him, and then there were two black kids. His mother, Judy Henderson, signed him up to play baseball because he needed something to do while she worked overtime as a nurse to support the two of them. That he wound up being good at it was a happy by-product. His Little League teammates nicknamed him "the Big Little Hurt," after the Hall of Fame slugger Frank Thomas, who was known as the "Big Hurt" both for the number of home runs he hit and for his enormous thigh muscles. (Kemp believes that in retrospect his friends might have just called him that to tease him, because he was chubby.) But as Kemp reached adolescence, the baby fat melted from his frame like candle wax. By the time he was a sophomore in high school he was a smidge under six foot three and chiseled, with electric green eyes on a face that eventually earned him fashion endorsements.

But Kemp never wanted to be a professional baseball player. No. He was going to play in the NBA. Baseball may have been cool for suburban white boys, or Latin American kids looking to move their families to the United States to enjoy a better life, but it was not Matt Kemp's first choice. Besides, he was always better at basketball than he was at baseball, and starred for Midwest City High next to future Duke and NBA player Shelden Williams. He thought he had a good shot at making it just as far as Williams. But Williams grew to be six foot nine in high school, while Kemp graduated at six two and a half. So unlike Mattingly or Kershaw or even Ned Colletti, Matt Kemp didn't choose baseball as much as baseball chose him. Or, more specifically, the Dodgers chose him in the sixth round of the 2003 MLB draft, and offered him $130,000 to sign. That was more money than he and his mother had ever seen. Years later, after he became an all-star and companies fell over themselves to get him to use their products, he sat at his locker thumbing through boxes of nonslip astronaut-ish socks that an eager sales rep had dropped off for him, unsolicited, and shook his head: "It's only after you're rich that people start giving you free shit," he said. "There wasn't nobody around to give me stuff when I was a kid when we couldn't afford anything."

Kemp finished his 2005 season with the Dodgers in high-A ball. But his development was so rapid that two months into the following season he was promoted to the big leagues—a remarkable achievement for someone who had been playing baseball full-time for only three years. In 2009, he hit twenty-six home runs and stole thirty-four bases, earning himself a Silver Slugger, winning a Gold Glove, and finishing tenth in National League MVP voting.

Then everything fell apart.

Even though Kemp had proven he was good enough to make it to the big leagues and emerge as a star, in his darkest moments during that nightmare 2010 season, he started to feel again as though he had never belonged. His caliber of play in center field seemed to be affected by however he'd done in his last at-bat, making it even more difficult to shake things off. When he struck out, the sting of it seemed to linger in his eyes until his next at-bat, clouding his vision in the outfield until he could somehow redeem himself on offense. That blindness caused him to fall deeper into the abyss. Sometimes, Kemp forgot to back up second base when the Dodgers' catcher attempted to throw out a runner from stealing, and he appeared to sulk after fly balls he misjudged, allowing them to sail over his head. He spent his days standing alone in the center of a huge field of grass, painfully exposed, as if the handsome man who now posed for Gap ads was still the pudgy, self-conscious boy. Baseball is a meditation on failure. Even Ted Williams, the best hitter in the game's history, failed to make it to a base more often than succeeded. Besides a bat and a glove, the other tool the game requires most is a short memory. Matt Kemp didn't have that. "So many nights I just went home and cried," Kemp said later, of that season. He couldn't shake the boos. He cared too much what others thought.

It was true that a change of scenery might have done the young outfielder some good. While Kemp hadn't yet reached his full potential on the field, as the boyfriend of the global pop star Rihanna he needed no help realizing the full scope of what playing in Hollywood had to offer. As his relationship with Torre soured and Colletti blasted him publicly, his agent could have demanded a trade, all but forcing Colletti's hand. But Kemp had a warm relationship with Mattingly, whom he affectionately called Donnie B., and when the Dodgers brass reassured Kemp's inner circle that Mattingly would succeed Torre, Kemp breathed a sigh of relief.

When Colletti ultimately decided to stick with Kemp and ownership promoted Mattingly, the new skipper knew one of his main objectives was to save the troubled slugger from himself. For outsiders, it was difficult to figure out what the problem was. Kemp was a good-looking, healthy, twenty-five-year-old man dating one of the most beautiful women in the world, getting paid a ridiculous amount of money to play center field for a famous baseball team. But he was miserable. And when Matt Kemp was upset, there was no hiding it. When he played well, he was a great teammate, all smiles and high-fives, perched on the top step of the dugout, snapping off enormous chewing gum bubbles night after night. But when he struggled his misery had a unique way of infecting everyone around him, like some kind of hellacious airborne virus resistant to antibiotics or pep talks. He was not an easy man to read. One night, he might notice a sick child in the stands, jog over to him unannounced after the game ended, and hand him his cap, cleats, and the jersey off his back. The next day, he might stroll into the clubhouse, notice his name wasn't written on the lineup card, and yell: "Trade me to the fucking Astros!" in frustration in front of his teammates.

Still, Mattingly's relaxed presence and exhausting patience had a better chance of soothing Kemp than shouting him down did. Kemp returned to spring training in 2011 with a renewed focus, having spent the entire off-season in Phoenix—some four hundred miles from the clubs on the Sunset Strip—hitting, lifting, and running every day. It worked. Kemp obliterated National League pitching that year, leading the league in runs, home runs, runs batted in, and total bases. Any pitch thrown to him on the inner half of the plate was a mistake. That year, twenty-two different pitchers looked at him standing there in the batter's box and thought, To hell with this, and intentionally walked him, figuring that giving him a free base was better than risking surrendering four. Kemp also stole forty bases, and finished the season just one home run shy of forty homers and forty steals—a feat that has been accomplished only four times in the game's history.

After his huge 2011, Colletti rewarded Kemp with an eight-year, $160 million contract extension before the 2012 season. And even though it was the largest deal in the club's history up until that point, at the time it seemed that the Dodgers were getting a hometown discount. He had just turned twenty-seven, and Los Angeles had sewed up the rest of his prime. A few months after Kemp signed that contract, the Guggenheim group bought the Dodgers. Kemp had grown up idolizing Magic Johnson and was ecstatic. At the start of the season, the two men appeared on the cover of *Sports Illustrated* together, announcing the triumphant liberation of the Dodgers from bankruptcy.

In 2012 Kemp picked up right where his 2011 campaign left off, homering on opening day and clubbing a Dodger-record twelve home runs in April, on his way to being named the NL's Player of the Month. Around that time, Scott Boras stood in the front row at Dodger Stadium during batting practice and watched Kemp hit; he marveled at his prowess. But Boras turned to a reporter and mentioned how the Dodgers ought to consider moving him out of center field or they'd run the risk of his legs crumbling underneath him, like Ken Griffey Jr.'s. Griffey had enjoyed one of the best decades ever to start his career, and seemed poised to shatter Henry Aaron's all-time home run record, before a series of hamstring injuries robbed him of the chance. Of course, it was also possible that Boras's concern for Kemp's health was really just a clever way to clear a position for his client Jacoby Ellsbury, Boston's center fielder, who was about to hit the free agent market. Boras knew the new Dodger owners were rich, but he had yet to taste that Guggenheim dollar. A few weeks later he was proven right. In the Dodgers' thirty-fourth game of the season, Kemp hit the ball to short and pulled up lame on his way to first base. Mattingly removed him from the game with a left hamstring injury. Despite his protests, he was placed on the disabled list, snapping his consecutive-games-played streak at 399, the longest in baseball. Unable to handle being sidelined, he sat out for the minimum of fifteen days before returning. But it was too fast. He came back for two games, injured it worse, and missed another five weeks. He returned in mid-July, but he wasn't the same player. The club kept him in center field, and on August 28 he crashed into the outfield wall at Coors Field in Colorado so violently he writhed on the ground for several minutes. The team called it a knee contusion. Kemp sat out for two games, then played nearly every day in September. But he endured lingering shoulder pain from the collision, and hit .220 in the season's final month. The Dodgers knew his shoulder was injured. But when they cut him open after the season ended, they discovered a torn labrum and rotator cuff damage. Kemp was stunned. He should not have been playing at all.

Entering 2013 with a surgically repaired shoulder, Kemp told reporters he was healthy, confident, and ready to go. But on the inside he was terrified. He could not lift his left arm above his head to reach the top shelf of his locker, let alone extend his heavy wooden bat high enough to drive a baseball with any authority. His new teammate Adrian Gonzalez had undergone the same surgery for a torn labrum two years earlier, and afterward declared that he was no longer a power hitter. Kemp approached Gonzalez and confided his fear that he would never hit another home run.

It only got worse for him. In mid-May the Dodgers were in Atlanta to face the Braves, and Kemp still had only one home run on the season. An opposing fan began heckling him, telling him that he was horrible at baseball. After a couple of innings of enduring his taunts, Kemp sassed the fan back, retorting that, basically, he was laughing his way to the bank. A few of Kemp's teammates heard this and became enraged. It wasn't just that he was struggling at the plate. Even the best hitters go through slumps, and everyone knew he was coming off a major injury that impacted his ability to hit. It was his effort in center field that drove them nuts. He'd fallen back on old habits, and his terrible at-bats were bleeding into the next half inning and poisoning his ability to concentrate in center field. Some coaches wondered if he just didn't care about defense. Since repeatable pitching and hitting mechanics are an important key to success, every team's video department offers playback that can be broken down into milliseconds, so that players can pinpoint the tiniest of hitches that can derail an at-bat, or, in some cases, a career. To amuse themselves, when Dodger pitchers watched game film they began counting the number of clicks it took Kemp to move when a ball was hit in his general direction.

His response to that Braves fan made a bad week worse. The Dodgers were in last place, and struggling to field nine healthy players each night. And now Matt Kemp, the supposed face of the franchise, was pointing out to some drunk guy that sticks and stones would never break his bones because he would always be rich. A teammate yelled at Kemp to shut up. Kemp did not. More words were exchanged. At a loss for how to curb their center fielder's downward spiral, the Dodgers' front office dispatched a club executive to speak with Kemp's mother, who attended almost every home game, about what the team might do to help her son. Was he having girl problems? they wondered. Was there something else going on? Whatever it was, they just wanted to help. When his mother told him that a team employee had approached her, Kemp exploded. "You don't know me!" he screamed at the executive, in front of stunned teammates. "You don't fucking know me!

Don't go talking to my mom!" In their attempt to support Kemp, the front office had poked at his deepest, most paranoid fear: that he was alone and the world was against him. With the situation deteriorating fast, the Dodgers panicked. Magic Johnson was in New York fulfilling his duty as a television analyst for ESPN during the NBA playoffs. Feeling that perhaps Johnson was the only one who could calm Kemp down, the team flew him to Los Angeles to meet with the brooding slugger.

After getting swept during that disastrous Atlanta series, the Dodgers set off for Milwaukee looking to turn things around. "Hopefully we'll get drunk on the plane and tell each other how we really feel," said one player. Don Mattingly felt sick. His job was to facilitate a winning season by keeping the locker room from imploding, and that wasn't going very well. It didn't help matters that after each loss Mattingly knew he would have to return to the stadium the following afternoon, sit in the dugout surrounded by cameras fixed on his face, and answer questions from reporters about whether he thought he was going to be canned. It reached a boiling point when a respected national columnist wrote a piece speculating that Mattingly's firing was imminent. Even members of Mattingly's own family thought he was out. The injuries weren't Mattingly's fault; the ghost of Earl Weaver couldn't have led this wounded club to a championship. But the Guggenheim group did not spend billions on a baseball team to watch it flounder in last place.

Mattingly had proven he could keep his team from rioting during the upheaval of the franchise under McCourt, but his in-game decisions baffled observers. He and Hillman seemed so transfixed by the double switch that they employed it as much as possible, often pulling bats from games that weren't yet decided to move a relief pitcher down a few slots in the batting order, only to watch it backfire later. As the noise around his potential firing grew louder, Joe Torre called to console him.

Mattingly had been around the game long enough to know that

any day he pulled on his Dodger uniform could be his last. Milwaukee was his make-or-break series, and he knew it. Colletti flew to Wisconsin, and many wondered if he packed his hatchet in his carry-on. Dodger players felt awful. They loved their skipper and didn't want him to be punished for their poor performance. With Mattingly's job hanging in the balance, Kershaw took the mound. The southpaw tossed a complete game, giving up just three hits and a run. Kemp homered for the first time in weeks, and Ethier added another solo shot and a triple.

Then the Dodgers got an unexpected lift. When Greinke hurt himself, the training staff told him he'd miss eight weeks. He replied that he'd be back in two. They split the difference. While Greinke admitted he wasn't 100 percent, he returned to the mound after being away for just four and a half weeks because he knew the Dodgers needed help. He took the ball in the second game of the Milwaukee series, but wasn't sharp, giving up five runs on nine hits in just four innings. "I just had no feel out there," Greinke said afterward. "I made no adjustments. It started out bad and never really got better." The Dodgers lost, 5–2.

After the game, Colletti huddled with Mattingly and the rest of the coaching staff at Miller Park until 1 a.m. The men agreed the Dodgers had sleepwalked through the first seven weeks of the season, and that it was time to shake things up. Maybe it was because he knew his job was at risk, or perhaps he was just sick of watching his guys go through the motions with little regard for the consequences, but Mattingly showed up to the field for the final game of the Brewers series seething with anger. His $214 million roster had won eighteen games and lost twenty-six. If their malaise was going to cost him his job, he wasn't going to go down without a fight. Lou Piniella had left a lasting impression on him when he managed him in the Bronx. Despite his placid demeanor, Mattingly liked to think that when the situation called for it, he could conjure a little Piniella. When he filled out his lineup card, he penciled in reserve Scott Van Slyke for Andre Ethier. It was a puzzling move. Van Slyke, son of former Pirates star Andy Van

Slyke, feasted off left-handed pitchers, while Ethier struggled against them. But the Dodgers were facing righty Wily Peralta that day. A reporter asked Mattingly why Ethier was out of the lineup. "I just want to put a club on the field that is going to fight, to compete the whole day," Mattingly replied. His answer was somewhat surprising. While his outfield mate Kemp had taken criticism for his lack of hustle in the past, this was a new knock on Ethier. The right fielder had homered and tripled in the first game of the series on Monday, but he'd also been ejected from the game in the eighth inning for arguing balls and strikes. The following day, he missed the sign for a safety squeeze play and was thrown out at home.

With Ryu on the hill, the Dodgers clobbered the Brewers in Mattingly's tantrum game, 9–2. Some players attributed their offensive outburst to the spark Mattingly lit before the game, saying that for the first time all season those seated on the bench seemed fixed on every pitch, and those on the field played with a sense of urgency. Maybe it was Ethier's benching that woke them up. Or maybe they knew they had to play better to save Mattingly's job. After the game, Ethier was asked about his manager's comments: "Yeah, I take offense to that, without approaching me first," he said. "Other than that, I show up every day and find ways to compete, to work hard whether I'm going good or bad."

It wasn't just Ethier's miscues during the Milwaukee series that chafed Mattingly, however. His frustration with his right fielder had been bubbling for at least ten days. When Ethier showed up to a Sunday matinee game versus the Marlins on May 12 and noticed his name written on the lineup card, he complained to his skipper that, at thirty-one years of age, he was too old to be playing in day games after night games. The banged-up Dodgers had lost seven straight entering their series with Miami, and had dropped their first game against the Marlins. With Gonzalez nursing his neck strain, Mark Ellis shelved with an injured quad, and Kemp dealing with a sore shoulder, the Dodgers needed Ethier more than ever. Mattingly was incensed that Ethier, one of the club's few starters who was still able to stand upright—who had also gone 4-for-4 the day before—would ask for a break while the team was melting down. Especially when he'd be facing Tom Koehler, a young righty making his second career start in the major leagues. So Mattingly left Ethier in the lineup, and he went 0-for-3. After popping out to third base in the fifth inning, an irked Ethier could be heard saying that everyone knew he didn't hit well during day games, because it was too bright for him. Whether it was a coincidence, or there was something to his theory that the sun blinded him, Ethier wasn't wrong: his career batting average was thirty-five points lower in day games than in night games, while his on-base plus slugging percentage (OPS) was eighty points worse.

Andre Ethier had always played with a chip on his shoulder, real or imagined. Hailing from Phoenix, Ethier signed on to play baseball at Arizona State out of high school. But when his coaches told him after his freshman season that he wasn't talented enough to play Division I ball, he was forced to transfer to a nearby junior college to keep playing. And though he proved them wrong by smashing the ball at the JC level, reenrolling at ASU, and continuing his torrid hitting there before being drafted in the second round by the Oakland A's, that feeling that he was always being underestimated and overlooked never left him. In one of Ned Colletti's better moves as GM, he traded troubled outfielder Milton Bradley to Oakland for a twenty-three-year-old Ethier a month after he was hired. Ethier was called up to the big leagues with a crop of young hotshots—including Kemp, Billingsley, James Loney, Jonathan Broxton, and Russell Martin—who were all projected to be better than he was. He used the bitterness he felt about being an afterthought as motivation, and it worked. Ethier hit thirty-one home runs and finished sixth in NL MVP voting in 2009, and made the 2010 and 2011 all-star squads.

Some hitters' postgame moods were determined by whether their teams won or lost; others were dictated by how they did at the plate that day. Some saw Ethier as a guy who seemed to be in a better mood after a loss in which he'd collected three hits than after a win in which he'd gone 0-fer. In late July 2008, the Dodgers were a game back of the Arizona Diamondbacks for first place in the NL West, and tied 0–0 with the Giants in the bottom of the sixth inning. Kemp led off the inning with a single, then stole second base. Up next, Ethier worked a nine-pitch at-bat before grounding out to second. Kemp hustled over to third. When Ethier returned to the dugout, his teammates lined up to high-five him for advancing the go-ahead run ninety feet in such a crucial game. But Ethier was angry. "That's not gonna help me in arbitration," he said, as he slammed his bat into the rack. Veteran third baseman Casey Blake had just been traded to the Dodgers from the Cleveland Indians earlier that week when he heard Ethier's remarks. At first he thought his new teammate was joking. When he realized Ethier was serious, he couldn't believe it.

Blake shouldn't have been surprised. Though teams that stick together are praised as ideal, the reality is that baseball is the most individual of any of the four major team sports. The 2013 Dodgers were less a team than they were twenty-five separate corporations. Assuming he is healthy, an everyday player notches somewhere in the vicinity of six hundred plate appearances each season. "So at that number, you're looking at about five hundred and fifty at-bats for yourself, and fifty for the team," said Diamondbacks pitcher Josh Collmenter, who had given this issue a lot of thought. In close games, a walk, a long flyout, or a ground ball to the right side can be critical to victory. This, in Collmenter's estimation, would qualify as an at-bat for the team. In these situations, a hitter might be better served shortening his swing so he has a better chance to make contact and advance the runner, rather than aim for the fences and risk striking out. This calculated approach was one of the reasons Adrian Gonzalez was so good at driving in runs year after year. With the bases empty, Gonzalez and Ethier were almost identical hitters over the course of their careers entering the 2013 season:

Ethier: .283 batting average/.348 on-base percentage/.478 slugging/ .825 OPS
in 1,921 at-bats

Gonzalez: .283 batting average/.345 on-base percentage/ .493 slugging/.838
OPS in 2,410 at-bats

But with runners in scoring position, Gonzalez was much better:

Ethier: .290 BA/.385 OBP/.482 SLG/.868 OPS in 937 at-bats

Gonzalez: .329 BA/.437 OBP/.559 SLG/.996 OPS in 1,080 at-bats

Why? Old-school analysts might call Gonzalez more "clutch," and it was true he had a gift for focusing in high-leverage at-bats. But a better explanation might lie in their differing approaches. With no runners on, Gonzalez considered it his duty, as one of the Dodgers' butter-and-egg men, to hit a home run or a double. "And when you try to hit home runs sometimes you pop out," said Gonzalez. But with runners on second or third, he simplified his approach and focused on roping line drives to knock them in. Runs batted in have become a controversial success metric in baseball, since a hitter has no control over whether he comes to the plate with a runner on base. But Gonzalez loved to use RBIs as a measuring stick, and cited it at the end of the 2013 season as one of the reasons why Arizona first baseman and Collmenter's teammate Paul Goldschmidt should win the MVP award over Pittsburgh center fielder Andrew McCutchen. The irony was that when Gonzalez didn't try to do too much he did more than usual: his career slugging percentage with runners in scoring position (when all he needed was a single to plate a run) was sixty-six points higher than it was with the bases empty (when he swung out of his cleats in hopes of parking one in the bleachers). "I think that's because when you're not thinking home run it's easier to square the ball up," said Gonzalez. "So yeah, in that sense it might be easier to hit a home run when you're not trying to."

Perhaps it was the constant pressure Ethier felt to prove himself that led him to be less willing to sacrifice his own at-bats for the team, at least earlier in his career. And who could blame him? All he had heard was that Kemp was a future MVP and Loney was a future batting champion. Could he really afford to give away outs to keep up? Regardless of his success against right-handed pitching he often felt like his struggles against lefties was all anyone ever talked about.

But while Kemp tended to bristle whenever an authority figure called him out, Mattingly's words worked like smelling salts for Ethier. He began hustling out every ground ball and showing up early to take extra batting practice and reps in the outfield. And after Kemp reaggravated the hamstring strain that derailed his 2012 season, Ethier shifted over to center and handled the difficult position admirably even though he'd never played it in the major leagues before. With Kemp on the DL, Mattingly didn't have a true center fielder on his roster. Ethier stepped up, and his teammates loved him for it. His rejuvenated attitude and effort won over the locker room. Perhaps Ethier felt he had a bigger, more important role on the team as the new captain of the outfield. In terms of status, center field was like the aisle seat on an airplane. Right field was the window, and left was the middle. Switching positions in the middle of a season can be mentally exhausting, and many players hate doing it. Ethier accepted his new assignment with a positivity his teammates hadn't seen before. He wasn't as athletic as Kemp, but he appeared to make more of an effort, to the delight of the Dodgers' pitching staff, who did not count the clicks it took him to move when a ball was hit to him. Ethier started hitting better, too. In his seventy-four games as the club's center fielder, his batting average and on-base percentage were each more than forty points higher than when he was in right, and his slugging percentage was eighty points better.

The scapegoating of Ethier one minute and praising him as a team savior the next underscored just how fickle a baseball locker room can be. The amount of time these grown men spent in closed quarters with each other was so unnatural that every loss made otherwise harmless habits, from grooming tendencies to music preferences, that much more grating. That claustrophobia extended off the field, too. The lives of Dodger players were so intertwined that it wasn't uncommon for one player's family to rent a home that his teammate's family had lived in the year before.

Nevertheless, Ethier's move out of right field was supposed to be temporary. No one knew that he would never be the Dodgers' starting right fielder again.

After the Dodgers left Milwaukee, they flew home for a series versus the St. Louis Cardinals, the National League's model organization. Though the size of their media market limited their payroll, the Cardinals had won two world championships in the past seven seasons by hoarding young talent via the amateur draft, which their analytics department seemed to crush each year. It wasn't just that their top picks panned out—many of the guys who wound up being stars were snagged by the Cardinals in the lower rounds of the draft after being overlooked by everyone else. They selected their second baseman, Matt Carpenter, in the thirteenth round of the 2009 draft and signed him for a thousand bucks. He would finish fourth in the 2013 MVP balloting. In that same draft, they picked pitcher Trevor Rosenthal in the twenty-first round. When his fastball began touching triple digits he became the club's dominant closer.

When the Cardinals took the field to stretch before the first game of that series at Dodger Stadium, a clutch of L.A. players watched them stream out of the visitors' dugout with envy. Nick Punto and Skip Schumaker had played for the Cardinals team that won the World Series in 2011, and Colletti brought both utility players to Los Angeles to help build a winning culture. St. Louis had selected Schumaker in the fifth round of the 2001 draft, and he spent twelve years in that organization before coming over to the Dodgers in a trade the winter before. He remained close to many of his former teammates, especially to ace Adam Wainwright, who convinced him to turn his life over to God.

Colletti was right about Schumaker and Punto. The two veterans were vital to keeping the clubhouse loose during the Dodgers' dreadful first half of the 2013 season. At thirty-five and thirty-three respectively, the light-hitting Punto, an acolyte of the headfirst slide into first base, and Schumaker, of similar grit, were not expected to start for the Dodgers. But injuries pressed them into full-time service. The humble duo became the club's spiritual leaders, and also offered the most comic relief. Perhaps the highlight of the Dodgers' twelve-week-long slump to begin the season was Schumaker taking the mound to pitch the ninth inning of a game in which his club was getting drubbed by the Rockies. Schumaker hit ninety on the radar gun and held Colorado scoreless in his inning of work. The next day, he joked that he had practiced shaking off his catcher before he entered the game to play mind games with the batters he faced. When asked if he would consider converting to pitcher, Schumaker replied: "Believe it or not, there was actually a time when I could hit a baseball. Becoming a pitcher isn't a bad idea, considering I already hit like one."

Schumaker and Punto would tell some of their teammates who had only ever been Dodgers about how much different it was to play on a team like the Cardinals, where everyone liked everyone else. St. Louis didn't hand out hundred-million-dollar contracts like Snickers bars on Halloween, but somehow they kept winning, even after they let their superstar first baseman, Albert Pujols, walk out the door. Part of the reason the Cardinals' deft general manager, John Mozeliak, felt comfortable letting Pujols sign with the Angels was that he was confident the organization's farm system could produce an adequate replacement. Sixteen of the twenty-five men who dressed for St. Louis on the first day of the 2013 season had been drafted by the club; only five Los Angeles players were homegrown. St. Louis's player development system was so superior to the rest of the league's that the new Astros owner hired the architect of it, Jeff Luhnow, to remake the organization in the Cardinals' image. Kasten had made it clear that the Dodgers' unlimited payroll had a shelf life: as soon as their minor-league system was nursed back to health they would rein in the excessive spending.

The Dodgers' pipeline was supposed to work like this: Scouting guru Logan White and his group would find talented young players and draft them, farm director De Jon Watson and his team would develop them, and Colletti and his assistants would decide whether to promote them, release them, or trade them. The factions functioned like a three-headed form of government, with all the checks, balances, and finger-pointing that went with it. If Colletti's crew was criticized, they could argue the failure of turning prospects into ballplayers was Watson's; when Watson caught heat, he could shift blame to White. As the major-league team sputtered out of the gate in April and May and it became obvious just how thin the team's farm system was, no one's job was safe. Even the club's training staff feared they were on the verge of being fired, as if they could somehow stop aging hamstrings from fraying, or angry opponents from tackling their pitchers.

It was no secret that White loved the risk and the upside inherent in drafting high school players. Since he began running the Dodgers' drafts in 2002, twelve of the club's eighteen first-round picks were selected out of high school, including Loney, Billingsley, and Kershaw. While White was respected as one of the sharpest scouting minds around baseball, the problem with taking teenagers, besides the greater likelihood that they will blow out, is that even when they do meet expectations, it takes them years longer to reach the big leagues than college kids, who might be called up months after being drafted, as reliever Paco Rodriguez was in 2012. As the club sat in last place in early June, rumors swirled that Kasten had ordered White to use the Dodgers' highest picks to draft college players because they would be closer to helping the big club. Though Kasten denied he ever gave such a directive, White took college athletes with the Dodgers' first three selections for the first time in his career.

The Houston Astros had opened the 2013 season with a $26 million payroll. The Dodgers would pay all the men who played for them that year almost ten times that amount. Comparing victories between the two teams became a running joke in the Los Angeles clubhouse. "Hey, we've got one more win than the Astros!" players would often say, in mock celebration. Unsure of what else to do, an anxious Colletti emailed leadership surveys to Punto, Schumaker, Hairston, Kershaw, and Mark and A. J. Ellis. The front office also called an emergency meeting with Kershaw's representatives, terrified that the stench of the season would push him toward free agency.

Colletti knew he had to do something drastic. So at the end of May he flew to Chattanooga to see about a young outfielder.

6

PUIGATORY

Ned Colletti landed in Tennessee with his job on the line.

He had somehow survived the chaos of the McCourt era, which was no small feat since the thing his former boss loved most after suing people was firing them. Then, against even longer odds, Colletti hung on to his job as GM when the Guggenheim group took over, because Walter and Kasten wanted to see him in action before deciding what to do with him. So far, his audition wasn't going very well. Even though ownership understood that the club's injuries weren't his fault, last place was embarrassing. And for the hundreds of millions ownership had spent on player salary, when the Dodgers flew home from Milwaukee on May 22 to face the Cardinals and Angels their roster appeared to be as deep as a paper cut.

A couple of young outfielders on the Dodgers' Double-A affiliate in Chattanooga were hitting well, so Colletti went to watch them play in person. One of those players was Yasiel Puig. He stood six foot three and weighed 240 pounds but carried it high in his chest and shoulders, like a wild animal that raised its hackles to look bigger to enemies. Except Puig's enemies were everywhere. He was shaped like a sinewy funnel, with quick, strong hands that could snap the handle of a wooden bat in half on a check swing that didn't even touch a baseball, and black eyes as endless as the season itself. Despite his size, he could beat any teammate in a footrace around the bases, an event that, were it up to him, would take place in batting practice every single day.

Puig hailed from Cuba but he may as well have been from Mars. When he showed up to the Dodgers' spring training complex in Glendale, Arizona, that February he didn't speak a lick of English. On his first day in major-league camp he stood in front of a water cooler and shook his head in disbelief at the blue liquid spewing out of it. He didn't know Gatorade existed in more than one color. As the season wore on, the rest of the baseball world looked at him in much the same way. No one had heard of Puig a year ago, but in 2013 he would be the game's most talked-about player.

Though it had been almost a century and a half since Major League Baseball was invented and declared America's pastime, the game had changed more in the last twenty years before Puig's call-up than in the hundred before that. In many ways, the advent of the Internet transformed baseball from a children's game to a chew toy for adult control freaks and obsessive-compulsives. The brightest minds in front offices around the league now tied their livelihoods to predictive statistics and computer spreadsheets, safe in the knowledge that in the post-Google era, superstar ballplayers didn't just materialize out of thin air anymore. The best (and worst) thing about scouting in the Information Age was that there were no more secrets: if any teenager, anywhere in the world, could hit a baseball five hundred feet or throw one 99 mph, then video evidence would, at the very least, be posted by a relative on YouTube. Because of this, and the United States relaxing its Cuba embargo shortly after Puig's arrival, he was perhaps the sport's last buried treasure.

Few MLB scouts had known what to make of the young refugee

when he took the field to showcase his talent in Mexico City eighteen months earlier. Most professional baseball players who blossom into stars have been studied under microscopes by talent evaluators since adolescence. But since Puig grew up in a country whose government not only controlled what went on the Internet, but was also especially keen to keep its young, exceptional ballplayers hidden from the prying eyes of American agents who might steal them away, his skill set was unknown. Some major-league scouts had seen Puig represent Cuba in a few international tournaments over the years, but he hadn't even played for his country's "A" team with the Cubs' uber-prospect, Jorge Soler, or Yoenis Cespedes, the star outfielder who defected the year before and signed with the Oakland Athletics.

After several attempts to flee Cuba, in June 2012 Puig left by boat in a harrowing 350-mile escape that landed him in Cancún. He showed up to Foro Sol Stadium in Mexico City a week later, fat and out of shape, having not played ball for a year after Cuban baseball officials had banned him from the game when they had foiled an earlier defection attempt. His showcase had been a fiasco. Major-league scouts were first told Puig's tryout would be held in Mexico City. Then they were told it would happen in Cancún. After another round of phone calls, Puig showed up in Mexico City after all; the confusion stemmed from the fact that two separate management groups were trying to claim him as their client.

The Guggenheim group had assumed ownership of the Dodgers just weeks before Puig's showcase. And in the midst of the chaos of a regime change, Logan White had taken over running the club's international scouting department as well as the draft. When White received a call from Puig's agent, Jaime Torres, asking him to come to Mexico to see the young right fielder, he was intrigued. White had never heard of the kid. Players born in the United States were subject to baseball's amateur draft, and teams picked in the reverse order of where they finished in the previous season's standings. The system was set up this way to help the weakest teams land the best prospects for competitive balance. But most foreign players were free to sign with the highest bidder. Now that White was working for men who were willing to pay a premium for the best players, he flew to Mexico City excited to finally have license to outbid other teams if Puig was a stud.

White arrived alone in Mexico City for the second day of Puig's tryout. Puig took four rounds of batting practice in front of him and scouts from a dozen other teams. Because Puig was so out of shape, forty-five pitches took forty-five minutes. He bent over his knees between pitches to catch his breath and took long breaks between rounds. Scouts from other teams didn't seem very impressed. By day three of his tryout, only four other teams stayed to watch him hit again. But White couldn't believe what he saw in the kid. Puig was raw, yes, but his mechanics were flawless. The path the barrel of Puig's bat took to meet the ball was so optimal that White believed he could hit for power and average. His hands were so fast that he could stay back on the ball for an unusually long time before he decided whether to swing, which gave him an advantage. They also appeared strong enough to flick baseballs over the fence even without the use of his legs. And his hands didn't panic or flail: they stayed between his body and the ball with so much consistency that he usually drove inside pitches to right-center field, a marked difference from young, overanxious hitters who try to pull everything. White had seen thousands of players swing bats over his three decades in the game, first from the mound as a pitcher in the Mariners' minor-league system, then as a scout for San Diego, Baltimore, Seattle, and finally Los Angeles. He knew Puig was an exceptional talent. He was certain he would be a star.

White wanted him, bad. But there were a few problems. First, new international signing rules were about to go into effect in a few weeks. Because MLB worried rich teams had too big of an advantage under the current free agency system, it decided to give each club an allotment of money to spend on international players, with respect to where they finished in the standings. (The worse the team was, the more it would be allowed to spend.) If a team went over its bonus pool money, it would be fined and prohibited from signing a foreign-born pro for more than $250,000 for the next two years. Under the new system, the worst teams might get only $5 million to spend on players, the best might get only $2 million. White thought Puig was worth many times that sum, and he worried the other teams who stayed to watch his tryout did, too. Since major-league clubs still weren't allowed to sign players out of Cuba, Puig would first have to establish residency in Mexico, then reach a deal with a team before the new rules went into place to avoid any penalties. While White wanted Puig, he didn't want to put the Dodgers in a situation where signing him would prevent the club from inking talented foreign players for two years—especially now that he was working with owners who were willing to spend money.

The other hurdle White faced was getting Kasten to say yes. Even though he loved Puig, signing him was still a huge risk. White had only seen Puig swing at 45 mph batting practice fastballs. Puig hammered the ball, sure, but Mexico City sits at 7,300 feet, and baseballs tend to rocket through thin air. White never saw Puig swing at a breaking ball, or run the bases, or field his position in right, or throw home from the outfield. Puig had been away from baseball so long and was in such a hurry to sign that his handlers didn't want him to hurt himself. The Dodgers had bid aggressively on the much-hyped Soler, but had lost out to the Cubs. White believed Puig was better. To help reassure himself that he wasn't crazy, he called two of his scouts in Los Angeles and asked them to hop on the first plane to Mexico City to watch the kid hit. The scouts did and agreed that Puig was the real deal.

Talent evaluators from other teams weren't as impressed. Some thought that Puig's refusal to run or throw or field demonstrated laziness or arrogance. Rumors flew about his temper. The stories the evaluators traded only added to his myth. Baseball scouts are known for gossiping like teenagers, but the veracity of these stories didn't matter because Puig's past was impossible to check. Nonetheless, the salacious tales scared off many potential suitors.

White knew about Puig's anger issues, and he told his bosses. But he also knew the kid was smart and quickwitted. They went to dinner together and Puig fixed White's computer so he could get online abroad. White believed that the Cubs and White Sox also coveted Puig, so he joked with the kid in broken Spanish that he didn't want to live in Illinois because Chicago was *muy frio and windy,* while Los Angeles was full of sunshine and the girls were better looking. Puig laughed. He understood.

While his future as a major leaguer was almost impossible to project based on a couple of days of BP at high altitude, the fact that he was such a mystery made White want him even more: his potential upside was much higher than that of an American prospect who'd been put through a battery of tests, both physical and psychological, by every other team. White looked at signing Puig like buying a lottery ticket. So he called Kasten and told him that the kid had a chance to turn into the kind of five-tool player who came along once in a generation. The Cubs had paid $30 million for nine years of Soler. White told Kasten the Dodgers should offer Puig $42 million, just to be safe. Kasten about choked on his phone. Since no one else seemed to know who Puig was, it was perhaps the biggest gamble of Kasten's career. He tried to call Mark Walter but couldn't reach him. With very little time to wait, Kasten knew he had to make the decision himself. Remembering that Walter had told him he wanted the Dodgers to be overaggressive in paying for international talent after they missed out on Soler, Kasten gulped, called White back, and gave him the go-ahead. The club's race to sign Puig before the deadline was so frantic they had to scramble to find a reputable doctor in Mexico City to examine him because they didn't have time to fly him to Los Angeles for a physical. When that doctor found no hidden problems, the Dodgers got their man.

Before Puig ever set foot in big-league camp, his legend preceded him. The Dodgers' longtime clubhouse manager, Mitch Poole, had heard about Puig's hellion reputation, so he assigned him number 66 in spring training as a joke. "I thought it'd be funny to give him number sixty-six to reference 666, like he was Diablo," said Poole. Puig wanted to wear 14, but that number belonged to Mark Ellis. Poole told Puig that after the regular season started he could pick a different number whenever he was promoted to the majors. Puig wasn't expected to make the Dodgers' twenty-five-man roster out of camp in 2013 because he had yet to play a full season in the minors. But he clobbered opposing pitching from the start, collecting thirty hits in twenty-seven spring games, and accounting for more hits than outs en route to a .517 average—best in the Cactus League among players with at least fifty at-bats. Though he was the Dodgers' best hitter during camp, he was sent to Double-A Chattanooga to get more experience. On his way out, he approached Poole with a new request. "Papi," he said with a smile. "Can I keep sixty-six?" He believed the number had brought him luck.

What began as a joke turned into an omen. Puig lived his life like the present moment was the only place safe enough for him to be. He rarely fell asleep before dawn, and when he did, he told friends he slept with one eye open so that he might see evil approaching. He wore the two sixes on his back like a crucifix to ward off the devil.

Puig had a gift for turning mundane baseball tasks into exciting ones. Routine fly balls became circus basket catches. If he was on second base and a ground ball was hit to an infielder, he might try running all the way home. People searched for other baseball players to compare him to, but Puig's style was more comparable to Michael Jordan's, or to his hero's, the Portuguese soccer star Cristiano Ronaldo. For starters, he seemed offended by the idea of hitting singles. Every time he whacked a baseball into the outfield he charged out of the batter's box as if he could make it to second before anyone caught him. He didn't just round bases, he blew past them, daring fielders to throw at him to make him retreat. And when he fielded the ball in right and the other team's runners were circling the bases, he didn't bother with relaying the ball back toward home plate via a teammate. He believed, with all of his heart, that he could throw a ball four hundred feet faster than any human could run ninety. To take your eyes off Yasiel Puig was a mistake, because he might do something you'd never see again. Because of its slower pace, Major League Baseball had been having a hard time attracting young fans who were more entertained by football and basketball. Puig was just what the game needed.

Opposing teams who saw how big and strong he was—how he could fling his bat at a baseball traveling 95 mph and three feet out of the strike zone and send it over the outfield fence—swore he was thirty years old. People who engaged him in conversation wondered if he was fifteen. His loud, booming voice entered rooms before he did. It wasn't uncommon for him to sit in his corner locker and yell "Pow! Pow! Powpowpow!" like machine-gun spray in a video game when he thought that he was not getting enough attention.

Though he hit the ball better than anyone else on their squad during spring training, the Dodgers had no intention of putting Puig on their opening day roster because he wasn't mature enough emotionally. In a perfect world, the young outfielder would have stayed in the minor leagues for the entire 2013 season so that he could make whatever mistakes he needed to make as far from the limelight as possible and arrive in L.A. the following April a year wiser for it. Some players could handle the pressure of being called up while they're still young enough to be playing college ball. Kershaw had made his major-league debut in 2008, two months after he turned twenty. But the self-possession Kershaw displayed as a teenager was exceptional; he handled pressure better than many players who were ten years older. Puig was still a kid: his favorite television show was the cartoon *Teenage Mutant Ninja Turtles*. During the first week of the season, Don Mattingly was asked why Yasiel Puig didn't make the Dodgers' opening day roster despite his obvious talent. "I heard a guy say one time, you feed babies baby food," Mattingly said. "You don't give them steak when they're six months old."

A Dodger executive explained it this way: "Go to YouTube and type in 'Puig bat flip' and you'll see why."

He was talking about the way Puig disposed of his bat after he hit a baseball with positive results. When he smacked home runs (or sometimes even singles), Puig flipped his bat high in the air behind him, handle up, barrel down, like a Spanish exclamation point. Opposing pitchers hated the way he celebrated his success against them and often retaliated by buzzing him with high fastballs during his next at-bat. The Dodgers saw it as an annoying extension of the youthful exuberance that made him great. Their tricky task was to get him to cool off the showboating without watering him down into a lesser player. But there was an even greater challenge when it came to Puig, with more serious ramifications: his joy turned to rage at a terrifying rate that he seemed unable to control. When opponents vented their exasperation with his antics, Puig puffed out his chest and hollered back. In the minors, he even dropped his bat to the ground in disgust after a called *strike two*. He was a man of high highs and low lows, the kind of player whose changing moods terrified coaches. It didn't help his cause that he pouted when he was assigned to Double-A out of training camp.

But with their backs to the wall and their season already circling the drain, the Dodgers in their desperation considered promoting Puig just weeks after Mattingly compared him to an infant. Team officials decided to delay his call-up, however, after he was arrested in the early morning hours of April 28 for doing 97 in a 50 mph zone, and charged with reckless driving, speeding, and driving without proof of insurance. The next day the Dodgers were embarrassed by the Rockies at home, falling 12–2 in the game that Skip Schumaker pitched in relief. Almost a month had passed since Puig's brush with the law when Colletti went to see him, and perhaps he had endured enough overnight bus rides and Double-A cold-cut spreads to atone for his transgression. While Puig might have done his penance, the Dodgers' front office was reluctant to promote him unless he was in line for significant playing time. What the young right fielder needed most were at-bats; a warm seat on major-league pine would just delay his maturation by another year.

• • •

That's where Mike Trout came in. In the year and a half he had been in the big leagues, Trout had already established himself as the best player in baseball. In his first full season with the Angels, the twenty-year-old center fielder became the first player in MLB history to hit 30 home runs, steal 45 bases, and score 125 runs in a season. He reminded many of Mickey Mantle. But at six foot two and 230 pounds, Trout was three inches taller and thirty-five pounds heavier than the Mick. As if his personal accomplishments weren't enough, he also collected the hit that forced the Dodgers to call up Yasiel Puig.

During the last week of May, the Dodgers and Angels played four straight games, two in Los Angeles then two in Anaheim. The Dodgers had taken the first two games of the series at home, but were trailing in the seventh in the third game, 3–1, when Trout stepped into the batter's box to lead off the inning.

Maybe it was because Trout was up to bat, or maybe it was just a coincidence. But while Kemp was slowed for most of 2012 with injuries, Trout had established himself as the best center fielder in Southern California, winning the American League's Rookie of the Year award and finishing second in MVP voting. When Trout whacked a 1-2 fastball from Dodgers reliever Javy Guerra toward the wall in right-center field, Kemp took off sprinting after it with more ferocity than usual. His first two steps toward the ball were fine. But when he took his third stride he pulled up lame and slowed into a trot. At first glance it wasn't clear what was wrong with Kemp; his face registered no pain, and he didn't grab at any part of his body. The ball ricocheted off the top of the wall and bounced into his glove, and he chucked it back into the infield well after Trout had arrived at second base. It wasn't until Guerra was removed from the game two batters later that anyone knew Kemp was injured. He motioned toward the dugout, and one of the Dodgers' trainers jogged out to talk with him during the pitching change. After some discussion, Kemp left the field, keeping his eyes on the ground in front of him. Someone in the Dodgers' dugout yelled out to Schumaker, who was playing second, that they needed to move him to center, so he had better grab an outfielder's glove.

"What happened?" Schumaker asked Dodgers hitting coach Mark McGwire as Schumaker approached the dugout.

"I don't know," said McGwire as he handed him a bigger glove. Schumaker shook his head. If Kemp's injury was bad enough to require a trip to the disabled list, he would become the twelfth Dodger to land on the DL in the club's first fifty-one games. The team had only twenty-five men on its roster: the wounded almost outnumbered the well. The Angels held on to win the game, 4–3. The Dodgers remained in last place, trailing the division-leading Arizona Diamondbacks by seven and a half games.

When the club announced that Kemp pulled a hamstring, yet again, the postgame locker room gave off an even more morose vibe than usual. "It's not as bad as last year," Kemp said after the game, and he may have believed it. "But you've got to take it easy and make sure you're careful with it because it can get worse. I'd rather maybe miss a couple days or whatever and not miss a month like I did last year." When Kemp hurt himself chasing down Trout's hit, he could not have imagined it would trigger a sequence of events that threatened his job.

At first, Mattingly tried to deny Puig was on the way to L.A. by suggesting instead that the Dodgers needed someone who could fill Kemp's position. "Obviously we'll need a player who can play center," Mattingly said. That was true: the loss of Kemp meant Los Angeles didn't have a true center fielder on its roster, as Puig's natural position was right. The Chattanooga Lookouts also featured a young center-field prospect named Joc Pederson, who had been the Dodgers' eleventh-round pick in the 2010 draft out of high school. He was better than where he was selected, though, and the club gave him the second-highest bonus of any of the players they drafted that year, hoping he would sign with them instead of going to play ball at the University of

Southern California, as his father had. A year and a half younger than Puig, Pederson entered the 2013 season as the Dodgers' fourth-best prospect according to *Baseball America*, and the youngest member of the Lookouts. Pederson was a better defender in center than Kemp was, and his arm was just as good. But he appeared overmatched in the batter's box and was striking out in 25 percent of his plate appearances versus Double-A pitching. To give themselves more time to mull their decision on Puig, the Dodgers promoted outfielder Alex Castellanos from Triple-A Albuquerque as a stopgap and headed off to Colorado for a series with the Rockies on the first weekend of June.

Privately, the front office had settled on Puig. The week before the club called him up, Kasten flew to Chattanooga and pleaded with the young outfielder to behave. "Please," said Kasten. "Do it for me." While there were doubts that Puig was ready to become a starting out-fielder in the big leagues, the club had little choice but to rush him. The Dodgers were not only losing, they were playing the kind of snoozy, uninspired ball that horrified their new owners, whose main objective was to showcase stars on their upcoming multibillion-dollar cable net-work. Puig was raw, sure, but he played like he had bumblebees in his pants. Even if he failed, he would not be boring. The front office had hoped he would roust the club from its season-long dirt nap. The decision to promote Puig was made even easier three days later when Carl Crawford reached out and slapped a ball down the left-field line at Coors Field, sprinted around first base, and grabbed the back of his right leg on his way to second. Hamstring injuries were now spreading through the Dodgers' clubhouse like a nasty flu bug. On the morn-ing of May 29, there had been no roster spot for Puig. But in the span of seventy-two hours, the Dodgers lost both Kemp and Crawford to the disabled list. Puig flew in to Los Angeles while the club was still in Colorado, and was told to keep his promotion a secret until it was made public the following day. For the next twenty-four hours, Puig referred to himself as "El Secreto." As an homage to the secrecy sur-rounding his call-up, when he was asked to pick a song that would play in the stadium whenever he walked up to bat, Puig chose a tune by Dominican musician Secreto El Famoso Biberon.

Three hours before his first major-league game on June 3, Puig stood behind home plate during batting practice and fastened white batting gloves tight on his hands as he took in the scene with Mark McGwire. Dodger Stadium hadn't yet opened its turnstiles to the public for that evening's game, which meant he was still a mystery to fans. But by the time the last out was recorded, few in the crowd would remember the Dodgers before Puig existed. He had come a long way since Logan White first saw him on that field in Mexico a year earlier when he was overweight and out of shape. Where his body used to contain curves, there were now right angles. The fat around his belly, thighs, and backside had fallen away and been replaced by muscle.

McGwire, who would become a sort of father figure to Puig over the course of the season, quickly ran through basic English with him, making sure the young Cuban knew how to say "fastball," "change-up," and "curve." As the two sluggers conversed in a language they cobbled together on the fly, Mattingly addressed the media and admitted he had lied about Puig's call-up. "I was basically bullshitting the whole time," Mattingly said of his comments the previous week that the team would promote a center fielder instead.

A few hundred thousand people may one day boast that they attended Yasiel Puig's first game, but the truth was the club had been playing so badly that Dodger Stadium was only half full that night. At first pitch, about 75 percent of the seats were empty. A reporter joked that there were as many media members in attendance for Puig's debut as there were spectators. It was hard to fault Dodger fans for staying home. Until Puig's call-up the team's lineup consisted of a hodgepodge of bench players thrown into starting duty in place of injured regulars. When Puig was promoted, the Dodgers had $87 million worth of players on the disabled list. (Fifteen teams had opened the season with payrolls lower than that.) As such, the Dodgers' lackluster line-up for Puig's first game looked like this:

RF Yasiel Puig (first major-league game ever)

2B Nick Punto (subbing for the injured Mark Ellis)

1B Adrian Gonzalez (regular starter)

C Ramon Hernandez (Subbing for the injured A. J. Ellis. Hitting cleanup.
  Would be cut eleven days later and never play in the big leagues again.)

LF Scott Van Slyke (subbing for the injured Carl Crawford)

CF Andre Ethier (Subbing for the injured Matt Kemp. Only third game in his
  eight-year career that he started in center.)

3B Jerry Hairston (Subbing for Luis Cruz, who had to move over to shortstop
  to fill in for Hanley Ramirez. Four months from retirement.)

SS Luis Cruz (Subbing for the injured Hanley Ramirez. Hitting .120. Three
  weeks from being cut.)

P Stephen Fife (Called up from Triple-A earlier that day to replace injured
  Chris Capuano in rotation. Making seventh career start.)

Mattingly opted to bat Puig leadoff for a couple of reasons. First, he wanted to get Puig as many at-bats as possible, especially given how decimated the Dodgers' lineup was. Second, he was wary of a roadkill situation. Puig was so fast around the bases that the skipper worried that if he batted a slower runner in front of him, the young right fielder might run over him. Guys who hit first in a major-league lineup tend to be quick and small, with their primary job being to get on base so the power hitters slotted third, fourth, and fifth can drive them in. Puig was one of the largest leadoff hitters in the game's history. If he was nervous, he hid it well. But that didn't mean he knew what he was doing.

His first at-bat was straightforward, but the Dodgers' coaching staff had to remind him to take his time walking up to the plate before his second at-bat so that he might give the pitcher, who hit in front of him when the lineup turned over, a chance to get back to the dugout. They also told him not to argue with umpires. After running through the simple vocabulary with McGwire during batting practice, Puig went and stood on first base while a member of the club's coaching staff mimicked the pickoff move of Eric Stults, the Padres' starter that night.

Even though Puig was fast, he lacked basic survival instincts, punctuated by his inability to slide. Watching him run the bases reminded some in the organization of handing the keys of a Ferrari to someone who couldn't drive stick. The coaches did not rehearse Stults's move so that Puig might try to run on him. Stealing bases was too advanced. The objective was just to help him avoid getting picked off.

Vin Scully told listeners that night that Puig's pregame pickoff tutorial was something he'd never seen before in his sixty-four seasons on the job. Scully, eighty-five, had been around the game his whole life. Born in the Bronx, he played center field for Fordham University and once even suited up against a Yale squad that featured George H. W. Bush at first base. "I could run, I could throw, but I couldn't hit," Scully would say about his ballplaying career. Upon graduation he began his career as a fill-in for a CBS affiliate in Washington, D.C., focusing on college football. Impressed by his professionalism, legendary Brooklyn Dodgers broadcaster Red Barber invited Scully to join him and Connie Desmond in the booth a year later, in 1950. Like Puig, Scully was just twenty-two years old when he began his Dodger career. When Barber left the club for the Yankees three years later, Scully became the team's lead announcer, at age twenty-five. Going into the 2013 season he was the second-longest-tenured team employee, after former manager Tommy Lasorda, who became a vice president, then a special advisor to the chairman after he retired.

As Scully put on his gray sport coat and fixed his silver and white striped tie before leaving for Dodger Stadium for Puig's first game, even he could not have imagined what was about to unfold. Vin Scully loved baseball, but what he loved even more were the stories of the men who played it. If a player's mother's cousin was a descendant of John Wilkes Booth or related to the astronomer who had discovered Pluto, Scully would figure out a way to weave that fact into the broadcast. One of the best stories he told was about racing Jackie Robinson on ice skates. The two men, along with Robinson's wife, Rachel, had gone to a resort in the Catskills one winter and Scully told them he was going to go skate. The couple asked if they could come along. "When we get there I'd like to race you," Robinson said.

"Jack, I didn't know you skated," Scully said, knowing Robinson had grown up in Southern California.

"I've never skated in my life," Robinson replied. "But I want to race you because that's how I'm going to learn."

Sure enough, when Robinson laced up his skates he could barely stand on the ice. He raced Scully anyway, running on his ankles.

Scully told this story, some fifty years after it happened, with the same sense of wonder that must have overtaken him on the day it took place. The legendary announcer was blessed with the rare combination of a child's enthusiasm and a poet's tongue.

Hours before Puig's first big-league game, Scully and his wife of forty years, Sandi, ducked into the car that waited outside their home in Thousand Oaks and began the forty-mile ride to Dodger Stadium. When he was younger, Scully drove himself to the park every day. But as he grew older a chauffeur shuttled him. During the drive to the stadium, which could take anywhere from forty-five minutes to an hour and a half, Scully and his wife liked to listen to show tunes and standards. Sometimes on the ride home he'd berate himself over mistakes he made during the night's broadcast. Though he was in the middle of his seventh decade working for the Dodgers, because of his advancing age he approached his job like a man employed on a year-to-year basis. For decades, he did every Dodger game, home and away. Then he began to scale back. First by calling away games only within the division, then by not traveling any farther east than Phoenix. Each August, he would announce whether he would return the following season. In 2012 he got so sick during one of the team's trips to San Diego that he thought it might be time to walk away. But he recovered and kept on going.

The Scullys' driver would arrive at Dodger Stadium around four o'clock every day and drop the couple off at the players' entrance near the top of the park. Like Puig, Scully's voice usually entered rooms before he did. He could be heard saying hello to every security guard and usher he passed, calling each of them by name on his way to the elevator, or whistling a standard like "Singin' in the Rain," his all-time favorite song. He and Sandi would then descend three floors to the media level and enter the press box named after him. He'd go over his game notes, film any pregame spots that were needed, then retreat to the press dining room for dinner with his wife. After he finished eating, he would often sidle up to the table with the writers on the Dodgers beat and trade stories about baseball and current events. Young reporters would ask him about watching Sandy Koufax in his prime, and he would never tire of telling them what a marvel he was, how it was impossible to compare any modern-day pitchers to Koufax because he took the mound every four days instead of five, and how he threw twenty-seven complete games in each of his final two seasons because there was no such thing as a pitch count. He would also say that out of everyone he saw in all the games he covered or attended as a fan, watching Willie Mays patrol center field at the vast Polo Grounds was perhaps the most remarkable.

Red Barber had told Scully when he began his career to refrain from being partial to the home team. And though Dodger fans claimed him as their own, Scully never referred to the Dodgers as "we," as in "We need to score some runs," or "We need to not get blown out tonight." He was so good at remaining impartial while broadcasters from other towns descended into homer-ism that it wasn't uncommon to hear a Dodger player wonder if Scully was in the tank for the other team. Scully, of course, was not, but it was the best possible testament to the fairness of his calls. His wife used to watch the games from the owners' suite, but in recent years had taken to sitting behind Scully during his broadcasts because he liked her company. Aside from the odd tech engineer and producer, Scully worked alone. Within sixty seconds of the final pitch of every home game, the Scullys were whisked out of the press box by security, through a crowd of fans hoping to catch a glimpse or a wave, and into the elevator, which was held for them. Then their driver took them home.

Vin Scully had called thousands of Dodger games before Yasiel Puig came into his orbit. In that time, he'd witnessed fourteen Rookies of the Year, ten Cy Young winners, and eight MVPs. But after watching Puig run and hit and throw and revive the energy around Dodger Stadium for two weeks, Scully was just as dumbfounded as everyone else. "He is not to be believed," Scully said. "Because this game is not that easy."

The buzz surrounding Puig was defeaning, but no one knew what to expect. Though the Dodgers desperately needed to change the course of a disastrous season to give fans something to cheer about, club officials asked the team's social media coordinator, Josh Tucker, not to hype Puig too much on the team's Twitter and Instagram feeds, because they didn't want to put even more pressure on the kid.

The Dodgers were playing San Diego at home on June 3, just eight weeks removed from the brawl that had cost them Greinke. They sat in last place in the NL West, with a 23-32 record. Only the Brewers, Mets, Marlins, and Astros had fewer wins—and the latter two clubs entered the season with the lowest payrolls in MLB, at $39 million and $24 million, respectively. When Puig ran onto the field, his crisp white uniform appeared brighter than those worn by his teammates, having not yet been muddied and ripped and colored by dirt and grass stains. He stood in right with the manufacturer's sticker still stuck to the underside of his blue cap. As he stepped up to the plate for his first major-league at-bat, the sparse crowd granted him a valiant ovation. Greinke and Kershaw moved toward the end of the dugout nearest the plate and leaned over the railing to get a better look. Kershaw worked on an enormous wad of bubble gum while Greinke spit sunflower seeds into a paper cup.

Puig stepped up to the plate carrying a two-toned bat with a wood-colored handle, the barrel painted black, and his name carved into it in capital letters. How many hits would it have in it? So many prospects advanced to the major leagues with breathless hype they never lived up to. Would Puig be one of them? He looked out at Eric Stults on the pitcher's mound as though he was already mad at him. One of the most terrifying things about Clayton Kershaw was that his face remained kind while he dominated hitters, like that of a sneaky executioner. Puig more closely resembled Greinke on the diamond: he glared at his opponent with cold eyes that steeled against any human inclination toward empathy. The young Cuban took the first pitch he saw from Stults low for a ball. He was fooled by the next pitch, swinging way ahead of a changeup as if he were trying to hit the ball to the moon. He took Stults's third offering for a ball, then fouled off another changeup. With the count even at two, Stults delivered the perfect pitch to any anxious rookie in his first major-league at-bat: soft, low, and away. Puig surprised everyone by waiting on it, and then reaching out and extending his bat until it almost touched the dirt to hit it. The ball looped over the shortstop Everth Cabrera's head and dunked into left-center field for a single. It wasn't a home run, but he was happy to take the hit. Puig rounded first, shrugged, and smiled. He was erased from the base paths a batter later when Nick Punto grounded into a double play. Up next was Adrian Gonzalez, who yanked a home run into the right-field bullpen, close to the spot where he had hit the ball in his first at-bat with the Dodgers eight months earlier. Gonzalez circled the bases and ran down the length of the dugout looking for Puig, to congratulate him on his first hit. When he found him, he pointed at the kid. They embraced.

In Puig's third at-bat, he hit a chopper to the right side of the infield that deflected off first baseman Kyle Blanks's glove and bounced into the outfield. Puig sprinted to first out of the box, rounded the base, and took an enormous turn toward second, daring the Padres' right fielder, Will Venable, to choose which base to throw to. It was a reckless move that Puig would employ over and over again in his first year with the Dodgers. Sometimes it would result in a rushed throw that sailed into the stands and awarded Puig two extra bases. Other times, he'd be thrown out by thirty feet. Puig played the game the same way he lived his life: gambling on his ability to stay one step ahead of whatever was chasing him.

Like many of his baseball-playing countrymen, Yasiel Puig had tried several times to defect from Cuba before he made it to the United States, including an attempt in April 2012 that was foiled by the U.S. Coast Guard on an open stretch of water between Cuba and Haiti. To finally make it out, he relied on a powerful Mexican drug cartel called the Zetas to smuggle him by speedboat from Cuba to Isla Mujeres, a four-mile-long island near Cancún, just off the coast of the Yucatán Peninsula. Miami investors who had heard of Puig's talents and wanted to cash in on his potential agreed to pay the smugglers $250,000 to get the young Cuban to Mexico, where he could establish residency and then be eligible to sign a free agent contract with an MLB team.

But according to a lawsuit filed against Puig by one of his traveling companions, a boxer named Yunior Despaigne, when the group landed in Mexico the smugglers changed their minds and decided Puig was worth $400,000. Puig, Despaigne, and three others were then held hostage in a Cancún hotel room for a month while the two sides haggled. According to Despaigne, Puig's Miami advisors solved the standoff by finding another group willing to whisk the young slugger to Mexico City, where he could hold that open tryout for interested MLB teams. If Despaigne was telling the truth, Puig's journey to the United States began with stiffing the drug dealers who had snuck him out of Cuba. Despaigne alleged in his lawsuit that he feared for his life because a smuggler named Leo found him in Miami, held a gun to his stomach, and told him to tell Puig that if he didn't pay the Zetas the money they were owed they would kill Despaigne and Puig both. A month later, Despaigne discovered that Leo, whose real name was Yandrys Leon, had been shot to death in Cancún.

This story wasn't unique to Puig. Rare is the Cuban Major League

Baseball player who didn't face the possibility of death, or worse, while fleeing the communist regime. When Puig signed with the Dodgers, no reporters knew for sure how he had gotten to Mexico, though the drug cartel rumors flew around him from the start. His teammates were aware of that theory; they spoke of it to each other in hushed tones, but most thought of it as one of the tall tales that added to the lore that surrounded him. The seriousness of his situation didn't hit them until later, when a team meeting was called in Pittsburgh ten days after Puig's call-up, in mid-June, and players were told that they were going to begin traveling with private security. No one ever told them that the added guards were for Puig, but his teammates soon noticed that the four hired men who took turns sweeping hotels before they arrived seemed concerned only with the young right fielder.

Puig never discussed with teammates or reporters his terrifying journey to the United States. In fact, in his first year in the big leagues he mostly stonewalled the media altogether. "I don't really like the press," he explained in one of the rare one-on-one interviews he gave. It was hard to blame him. Back in Cuba journalists were government spies. Puig didn't trust anyone whose job was to uncover truths, especially now that he was harboring dark secrets about how he had escaped his home country. At the end of Puig's first week, Luis Cruz took a roll of masking tape and cordoned off a small section of carpet in front of their adjoining lockers. Puig got down on his hands and knees and wrote "No Reporters" in Spanish with a blue Sharpie pen on the tape. "He likes playing," said Cruz. "He doesn't like all the attention."

But that attention was inevitable after the way his first game ended. In the top of the ninth the Dodgers were leading the Padres 2–1 when they brought in Brandon League to close out the game. Colletti had traded two middling prospects to Seattle for League at the deadline in 2012, and the twenty-nine-year-old right-hander did well in the final two months of the season for Los Angeles, posting the best numbers of his career. As a reward, Colletti gave him a three-year contract for $22.5 million. Despite his success in Dodger blue, the deal looked like a mistake from the day it was signed, just like the contract Colletti had given Andre Ethier months earlier. The influx of cash Colletti had to play with was not without its downside. Outbidding everyone else for superstars like Greinke and Kershaw was one thing. Overpaying guys like Ethier and League was another. Each club had only twenty-five roster spots. It was much easier to cut underperforming players who weren't still owed eight figures. If a guy making the minimum struggled, the club could ax him from the roster with no real skin lost. But if a guy making a lot of money floundered, the Dodgers were hurt not only by his play on the field but also by the fact that they were stuck with him.

One of the most curious things about baseball is that men who pitch the ninth inning are paid way more than those who pitch the sixth, seventh, or eighth—even though they're responsible for the same number of outs. This is because most general managers believe that a player must possess a certain type of bravery to be a closer, because the last three outs of a game are the hardest to get, even when facing the bottom of a lineup. Colletti, in particular, had an affinity for pitchers who had amassed a pile of saves in the past, so much so that a player's career save total seemed to trump better, more accurate measures of his ability. First and foremost, closers need to strike out hitters. This is because when a batter makes contact with a baseball, even when he is fooled, it has a chance of falling in for a hit. A strikeout neutralizes bad luck. In 2012, the National League's most dominant closer, Atlanta's Craig Kimbrel, fanned 116 batters in 62 innings. In the four months with Seattle before he was dealt to Los Angeles, League had struck out just 27 batters in 44 frames. While League excelled at inducing ground-ball double plays with his sinker, he didn't make batters miss. And because of this, the Mariners had replaced him as closer with the second-year fireballer Tom Wilhelmsen.

What made League's contract even more perplexing was that the Dodgers had a twenty-five-year-old homegrown reliever who was much better. In 145 career innings, Kenley Jansen had struck out an incredible 236 batters, which was 41 percent of the men he faced. He did this while posting a 2.22 earned run average. And he did it with one pitch that everyone knew was coming. Jansen's cut fastball reminded many of the brilliant Yankee closer Mariano Rivera's, except that Jansen threw it harder. He stood six foot five and weighed 265 pounds. At nearly seven feet, his stride toward home plate when he threw a pitch was one of the longest in the majors and had the effect of making his 97 mph fastball seem even faster. But heading into the 2013 season, the Dodgers' front office didn't feel comfortable moving him into the closer's spot, as if he would somehow combust under the weight of it. Perhaps that was because they had signed Jansen—who hailed from the tiny Dutch Caribbean island of Curaçao—as a catcher, and converted him to pitcher only after they discovered he couldn't hit. In 2009, at age twenty-one, he had even served as the starting catcher for Team Netherlands in the World Baseball Classic. Jansen entered the 2013 season with only two and a half years of experience as a major-league pitcher, a statistic Colletti seemed to value more than his strikeout rate. The Dodgers' GM preferred League to close games.

That decision had been a disaster. On May 31, League owned a 5.31 earned run average and had blown three wins the struggling Dodgers could not afford to give away. Jansen pitched a clean eighth inning in Puig's debut game on June 3, striking out two. When Mattingly brought in League in the ninth, he fell behind to Padres second baseman Jedd Gyorko, before getting him to ground out to shortstop. Then, with one away, he walked the right fielder, Chris Denorfia, on pitches that weren't close to being strikes. Many fans in the stadium began to boo. League grimaced and paced behind the rubber, looking about as comfortable on the mound as if he were walking barefoot on cactus needles.

Kyle Blanks was on deck, which was significant, because with Carlos Quentin out of the lineup that day, if any Padres hitter could tie the game with one swing it was the six-foot-six, 265-pound Blanks. League's best skill was getting batters to hit ground balls, and a ground ball in this situation would likely result in a game-ending double play. League knew that to get the result he wanted he needed to keep the ball down, so his first two pitches were low and out of the strike zone. His third pitch was belt high. Blanks went with it, and hit it deep toward the right-field wall, over Puig's head. Puig sprinted back toward the fence, running an awkward banana route toward the ball. It looked like a home run off the bat. But before the ball could clear the fence the night sky knocked it down. With his momentum carrying him backward, Puig caught the ball one-handed on the warning track, took two steps to his left, and fired it toward first base across his body. Denorfia had been off with the pitch and now he was sprinting back toward first. The ball arrived a split second before he did for an improbable game-ending double play.

That game-winning throw from the wall was Puig's career highlight for less than twenty-four hours. In his second game he hit two home runs and drove in five. Most young players come up to the big leagues trying to pull everything, and opposing pitchers use that tendency to their advantage by feeding them a steady diet of pitches away. Puig surprised them by driving those pitches over the right-field fence. When Puig hit his third homer of the week in just his fourth game, a stunned Scully delivered this call: "And a high drive into deep right field—I don't believe it! A grand slam home run!" Then he stayed silent for ninety seconds through Puig's curtain call and two replays, letting the crowd's euphoric screams narrate the scene. "I have learned over the years that there comes a rare and precious moment where there is absolutely nothing better than silence," Scully said afterward. "Nothing better than to be absolutely speechless to sum up a situation. And that was the moment."

The mechanics of Puig's swing were as gorgeous as Logan White had described to Kasten back when he first saw him taking batting practice on that field in Mexico City. His arms were long and strong enough to cover the outer part of the plate. And because his hands hung particularly close to his body when he swung, he could stay back on inside pitches rather than flail over them. This meant that there weren't very many places where a pitcher could get away with throwing the ball to him. "If you catch too much of the plate you're basically fucked," said one NL West starter. For all the emotion with which he played the game, Puig was quiet in the batter's box and held his bat still until he began his swing. "Puig is a stud!" tweeted Braves perennial all-star third baseman Chipper Jones the day after Puig's grand slam against his former team on June 6. "Bat stays in the zone a long time."

Puig became the second batter since 1900 to hit four home runs in his first five games. For his efforts, he was named the National League's player of the week. A pitcher who gave up one of those home runs was heard saying after the game, "There's no way that guy is twenty-two." But it wasn't just his stats that got the rest of the sport talking. Mike Trout was the best player in baseball, but he went about his business on and off the field in such a calm and composed manner that he was almost boring. Puig was a human backflip. He stood in the batter's box and admired his home runs; he stared at pitchers who threw inside. He showed up to the ballpark when he felt like it, and ran through stop signs held up by the Dodgers' third-base coach, Tim Wallach, because he thought he knew better. Opposing players could not stand him. "If he's my teammate I probably try to teach him how to behave in the big leagues," said Diamondbacks catcher Miguel Montero a month into Puig's career. "He's creating a bad reputation around the league, and it's unfortunate because the talent he has is to be one of the greatest players in the big leagues." When told of Montero's comments before a game in Arizona, a Dodger pitcher nodded in agreement. "He's right," he said. "But I don't really care because he rakes."

After Puig nailed the runner at first to win his first game with the Dodgers, there was little hope of coaches getting him to hit a cutoff man ever again. "I always try to put on a show for the fans," Puig explained later. "They come to spend their time and lose sleep watching us play. To me, it is one of the more emotional things in baseball." And put on a show he did. In his first month with the Dodgers, Puig collected forty-four hits and was named the NL's player of the month. The only player to post more hits in his debut month was Yankee great Joe DiMaggio, who had forty-eight in May 1936. Puig had never even heard of DiMaggio. He had no context for the pace he set. Even though the coaching staff had seen him hit well in spring, they were stunned by the tear he was on. "I don't think any of us were really thinking this is something that could keep happening over an extended period of time," said Mattingly.

The mood around Dodger Stadium reminded some old-timers of the pandemonium surrounding Fernando Valenzuela's debut season in 1981, when he won the Cy Young and Rookie of the Year awards. The forty minutes or so between the young right fielder's at-bats felt like Puigatory. The club raced to stock concession stands with his number-66 jersey. "Every friend, celebrity and executive I know has been calling me for Dodgers tickets now!" tweeted Magic Johnson. "Dodger Stadium is the place to be!!" But the excitement in the crowd didn't match the energy in the Dodgers' locker room. While his teammates—the pitchers, in particular—were happy to receive the offensive boost Puig provided, the Dodgers still sat in last place.

Juan Uribe did his best to loosen the tension in the clubhouse. Though he still hadn't regained the starting third-base job from Luis Cruz, he was hitting much better than he had in his previous two years as a Dodger, and showed up to work every day in the same goofy mood. It was not uncommon for him to wear a bright red or purple suit on travel days, and walk to the team bus donning aviator shades with a cigar hanging from his mouth. He was the only teammate who could tease Kemp and get away with it. He would sometimes approach the sensitive slugger singing "Oh na naaa," which was part of the chorus from Kemp's ex-girlfriend Rihanna's hit song "What's My Name?" When the Dodgers were in San Francisco in September, a television in the clubhouse showed a game where Brewers center fielder Carlos Gomez hit a home run against Atlanta and barked his way around the bases, causing both benches to clear before he reached home plate.

Dodger players were glued to the fight. Kemp stood in the center of the room under the television, shaking his head and yelling, "Wow!" He could not believe how angry Gomez was. Uribe jumped up from his chair and grabbed Kemp by the shoulders, acting as though he were holding him back from a fight. "That's like you in San Diego!" he said, referring to Kemp's reaction during the Greinke-Quentin brawl back in April. "Hold me back! Hold me back!" The rest of the room laughed. And after realizing how silly he'd been, Kemp did, too.

It wasn't just Kemp whom Uribe goofed on. The Dominican-born player gave up on trying to pronounce Skip Schumaker's name, so he began calling him Chewbacca. He took Puig under his wing, too, and chided him when he hid from media in the shower or the commissary. While the Dodgers' front office loved that Puig's play helped revive an otherwise flatlining club, many of his teammates worried about putting so much pressure on a player who was so emotional and immature. His stellar play gave the coaches no other option; regardless of his mental lapses and temper flares, he was allowed to take up residence in the club's central nervous system because he hit like, well, DiMaggio.

A week after Puig's debut, the first-place Diamondbacks came to L.A. for a three-game set on June 10. A Dodgers sweep would cut Arizona's lead to four and a half games. But if the Diamondbacks won all three contests the Dodgers would trail them by ten and a half games with a little over half the season to go. With Kershaw on the mound for the first game, the club felt good about its chances of gaining some ground. The big lefty was his usual self, going seven innings and giving up one earned run before handing the ball to Jansen for the eighth. Jansen tossed a perfect frame, and the Dodgers took a 3–1 lead into the ninth. Brandon League walked to the mound to close it out. After striking out Montero, League imploded. He gave up a double, three singles, and a walk, and the Dodgers watched the Diamondbacks score four runs to win the game. In a season full of bitter losses, this one tasted the worst. Throughout their slide, the club at least believed that when they sent Kershaw to the mound, it would stop the bleeding.

League's waste of Kershaw's gem was devastating. After it was over and the players were left to dress in silence, one veteran infielder said he hoped a blogger would ask a dumb question so he could pop him.

The best managers understand that a baseball season is grueling and cruel, and slumps can gnaw away at the confidence of even the most talented players. When a guy struggles, often the worst thing a skipper can do is panic and change his role, especially if he needs something out of that player down the road. The Dodgers were committed to League for two and a half more seasons. The last thing Mattingly wanted to do was add to his self-doubt. Even though League was a millionaire many times over, the money didn't make the humiliation of public failure any easier. Dodger fans booed him at the stadium and cursed him on social media. The pain struggling players go through is rarely as bad as the anguish their families feel, sitting in their aisle seats at the stadium for quick exits or in front of their televisions at home, peering at the carnage through their fingers, helpless to stop it. Pitchers' next of kin had it the worst. Their wives are often as nervous during May games as the team's most die-hard fans are during the postseason: sometimes one pitch away from vomiting. In the middle of League's ninth-inning shellacking his wife, Sasha, burst into tears.

Most Dodger players loved how patient Don Mattingly was, except for when they needed him to hurry up and make a decision. "Leaguer's our guy," Mattingly would say over and over again whenever he was asked about the closer's status after a poor outing. Players respected Mattingly for his loyalty, but in this case his optimism was hurting the club. While management worried Jansen might come down with a case of the youth yips if Mattingly named him the new closer, his teammates thought the Dutch Caribbean righty had the best stuff in the bullpen and the perfect temperament to finish games. Jansen seemed to exist on island time, as if his growing up so close to the changing ocean tides taught him he could not stop the waves from breaking but he could learn how to surf. Jansen never got too high or too low and he spent more time living in his right arm than in his brain. His relaxed attitude was given away by his uniform pants, which he wore so long they often caught and ripped on his spikes. He never seemed to worry about tripping and falling.

While some closers grew enormous beards or sprinted into the game to the throbbing of heavy metal music, Jansen kept his hair a smidge longer than a buzz cut and jogged in to Tupac Shakur's "California Love," which mostly made the crowd want to get up and dance. He wore number 74 because it was the address of the house he grew up in back in Curaçao. His first big-league paychecks had gone toward paying off what his family owed on it, and he never wanted to forget his roots. Mattingly didn't want to make a closer change, but League's struggles didn't leave him much choice. The following day he named Jansen the new closer.

No one would remember June 11, 2013, as the day the Dodgers finally made Kenley Jansen their ninth-inning guy. No one would remember it as the day that Chris Withrow—a former first-round draft pick whose fastball touched 100 mph—was called up, either.

While the new Dodger owners packed their team with all-stars, the front office of their small-market division-rival Diamondbacks realized that their window for winning the NL West might have closed when McCourt was run out of town. Arizona had been interested in signing Hyun-Jin Ryu before the season, and submitted a bid to his Korean team during the auction process. Their general manager, Kevin Towers, told the press that the Dodgers had blown everyone away with their $25.7 million posting fee for Ryu, which was double the second-highest rumored bid for the lefty, which came from the Cubs. The Diamondbacks had been in on Puig, too, but didn't offer anything close to what the Dodgers paid to get him. "When you have that wherewithal financially it doesn't mean you're the best scouting organization," a frustrated Towers said in a radio interview in mid-July. "You just have the wherewithal to go out and buy whatever you want."

Determining an international player's value was a fool's errand, since overseas stats didn't necessarily translate. The Cubs never confirmed what they bid on Ryu, but they had been aggressive in the international market, inking Jorge Soler to the $30 million deal months earlier that inspired the Dodgers to sign Puig. If Los Angeles had outbid the next-highest offer for Ryu by tens of million of dollars in the blind auction, was it still bad business if Ryu was worth more than they paid? Mark Walter had already demonstrated that he didn't care that others thought he was overpaying when he bought the Dodgers because he believed everyone else was undervaluing the club. He was right. Perhaps because they did not want to miss out on another Soler or Puig, the Diamondbacks would change their philosophy and sign twenty-four-year-old Cuban third baseman Yasmany Tomas to a six-year deal for $68.5 million in 2014.

Because they would never have the cash to outbid teams like the Dodgers on the free agent market for players like Greinke, Kershaw, or Kemp, the D-backs embraced the philosophy that there was a right way to play the game, and a wrong way. The right way involved a strict adherence to baseball's unwritten rules: runners were to be advanced station to station, a man should play for the name on the front of his jersey and not the name on the back, the tallest weed was to be plucked, etc. In that way, the culture clash between the Dodgers and Diamondbacks was a microcosm of the battle between capitalism and communism. For Arizona, the team was more significant than any single player. And any opposing player caught celebrating a personal accomplishment for one second longer than necessary was to be greeted with a fastball to the numbers in his next at-bat. Towers made it clear the following off-season that if one of his pitchers shied away from throwing at opponents on purpose when asked, he would be traded. He even hinted that the club's pitching coach, Charles Nagy, was fired because his staff didn't do it enough. Whether it was jealousy of the Dodgers' new financial freedom, personality clashes, or a little of both, the Diamondbacks' front office seemed to resent the way the Dodgers did business. That anger trickled down to their coaches and players. Puig would push them over the edge.

The Diamondbacks were managed by Kirk Gibson, the man who had enjoyed the most famous at-bat in Dodgers history. Forget just Dodger history: the image of a hobbled Gibson limping around the bases after hitting that improbable ninth-inning pinch-hit home run off the Oakland Hall of Fame closer Dennis Eckersley to win Game 1 of the 1988 World Series was one of the more enduring moments in the history of baseball. It was so sweet a memory in Los Angeles that Gibson could have lived off it there for the rest of his life, like his manager, Tommy Lasorda. But Gibson wasn't the type. While his teammate Orel Hershiser allowed himself to be embraced by Dodger fans after his playing days were over by returning as a broadcaster, Gibson was never comfortable with the sentimentality of hanging around. He later sold his World Series trophy and NL MVP award from the 1988 season, and also his bat, jersey, and batting helmet from the at-bat that made him a Dodger legend. And when the Dodgers decided to do a Kirk Gibson bobblehead giveaway when the Diamondbacks came to L.A. in 2012, Gibson refused to be shown on the video board and tried to hide from the camera. "I think it's totally ridiculous," he said at the time.

The Dodgers should not have been surprised when Puig stepped into the box on June 11 and was greeted with a fastball to the nose. As Puig sat on home plate, team trainers ran through a concussion test, before stopping halfway through and realizing they needed a translator. The Diamondbacks' pitcher, Ian Kennedy, had not meant to hit Puig in the face but showed no remorse. Perhaps he meant to brush him back. The ball had left his hand in a straight line for Puig's head, and it was traveling too fast for the young right fielder to duck out of the way. Puig was lucky the ball glanced off the cartilage covering the tip of his nostrils. Had it tailed a quarter inch to the right the bones in his cheek and eye socket might have been shattered, similar to what would happen to Marlins slugger Giancarlo Stanton a year later. Puig stayed in the game and took his base.

When Greinke hit Miguel Montero in the back with a fastball the following inning in retaliation, the Dodgers thought it was over. The Diamondbacks disagreed. After Greinke stepped up to the plate in the bottom half of the inning, Kennedy threw a first-pitch fastball at his neck. Greinke held his ground and shrugged his shoulder high so that the ball hit it instead. The force of the blow was so hard that it knocked his helmet off. Greinke stood expressionless in the batter's box, then smirked as if to say, *Great, I'm going to be in the middle of a brawl again.* And instantly it was on. Every player and coach from both teams emptied onto the field until five dozen men were shoving each other near the visiting on-deck circle. Puig roundhouse-punched Arizona utility man Eric Hinske in the back of the head. Dodger reliever J. P. Howell pushed Diamondbacks assistant hitting coach Turner Ward over the railing that divided the crowd from the field, as if he were a WWF wrestler. Schumaker pushed his way into the middle of the scrum, looking for Kennedy. "I'd never seen a pitcher throw at two different batters' heads before," he said after the game. "He ran to the bench right after he hit Greinke." It had taken Puig only a week in the majors to incite a riot. But Puig was just a subplot in the bizarre drama that was taking place on the field. It seemed unlikely that Ian Kennedy thought of hitting Greinke all on his own, and after the game he didn't seem to care that he got Puig in the face. "He plays with a lot of arrogance," Kennedy said later of the Dodgers' young right fielder. But even if Puig's beaning had been an accident, that fastball to Greinke wasn't. There was no doubt in Mattingly's mind it had come from Gibson.

It wasn't the fact that Dodger batters were being hit that enraged Mattingly. The culture of the game dictated that if a player was plunked, his teammate had the right to retaliate and hit a batter on the other team. Macho tough-guy stuff was not only tolerated, it was celebrated. Anything from the backside down the legs was fair game. But Mattingly believed that if a guy couldn't throw inside without hitting someone on or near his head, then he shouldn't throw inside. In

1920, Cleveland Indians shortstop Ray Chapman had been killed by a beanball to the temple. Today's batters wore helmets but they weren't indestructible. Besides, the ball thrown at Greinke was headed for his neck, which could have severed an artery.

An angry Mattingly wanted Gibson. As he ran toward the D-Backs' manager, he pushed Arizona's bench coach, former Tigers great Alan Trammell, out of his way and to the ground. He felt bad about that later, saying he didn't even realize he had steamrolled his friend Tramm. Fights were not uncommon in the sport, but it was rare to see opposing coaches scrap. By the time Mattingly reached Gibson, McGwire had already grabbed a fistful of Gibson's jersey at the neck, and was screaming and cursing at him. When the Diamondbacks' third-base coach, Matt Williams, tried to intervene, McGwire grabbed him by the collar, too, and held them both by the throat at the same time. After both teams were separated, the Dodgers came back and won the game 5–3. Jansen pitched a perfect ninth to close it, striking out two. Some predicted that after two months of mediocrity, maybe the second brawl would be the catalyst to help the Dodgers turn the corner. It wasn't. Los Angeles dropped six of its next eight games.

Making matters worse, the following week news leaked that Kershaw had turned down a record-breaking contract extension. Kershaw was furious. The report lacked key details about the terms of the contract, including the fact that the Dodgers had wanted to lock him up for the next fifteen years plus an additional personal services contract after his playing days were over. He had not declined to sign the deal because he thought $300 million was too low a figure; he said no because the idea of signing a lifetime contract at twenty-five years old was terrifying. What if something went wrong? What if he tore his labrum or snapped his ulnar collateral ligament during the second year of a fifteen-year deal and could no longer pitch and was still owed all that money and his salary obligation hurt the team and the fans hated him for it? What if the Dodgers were terrible and he never got his shot at a ring? What if Colletti and Kasten filled the locker room with megalomaniacs who didn't care about winning? Kershaw thought about these things more than he thought about the money. He hated that the report made him seem greedy. But what he hated even more was the idea that someone had leaked the news to a reporter to make him look bad. Kershaw didn't play games through the media. He was as private a man as he was proud. The report felt like a betrayal. Some of Kershaw's teammates wondered if this was the sort of thing that would drive him to free agency. Between this leak and the way the team was playing, it was beginning to look as though Clayton Kershaw would walk when his contract expired at the end of the 2014 season.

Meanwhile the Dodgers' roster was still a mess. While Mattingly refrained from criticizing the front office to the press, friends said he was beyond frustrated by the construction of the team. Among other problems, with Kemp on the disabled list he had no center fielder on his roster. (How could he be expected to win more games than he lost with no one to play the most important outfield position?) Kasten did not want to fire Mattingly. "I don't think anyone thought he was the problem, or that making that change was going to magically fix everything," Kasten said later. "But as we were looking, searching, struggling for answers that was obviously a thing you think about."

Kasten knew the Dodgers' malaise wasn't Mattingly's fault. He hadn't hired these players, and he didn't run around taking a mallet to their arms and legs. Mattingly wanted young players who were hungry; Colletti kept stuffing his roster with washed-up veterans. The disconnect between the two men became obvious in their stalemate over the club's backup catcher. During the first week of the season, Colletti had traded Aaron Harang to the Rockies for the aging Ramon Hernandez with the idea that he would be A. J. Ellis's backup. Mattingly preferred twenty-five-year-old rookie Tim Federowicz. Because Mattingly didn't have the power to cut Hernandez, the Dodgers carried three catchers for nine games in May, instead of the usual two. Mattingly started Federowicz twice and used him as a pinch hitter in five other games. He didn't play Hernandez once. Colletti responded by optioning Federowicz down to Triple-A, to the ire of the coaching staff.

On June 22, the Dodgers sat in last place with an abysmal 30-42 record, nine and a half games out of first and trending downward. Mattingly woke up on that Saturday morning, the second day of summer, still the manager of the Los Angeles Dodgers.

He did not know if he would last the weekend.

7

THE RUN

On what Mattingly figured to be his day of reckoning, the ball found its way into Zack Greinke's right hand, as it always seemed to in the season's biggest moments. Though he'd been a Dodger for only three months, Greinke had already been at the center of mega-brawls with two division rivals. And now here he was, back on the same mound where his clavicle was snapped in one of those dustups just weeks earlier, pitching to save his skipper's job. While Puig had been awesome in his three weeks with the Dodgers, smacking home runs and gunning down runners and generally playing like an inspired maniac fans couldn't take their eyes off, he couldn't stop the club's free fall by himself. Heading into their June 22 contest at San Diego, Los Angeles had dropped six of its last eight.

Players knew Mattingly's job was at risk, so they scoured social media and texted their agents and traded gossip. One popular theory was that Gerry Hunsicker, whom Kasten hired in the off-season as senior advisor of baseball operations, would take over for Colletti and replace Mattingly with Rays bench coach Dave Martinez. Hunsicker had been the Astros' GM from 1995–2004 before going to work as an executive for Tampa, and was thought to be close with the popular, bilingual coach. Martinez would have made sense. The Rays were respected throughout the industry as a model organization that made the most out of their limited resources by adhering to the sabermetric vision of their bright young general manager, Andrew Friedman. Plus, Tampa's coaches and front-office executives had earned the reputation of being loyal to Friedman and to each other, which influenced the Rays' strong clubhouse chemistry. When Mattingly spoke of the need to get his players to rally around each other he liked to use the analogy of a group of men tugging on the same end of a rope, even though he knew it was corny. The Rays were famous for doing just that; so deep was the organizational trust that Friedman worked without a contract, despite being one of the most sought-after executives in baseball. Though their payroll had never crossed the $100 million threshold, the Rays made it all the way to the World Series in 2008. The rich Dodgers, meanwhile, were spiraling into chaos, with their coaches, players, general manager, scouting department, and player development executives pointing fingers at each other in an effort to stay employed.

Another rumor had both Mattingly and his bench coach Trey Hillman fired, with Tim Wallach promoted to interim manager. The veracity of the gossip didn't matter: the point was, it was getting louder by the day. No one knew for sure what Kasten and Walter were waiting for, but many players and staff members thought that if the Dodgers failed to win both weekend games in San Diego, Donnie Baseball would be gone.

While most of his players continued to like Mattingly, some covering the team wondered if the club might do better with another skipper in charge. Mattingly was a good man, but perhaps his innate kindness hurt his ability to lead. Maybe the club needed a screamer who didn't suffer superstar egos. And perhaps a guy with a weaker conscience wouldn't agonize over demoting a struggling player like Brandon League.

Though he was no pushover, Kasten was notorious for hating to fire people, as if the potential to upgrade a position wasn't worth giving off the impression that his organization was in turmoil. Maybe it wouldn't come to that. Looking at the starting pitching matchup, the Dodgers had the clear advantage in sending Greinke to square off against the erratic Edinson Volquez on June 22. But in a testament to Mattingly's rotten luck, Volquez took a no-hitter into the sixth inning. He then regressed to his usual self, however, walking the bases loaded and allowing a run to score on a Skip Schumaker groundout. The Dodgers hung four more on San Diego in the sixth behind an Adrian Gonzalez home run and two Padre errors. That cushion was more than enough for Greinke, who gave the Dodgers eight dominant innings, allowing just one run in his last frame of work. The next day Los Angeles beat San Diego 3–1 on back-to-back ninth-inning blasts from Gonzalez and Hanley Ramirez. Then they went home to play the Giants and won the next game and the game after that. And when Kenley Jansen fooled San Francisco's pinch-hitter Brandon Belt with a cut fastball that caused him to pop out to short to end the game the following night on June 26, the Dodgers completed the series sweep and took their fifth game in a row. The home crowd erupted with full throats usually reserved for playoff victories, as if sweeping their rivals meant that after months of misery the season was not lost. Mattingly's decision to make Jansen the closer had paid immediate dividends. Jansen had struck out twenty-eight since his last walk; he hadn't walked a batter in six weeks.

The mood in the Dodgers' locker room seemed to lighten a tick with each victory, as if someone were controlling the dimmer switch where players dressed. Kershaw had started the June 26 game and gave up two runs in eight innings before turning the ball over to Jansen. The Dodgers' ace had walked Giants second baseman Marco Scutaro to lead off the top of the fourth inning, then given up a home run to catcher Buster Posey. Under normal circumstances Kershaw would have berated himself post-game for walking a weak hitter before an op-posing team's best player. But after the game Kershaw stood in front of his locker and smiled. Because of how rotten the season's first eleven weeks were, this winning streak felt better to him than a shutout ever did. "Winning does a lot," he said. "It puts aside a lot of differences, it puts aside bad blood." He caught himself and added: "Not that we had any of that." By the time the Fourth of July rolled around, the club that had been left for dead had won ten of eleven. Meanwhile, the other teams in the division were collapsing. On June 22 the last-place Dodgers trailed the rest of the NL West by a combined 28.5 games. By Independence Day they had trimmed that deficit to 2.5.

As the Dodgers starters began to get well, the club's front office started cutting bait on players who weren't performing. After Hanley Ramirez returned from the disabled list the day after Puig's call-up, opening-day shortstop Justin Sellers played only one more game for the Dodgers' big-league club. They released backstop Ramon Hernan-dez and third baseman Luis Cruz, installed rookie Tim Federowicz as backup catcher, and put Uribe back at the hot corner. They designated reliever Matt Guerrier for assignment, then traded him to Chicago for Carlos Mármol. That move surprised many around the team, since Cubs president Theo Epstein was thought still to be smarting over Colletti's reneging on an agreement the two men made the previous summer to send pitcher Ryan Dempster to Los Angeles. Some insiders thought Epstein was so angry that he would try to avoid trading with Colletti again. But the Guerrier-for-Marmol swap was much smaller stakes, and it was executed at the behest of the Cubs' catching coach and Joe Torre's godson, Mike Borzello—the same guy who had en-couraged Kershaw to throw a slider years earlier when he worked for the Dodgers.

Then, on July 6, the Dodgers traded three minor-league pitching prospects to the Marlins for starter Ricky Nolasco. That move turned out to be deft. After trotting out middling bush leaguers to replace injured members of their rotation only to watch them get torched during the first few months of the season, the Dodgers were much better with Nolasco on the mound as their number-four starter. The club won ten of his first twelve starts. To help things along, the Dodgers got Matt Kemp and Carl Crawford back, too. Kemp's return was short-lived, however. After just ten games back from his hamstring injury, he felt something in his left shoulder pull, and landed back on the disabled list. But this time the Dodgers kept winning.

A month after their brawl with the Diamondbacks the Dodgers flew to Arizona on July 8 with a newfound swagger in their step. Perhaps Puig's confidence was rubbing off. He had good reason to be cocky. That day, he became only the second player since 1950 to hit over .400 through his first 130 major-league at-bats. When he collected his second hit of the game in the fifth inning, his average stood at .415. Each time Puig stepped into the batter's box at Chase Field, the Arizona faithful booed him louder than they cheered any of their own players.

While hecklers had no problems shouting Puig down, nobody in the Dodgers' organization wanted to be the bad cop. He often arrived to the ballpark late and wasn't punished for it. He made reporters stand by his locker and wait an hour to interview him, only to tell them through a PR person that he wasn't talking that day. He tested limits of behavior like a small child, and was smart enough to learn quickly that he could get away with a lot. Team rules became optional because breaking them brought no consequences. Some Dodger players who were frustrated with Mattingly's reluctance to discipline Puig wondered if he was not free to do so without the approval of the front office. Puig, it seemed, was Kasten's baby. After all, it was Kasten who gave the go-ahead to sign him for a hefty sum that was mocked by the rest of the league in what was turning out to be a genius move. Puig was the feather in the new ownership group's cap. Did the Dodgers really want to bench a guy they were building a marketing campaign around?

Mattingly had good reason to avoid being a disciplinarian when it came to Puig. He had witnessed firsthand what happened with Matt Kemp when Joe Torre went all tough love on him, and he couldn't afford to alienate Puig in the same way. "He's not a bad kid," Mattingly said before a game during that series in Arizona when a reporter asked him for a character assessment. While Mattingly's affection toward Puig seemed genuine, that warmth was no doubt influenced by the fact that the kid had helped him keep his job. As Mattingly defended Puig that day in the Chase Field dugout, Puig was taking batting practice some thirty feet away and launching home runs off the scoreboard.

Did it fall on Colletti, himself a former public relations man, to tell Puig to show up on time? One of the biggest misconceptions about Puig was that he was a dumb, naïve kid thrown into a new culture without a clue of how to handle himself. In reality, despite the language barrier, Puig was able to read situations well and manipulate those around him to get his way. Most rookies do what they are told because they're worried about making waves. But Puig never acted like a rookie in the clubhouse. When the Dodgers' PR staff asked him to do interviews, he often shrugged, knowing they were optional for him. He also seemed to have a photographic memory, especially when it came to slights. When an out-of-town reporter lobbed a question he didn't like at him after a game at Dodger Stadium, Puig looked at the man and said: "You asked me that question at Yankee Stadium a few weeks ago." It had been six weeks. He had not forgotten.

One reporter who had covered famous players on the Dodgers beat for decades—from Valenzuela to Piazza and Nomo and Manny Ramirez—said he had never seen anything like Puig's distaste for reporters. In fairness to Puig, the media demands were so excessive that if he had honored every request he would not have had time to eat or sleep or hit. But the club did him no favors with the press by allowing him to make up rules as he went along. When Fernando Valenzuela was a rookie, to help him deal with the onslaught of reporters the Dodgers made him available via press conference before the first game of every series, and after each of his starts. The media was to leave him alone the rest of the time, so that he might have room to breathe. This worked out well for everyone involved. If a writer complained about Valenzuela's unavailability, the club could say, "Well, you should have been there Monday when he talked." The Dodgers set no such parameters with Puig. But even if their public relations staff had tried to fix a schedule like that, it seemed questionable that Puig would do what they told him to. Most fans don't care if an athlete gets along with a newspaper reporter, and that's reasonable. But because Puig was now the most talked-about player in the game, and his past was such a question mark and he shared nothing about himself, the people he blew off were left scrambling to fill in the blanks. Puig's fear that the media would bury him became a self-fulfilling prophecy.

This became evident when a national television reporter went to San Francisco the weekend before the Arizona series to film an interview with Puig about his first month in the big leagues. Whether Puig had agreed to do it or club officials just hoped he might, when Puig backed out, the reporter was understandably upset. Later that day, Uribe chided Puig within earshot of reporters, saying he should be forthright with media so they could get what they need and leave the locker room. Every clubhouse is open to the press three and a half hours before the game until the team goes to stretch, and then again after the game. Players understood that reporters had to invade their space to do their jobs, but what they hated more than anything was when media stood around in there forever. "Who are you waiting for?" a team's PR person would ask a lingering scribe, as if to say, *If you aren't waiting to speak to someone in particular and are just loitering then get the hell out.* Puig making media wait by his locker for an hour after each game irked the rest of the team, who preferred being naked around as few strangers as possible.

The conversation between Puig and Uribe had been lighthearted, as Uribe usually took a humorous tack when trying to get his point across. The men were shocked when they learned that the journalist

Puig blew off reported that Dodger players were tired of Puig's act, as evidenced by the affable Uribe screaming at him. The story gained traction because Puig had been involved in a shouting match with the Giants' fiery closer, Sergio Romo, earlier that day. Romo had retired Hanley Ramirez to end the previous day's game, and mocked the Dodgers' shortstop by mimicking the celebratory hand gesture Ramirez made to teammates after someone did something good. Puig took notice. The next day, Puig flipped his bat after singling off Romo in the ninth inning, then taunted him five batters later as he jogged home to score the go-ahead run off an A. J. Ellis double. The drama between Romo and Puig was, for the most part, benign. Though both men often let their emotions get the better of them on the diamond, their actions toward each other were more annoying than malicious. The story about Puig and Uribe was different. Puig heard the report and was hurt by it. The reporter was fluent in Spanish, so he had understood the conversation with Uribe. Puig's friends say the incident ended any possibility of mending his relationship with the press.

The young right fielder's tiff with the reporter continued into Arizona, and got even more personal. Before the first game of the series, Puig was standing behind home plate waiting his turn during batting practice when a group including retired Diamondbacks great and Cuban American Luis Gonzalez walked up. Puig shook Gonzalez's hand and said hello, then walked off. Gonzalez was not impressed by Puig's lack of interest in chatting with him. The reporter then went on TV and said that some felt Puig had disrespected his legendary countryman. The "arrogant" narrative marched on. The Dodgers didn't hire a professional translator for Puig; they asked one of the farm system's English teachers, Tim Bravo, to do the job. Bravo became a guardian to Puig, living with him, teaching him how to order American food in a restaurant, grocery shop, and use an ATM. While Bravo was off working with Puig, his seven-year-old son, Zechariah, was back home in New Mexico battling a rare type of cancer. Puig was so grateful for Bravo helping him transition to life in the United States that he offered

Frank and Jamie McCourt at the press conference introducing them as the new Dodgers' owners in 2004. Five years later, the two began bitter divorce proceedings that drove the franchise into bankruptcy. *(AP Photo/Reed Saxon)*

From left to right: Peter Guber, Stan Kasten, Guggenheim Partners' CEO Mark Walter, and Magic Johnson walk up to the press conference introducing them as the new Dodgers' owners on May 3, 2012.

(AP Photo/Damian Dovarganes)

Mark Walter talks with Don Mattingly during batting practice at Dodger Stadium before a game versus the Giants on October 2, 2012. Even when Mattingly was rumored to be on the hot seat, he enjoyed Walter's support. *(Larry Goren/Four Seam Images via AP Images)*

The Dodgers' starting lineup remove their caps for the national anthem on opening day, April 1, 2013. *(Louis Lopez/Cal Sport Media via AP Images)*

Zack Greinke pitches to a batter at Miller Park in Milwaukee on May 21, 2013. As the first big free-agent signing of the Guggenheim regime, Greinke became the Dodgers' second ace, behind Clayton Kershaw, and a key to their championship hopes. *(AP Photo/ Morry Gash)*

Carlos Quentin (center) tackles Zack Greinke after being hit by a pitch, as A. J. Ellis (number 17) tries to stop him. Greinke would miss four weeks with a broken collarbone. *(AP Photo/Lenny Ignelzi)*

Yasiel Puig flips his bat into the air to celebrate a hit. Puig's bat flips would soon cause a lot of resentment among Dodgers' opponents. *(Dominic DiSaia)*

Clayton Kershaw stares off into space while preparing for Game 4 of the 2013 NLDS versus the Braves. *(Dominic DiSaia)*

Juan Uribe celebrates after hitting an eighth-inning two-run home run in Game 4 of the 2013 NLDS to help the Dodgers advance to the National League Championship Series. *(AP Photo/Jae C. Hong)*

Hanley Ramirez is hit by a pitch in the first inning of Game 1 of the 2013 NLCS. Ramirez, the Dodgers' best hitter, suffered a broken rib on the play, all but ending the club's World Series hopes. *(AP Photo/Jeff Roberson)*

Yasiel Puig and Adrian Gonzalez pose with posters that Cardinal fans created to make fun of them before Game 6 of the 2013 NLCS at Busch Stadium in St. Louis. The Dodgers would lose 9–0 and be eliminated hours later. *(Molly Knight)*

Ned Colletti (left) and Don Mattingly address the media after the Dodgers were eliminated two wins shy of the World Series in 2013. After the club failed to mention that his option for 2014 had vested a week earlier, a frustrated Mattingly told reporters he did not want to manage a team where he was not wanted. *(AP Photo: Nick Ut)*

Clayton Kershaw celebrates his first career no-hitter against the Rockies on June 18, 2014. He struck out fifteen and walked none, missing a perfect game only because of an error. *(AP Photo/Chris Carlson)*

Yasiel Puig and Matt Kemp celebrate after Kemp hit an RBI single to beat the Braves on July 30, 2014. The all-star outfielders had a tumultuous relationship in their two seasons as teammates. *(AP Photo/Mark J. Terrill)*

Clayton Kershaw (left) and A. J. Ellis celebrate the Dodgers' clinching the NL West for the second straight season after beating the Giants on September 24, 2014. San Francisco would enter the playoffs as a wild card and go on to win the World Series. *(Molly Knight)*

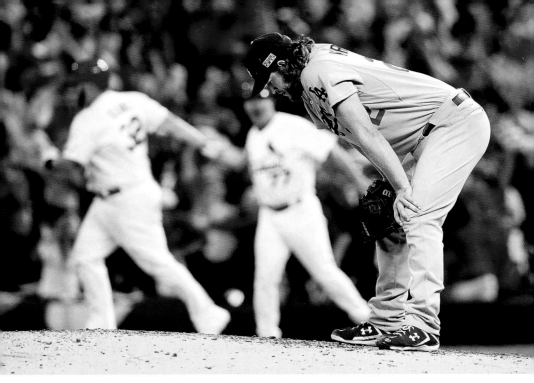

Clayton Kershaw reacts to giving up a three-run home run to Matt Adams in the seventh inning of Game 4 of the 2014 NLDS. The Cardinals would win the game 3–2, and eliminate the Dodgers. It was the second time in two years St. Louis beat Kershaw to end the Dodgers' season. *(Jeff Curry, USA Today Sports)*

Andrew Friedman (right) speaks with ESPN reporter Mark Saxon in the Dodgers' dugout before a game versus the Padres in San Diego on April 24, 2015. *(Molly Knight)* to pay for the boy's treatments and the family's living expenses. During the televised report about Puig disrespecting Gonzalez, the reporter also said that Puig often dispatched Bravo to collect phone numbers from women in the crowd during games. Bravo's wife saw the report and was furious. Though his family needed him during his son's illness, his wife was okay with him being away to help this extraordinary player assimilate. She knew her husband loved Puig, and that Puig loved him. Plus, it was his job. But now she was hearing on national television that part of that job was to be Puig's pimp? *No. If that's what you're doing you have to come home,* she told him. So Bravo quit.

The report about the phone numbers created even stickier problems for Puig, who had quietly been in an on-off relationship with the daughter of a Dodgers minor-league instructor for most of his year in the United States. The young woman was pregnant with his child. Whether or not Puig was carousing didn't matter. Puig's teammates thought the dispatch was unfair. Even those around the team who thought Puig's relationship with a coach's daughter was a potential train wreck agreed the report was unnecessary and offside. To Puig, this story hurt worse than the fastball he took off the nose from Ian Kennedy. Losing Bravo devastated him. What little trust he had left in the media was gone. The Dodgers beat writers paid the price. His petulance baffled many on the beat who felt they'd done nothing but praise him since his call-up. And it was true. While it would be hard to blame a guy for not wanting to talk about being in a slump, Puig was having the best first month for a rookie since the Great Depression, yet he seemed to detest the very people who reached for superlatives to describe his stellar play.

And it wasn't as if having an opinion on Puig was optional. The Luis Gonzalez incident was all the ammunition Puig's detractors needed to prove he had no respect for the game, which was the sport's gravest sin. Though baseball doesn't request that its players bash opponents' heads in, in many ways the game is more tribal than football, and rookies are expected to genuflect before old-timers to gain admittance to the sport's inner sanctum. It went back to the fundamental tenet on which the Diamondbacks were built: that the way one played the game was more important than the result. While Gonzalez is not a Hall of Famer, he is the best player in the young franchise's history. Puig's perceived disrespect of him infuriated the Arizona fans even more. One NL all-star pitcher summed up how the rest of the league felt about Puig in a text message to a Dodger starter. "I love him. I love watching him play. But I can't fucking stand him."

A debate raged between those who said Puig blew off Gonzalez on purpose because he felt like he was more important than anyone who came before him, and others who argued that the kid had no idea who the Diamondback legend was since he grew up on a communist island with limited access to Internet. Both sides were wrong. While it's true that Puig didn't know Gonzalez was Arizona royalty, he knew the guy being introduced to him was wearing a polo shirt with the Diamond-backs logo on it. After being bad-mouthed repeatedly by Arizona players and hit in the face with a fastball by their pitcher in his first week, Puig wanted nothing to do with any of them. In that way, Puig was more old-school than anyone on either team. He didn't care who you were: if you wore Diamondback red you were his sworn enemy.

That hatred was mutual. The only thing Yasiel Puig did better than hit baseballs was get under the skin of opponents. The preposterousness of his background made for no better hero. The way he carried himself on the diamond made for no better villain.

Eight men were suspended for their roles in the Dodgers-Diamondbacks brawl at Dodger Stadium, including Gibson, McGwire, and Mattingly. Ian Kennedy got the worst of it with a ten-game ban. Greinke, Puig, and Montero were fined but not held out of play. Skip Schumaker elected to begin serving his two-game suspension during the last night of the series in Arizona, on July 10.

Because he was suspended, Schumaker wasn't allowed to be in the Dodgers' dugout or clubhouse for the game. But since the team was flying home to Los Angeles right after the contest, he had to be at the ballpark so he could board the bus to the airport when the game was over. So, Schumaker decided to watch the game from the stands at Chase Field, moving around to different sections during each half inning so no one in the visiting crowd would recognize him. ("As if someone would recognize him!" Nick Punto joked later.) It seemed like a decent plan at first. He didn't anticipate the game going fourteen innings.

At quarter to midnight, with Schumaker sitting by himself on the aisle in the lower bowl trying not to draw attention, A. J. Ellis stood in the on-deck circle next to Hanley Ramirez, bleary-eyed and exhausted and hoping to break the tie. The game had just inched into its sixth hour, and Ellis's knees ached from squatting down behind home plate for all 211 of the pitches he had caught that night. The Dodgers had been chasing Arizona the entire season, and now they had a chance to cut the D-backs' division lead to one and a half games. On the mound for the Diamondbacks in the top of the fourteenth was Josh Collmenter, a long reliever and sometime starter who looked as though he could pitch another fourteen innings. Los Angeles had exhausted its bullpen, and only Jansen and League remained. Ellis knew that if his side didn't score soon, they'd probably be forced to burn the following day's starting pitcher.

Between innings, the Dodgers' catcher had received a scouting report on Collmenter from Mark Ellis. "If the ball's away, it's cutting," Ellis told him. "But if it's in it'll stay straight." A. J. Ellis was swinging a hot bat. In the ninth inning, he had collected the two-out, game-tying base hit. But few in the National League were as hot as Hanley Ramirez. For all the attention Puig got for bringing the Dodgers back, Ramirez was the real catalyst. The slugging shortstop would play in eighty-six games for the Dodgers in 2013. The club went 55-31 in those contests, and 37-39 without him. That he was more valuable than even Puig was due to the fact that shortstop tends to be an anemic position offensively. Ramirez hammered the ball. In the thirty games since he had returned from the disabled list on June 4, he hit .398 with six home runs and a .694 slugging percentage. Those gaudy numbers were no fluke. Ramirez looked like the player he was when he hit .342 and won a batting title at age twenty-five for the Marlins in 2009. Nobody had noticed that Ramirez was quietly the team's MVP because his return to health happened the day after Puig's call-up.

While the Boston trade had grabbed all the headlines in August 2012, the Dodgers' move to acquire Ramirez a month earlier seemed poised to have an even bigger impact. At twenty-nine years old, Ramirez was the second-best-hitting shortstop in the majors, just a smidge behind the Rockies' superstar Troy Tulowitzki. After coming to the Marlins in a trade that sent his future teammate Josh Beckett to the Red Sox, Ramirez flourished in Miami, winning the Rookie of the Year award in 2006, and finishing second in MVP balloting in 2009. But injuries and an attitude that could most generously be described as apathetic wrecked his final two seasons with the Marlins, who, in the end, became more than willing to dump him. Ramirez's time in Florida was both offense-happy and offensive. He hit .342 with twenty-four home runs one year, and stole fifty-one bases twice. He was also benched for loafing after baseballs on defense, got into regular screaming matches with coaches, and came to public fisticuffs with his double-play partner, Dan Uggla. In his last half season with the Marlins, he dogged his way into hitting .246. When he wanted to, Hanley Ramirez could hit a baseball as hard as anyone in the major leagues, except for maybe his former teammate Miguel Cabrera. The ball off his bat screamed like a shotgun blast. But when he was in a mood, the mercurial shortstop had a reputation for phoning it in. Coming into the 2013 season, no one was sure which Ramirez the Dodgers would get.

His Miami malaise was not without merit. After all, he'd suited up for the Marlins' controversial owner, Jeffrey Loria, for his entire career. Loria had given McCourt a fight in the worst-owner sweepstakes, persuading Miami taxpayers to buy his team a new stadium by promising to field a competitive team, only to slash payroll by selling off all his good players once he got his ballpark. With two and a half years left on his Marlins contract, Ramirez feared he would be left to rot. Sensing a rare opportunity to land one of the best hitters in the game for fifty cents on the dollar, the Dodgers gave up Nate Eovaldi, a solid but not otherworldly young pitching prospect, to get him. Colletti and Kasten were optimistic that a change of scenery would do wonders for the sulking shortstop.

Ramirez arrived in Los Angeles acting like a hostage who had been freed. He showed up every day with a grin on his face and often talked about how all he wanted to do was help his team win. He was affectionate with teammates, granted interviews to reporters, and even posted cheesy inspirational quotes under the headline "Attitude is everything!" on his social media accounts. Many wondered if this happy-go-lucky chap was the same guy who almost got decked in his own clubhouse in Miami more than once.

People had often asked Ramirez about his unusual first name. It was an accident. His mother had wanted to name him Juan Jose, and call him J.J. for short. His father objected. "Too many J's for him," said Ramirez. His grandmother had an idea. A voracious reader of Shakespeare, she loved the tale of a man who could never make up his mind about what he wanted to do. She told her son to name the baby Hamlet. So they did. But the clerk who filled out his birth certificate spelled it wrong. From that day forward, he went by Hanley. "I don't really know why they didn't change it back," said Ramirez. "But that's okay because I love my name. It's a good name, right?"

Before he suited up for the Dominican Republic in the World Baseball Classic, Ramirez had never played for anything meaningful before. The closest his Marlins had ever finished to the top of the NL East was six games back. In his final full season in Miami, his club wound up a pathetic thirty games out of first. But the WBC was different. When he buttoned up that red and blue uniform and took the field with his countrymen, he experienced a sense of pride on the diamond that he'd never felt before. Ramirez didn't know how different it felt to play in games that mattered. The Dominicans dominated the 2013 tournament, sweeping their way to gold, undefeated. Ramirez had a blast, and friends said it changed him profoundly. He remembered that baseball was supposed to be fun.

Ramirez was the rare athlete who was talented enough to perform in the top 20 percent of hitters in the league while putting in only half the effort. But if he busted his ass, really gave a damn about winning every single at-bat, he could be one of the best in the game. Under the bright blue Los Angeles skies, and with the promise of a fresh start, Ramirez had the best possible opportunity to move forward. But like his intended namesake, the famed fictional prince of Denmark, the choice was his.

The timing was ideal for Ramirez to snap out of his snit and re-discover his old form. He was entering the penultimate year of his contract, and he knew the Guggenheim group was handing out blank checks to superstars. All he had to do was hit. And even though hitting a baseball is the most difficult thing to do in sports, Ramirez didn't think it would be a problem. He was so locked in at the plate when he bothered to be, so naturally good at driving baseballs to the wall and over it, that many of his teammates thought he was somewhat of a genius, that annoying kid in school who aced every exam without ever studying. The Internet had created a never-ending trove of material for pitchers and batters to sift through to gain a competitive advantage. Ramirez never read scouting reports. He rarely even bothered to find out the names of the pitchers he would have to face in advance of a series, and didn't believe in watching any film, either of himself or of his opponent.

Every at-bat was like a blind date. His hands were so fast and his instinct so sharp it didn't matter. He had no use for any ammunition other than a bat—all that information, what the pitcher liked to throw against righties like him, how the ball spun out of his hand, what his ERA was—all of that was just noise that could confuse him. While his teammates reviewed charts for hours, Ramirez would spend that time in the training room prepping his body for battle, stretching, getting massaged, and hooked up to suction devices as part of an ancient Chinese medicine treatment known as cupping. His goals for the season were simple: he would show up early, he would hit, he would smile, and then Mark Walter would pay him a lot of money to stay in Dodger blue so he could do it all over again for years to come.

Unfortunately, his newfound attitude was challenged by bad luck. In the championship game of the WBC, Ramirez dove for a ground ball and jammed his right thumb. At first, the injury wasn't thought to be serious. But an MRI later revealed a torn ligament that required surgery. Effort had its consequences; Ramirez would be sidelined for two months. Still, when he was able to handle a bat again and take a few rounds of hacks with his teammates, they couldn't help but be excited by the way he stung the ball. Ramirez would start batting practice by spraying line drive after line drive to right, center, and left field, then encore with a home run exhibition. The Dodgers tumbled into last place without Ramirez. When he came back, the tenor of the season changed.

After Collmenter finished warming up to begin the top of the fourteenth, Ramirez began his slow walk toward the batter's box. Ellis called after him from the on-deck circle. "Show me why you're the best hitter I've ever played with," he said. Ramirez said nothing. Ellis didn't think he had heard him. A month earlier, a heartbroken Ellis had told his wife, Cindy, that because the team was so terrible it would be all right if she wanted to start making vacation plans for October. A lot had happened in the last thirty days, though, to bring the playoffs back into focus. But there was still work to do. Collmenter set his feet on the rubber and pumped a first-pitch cutter toward Ramirez. The ball was up and away, out of the strike zone. It wasn't a good pitch to hit but that didn't matter to Ramirez. His eyes widened, and he unleashed his black bat at the baseball. The ball screeched out to right field and cleared the fence on a line drive. Ramirez rounded the bases alone, and pointed to the sky with both hands when he crossed the plate.

Then he skipped toward Ellis and slapped him five. As Ellis began to walk toward the batter's box, Ramirez turned around and said to him, "That's why."

Mark Ellis's scouting report proved correct. Collmenter's seventh pitch to A. J. Ellis left his hand looking like it was headed toward the inner half of the plate. It stayed straight. Ellis whacked it for another home run. Of the few thousand fans who remained at Chase Field, the ones in blue began to chant *Let's go Dodgers! Let's go Dodgers!* Jansen closed out the game for the win. Later, after the players showered and dressed, no one said it out loud. They didn't have to. Though there were seventy-two games left, and the Dodgers' record was now at just .500, the NL West race was over. Los Angeles was playing like the team everyone thought it would be when the season began. The underdog Diamondbacks didn't build up a big enough lead while the Dodgers were wrecked by injuries, and they would not be able to hang with them now that their players were emerging from the disabled list. Arizona's lead was now one and a half, but it felt as if Los Angeles was up by ten. The Dodgers had won fifteen of eighteen, and there was the sense that they'd only get better when Kemp came back.

But some of his teammates wondered if the club might be better off without him. Though Kemp was happy the team was winning, it was frustrating to watch them succeed without him. While Kemp praised Puig in public, many of this teammates thought he was privately terrified of being replaced. The Dodgers were playing so well that as they headed into the all-star break they were perhaps the only team in baseball not looking forward to it. Fair or not, Kemp irritated some teammates by heading to Cabo San Lucas for the break instead of rehabbing his injury.

After the break, the Dodgers flew to Washington and activated their center fielder. He said his hamstrings felt good as new, and that his shoulder was continuing to heal. And he did well in his return versus the Nationals on July 21, collecting three hits and a walk in four at-bats with a home run that helped lead the Dodgers to a blowout 9–2 victory. But in the top of the ninth, Kemp was on third with the bases loaded and two out with Carl Crawford at the plate. Crawford tapped a slow roller to first and hustled down the line to beat it out. Because he didn't think he'd have enough time to get the speedy Crawford, Nationals first baseman Chad Tracy threw the ball home to try to force out Kemp. Not expecting the ball to be anywhere near him, Kemp had been trotting toward the plate. When he realized there would be a play at home, he hurried his pace and awkwardly dove, rolling his left ankle in the process. After being thrown out, he screamed, grabbed his foot, and tucked into a ball in the dirt. Kemp had been an active member of the roster for less than twenty-four hours, and he was about to be lost again.

If Kemp had been worried about being replaced, this game was the ultimate metaphor. With him back in the fold, the Dodgers enjoyed the luxury of having their four outfielders healthy on the same day for the first time all season. Puig had been given a rare game off. But with Kemp unable to take center in the bottom of the ninth, Puig subbed for him. An MRI later revealed an ankle sprain bad enough to land Kemp back on the disabled list. His failure to hustle in his first game back would cost him the next fifty-two.

The next day Los Angeles took over first place in the NL West for good.

The resurgent Dodgers went 19-6 in July. This run included five- and six-game winning streaks. They went a month without losing a game on the road. By the time the trading deadline arrived on July 31, they led the Diamondbacks by two and a half games. Colletti had made at least one trade on deadline day every year since he took over as GM before the 2006 season. Among other players, his July 31 haul over the years included Greg Maddux, Julio Lugo, Scott Proctor, Manny Ramirez, Octavio Dotel, Ted Lilly, Ryan Theriot, and Shane Victorino. Each man was added on the annual trade cutoff day in hopes that he might be the final piece to push the Dodgers to a championship. None ever was. At the 2013 deadline, the Dodgers circled a deal with the Angels for second baseman Howie Kendrick that would have sent pitching prospect Zach Lee, their first-round draft pick in 2010, to Anaheim. The club was also rumored to be sniffing out a Matt Kemp for Cliff Lee trade with the Phillies that would ease the Dodgers' outfield logjam and basically represent a salary swap of oft-injured players. But the club was playing so well that the front office decided against making any major moves. Colletti was able to keep his streak alive, however, by working out a small deal for Twins catching farm hand Drew Butera, who would provide insurance should Ellis or Tim Federowicz get hurt.

On July 31, the Yankees came to Dodger Stadium to face Clayton Kershaw. L.A.'s ace pitched eight scoreless innings, despite more than a few obstacles to his regimented pregame routine. Since the Yankees visited Los Angeles only once every three years in interleague play, the Dodgers' marketing department capitalized on the high-profile series and treated it like a playoff game. Normally, before Kershaw started warming up in the bullpen he would sit in the Dodgers' dugout alone, staring at the ground or off into space while he gathered his concentration. But the pregame festivities turned the dugout into a mess. Magic Johnson and Mark Walter stood on the top step, while dozens of media members crammed around them. Nicole Scherzinger of the pop girl group the Pussycat Dolls and her handlers weaved their way through the crowd toward home plate so that she might perform the national anthem. Before that could happen, the Dodgers paid tribute to retiring Yankee closer Mariano Rivera, with Walter and Johnson presenting him a giant deep-sea fishing rod after a video tribute blared through the stadium. Just before the Rivera ceremony, the soccer superstar Cristiano Ronaldo had been kicking a ball around on the infield grass with Puig. As Kershaw sat with his eyes fixed on the ground, the ball whizzed by his head, narrowly missing it. After Scherzinger finished singing, the actor Samuel L. Jackson read the starting lineups for the Dodgers and Yankees over the public address system. Then, new sports agent Jay-Z took his seat behind home plate a few rows from Scott

Boras, who had just lost the Yankees' star second baseman Robinson Cano as a client to the rapper-agent months earlier.

Jay-Z, Jackson, Ronaldo, and Scherzinger were exactly the kind of patrons the club's marketing department hoped to attract to their Dugout Club, the section that made up the ten rows behind home plate at Dodger Stadium. Folks who spent nine hundred dollars a ticket were treated to unlimited free food (gourmet and ballpark fare), wait service, televisions, and a private cash bar. Over the years, the Lakers had become known for their celebrity courtside clientele, and the Dugout Club was the closest thing the Dodgers had to the same starry incubator. If the new Dodger owners got their way, the club would become like the ultimate Hollywood lunchroom, with actors, pop stars, models, and studio heads mingling and mugging for the cameras. In some ways it already was: all the major talent agencies and entertainment law firms in town owned season tickets in the premium spot, and their clients popped in and out of those seats every night. The stars who attended the game versus the Yankees matched those on the field. Television ratings for the game that night were the highest for any MLB regular-season game in the Los Angeles market on record. This was no small thing, because the Dodgers were as much a media and entertainment company as they were a baseball team.

The Yankees were the closest business model the new Dodgers hoped to emulate, with a few caveats. Walter said when he took over that he didn't want to price families out of the stadium; that if the Dodgers were going to raise ticket costs he'd rather tax the rich down in the Dugout Club and surrounding seats than stick it to the people in the cheap seats. For the most part, he kept his word. It was still possible to buy season tickets in the upper deck for $5 per game.

Despite all the pregame pomp and circumstance, Kershaw delivered the first pitch at 7:11, just a minute behind schedule. It had been a long summer for the big lefty. Though the Dodgers' brass loved him best of any player, members of the club's front office were growing more exasperated with his contract situation. When the Dodgers were flailing in last place with a record comparable to the awful Astros, it was hard to blame Kershaw for being wary of signing on for fifteen more years. But the Dodgers were winning now. What did he want?

While the club's front office fixated on Kershaw, fans, teammates, and the press continued to obsess over Puig. The right fielder ate it up. Now that Bravo was gone, Puig had no handler to tuck him in at night and make sure he got to the stadium on time. The Dodgers traveling secretary, Scott Akasaki, sent regular group text messages to players about things like when to show up for a game and when to pack a suit for a travel day. A small whiteboard in the team's clubhouse next to Puig's locker also posted the same information. To help Puig with his chronic tardiness, McGwire told the kid to find out whatever time the Dodgers were due to begin stretching on the field that day and show up to the park two hours earlier. That advice didn't take. He arrived twenty minutes late for a team meeting in July and Schumaker told him to clean it up. Puig just glared at him.

When teams are at home, players are responsible for getting themselves to the ballpark. When they're on the road, the club organizes two buses to transport players and staff from the team hotel to the stadium. The league was pretty much divided between early bus guys and late bus guys. Puig fell into the latter group. Mattingly defended that. "I've seen guys that are in the Hall of Fame that came on the second bus," he said. "Rickey Henderson was a late bus guy. Dave Winfield was another late arriver. And honestly I wasn't one of those guys who was at the ballpark early. But in those days I guess there wasn't much reason to get there early. There weren't full batting cages in every city back then. There weren't full kitchens. There was just a candy rack."

The late bus was fine, as long as a player was on it. But during a series with the Marlins in mid-August, Puig—who made his off-season home in Miami—opted to sleep in his own bed and drive himself to the ballpark. He showed up thirty-five minutes late. A ballplayer missing stretch was a rare occurrence. Longtime Dodger beat writers couldn't recall a player ever showing up that late. Nick Piecoro, a reporter who had covered the Arizona Diamondbacks every day for seven seasons, said that he remembered a player missing stretch once, and that happened during spring training with a random reliever who had no shot at making the team anyway. "He said he was jet-lagged from flying in from Australia," said Piecoro. While Puig was prone to oversleeping and getting stuck in traffic, his constant tardiness was made more serious by the fact that the organization had arranged a private security firm to watch over him because of the drug cartel threats. Teammates wondered if one day Puig wouldn't show up at all.

Mattingly benched him that night but told reporters he had planned to give Puig the day off. Barring Puig from playing in Miami was enough to get the kid's attention. Since his defection from Cuba, many of his relatives had joined him in the United States, and made their homes in and around Miami. Puig's mother, sister, cousin, and many other friends were on hand to watch him play at Marlins Park. Not to get to run out onto the field in front of them was painful, and perhaps what Mattingly needed to do to get his young slugger in line. But the skipper ultimately decided he needed Puig's bat more than he needed to teach him a lesson. Since his call-up on June 3, Puig had led Major League Baseball in batting average, runs, hits, and total bases. In the eighth inning with the game tied 4–4, Puig came off the bench and hit the first pitch he saw for a mammoth home run to center field, giving the Dodgers a lead they would not relinquish. If any message was sent, it was that Puig could break rules and still be handed a bat, because winning mattered most.

And, oh, were the Dodgers winning. The club won fifteen of the first sixteen games it played in August, and would win twenty-three games that month—the most wins in any month in Los Angeles Dodgers history. June 22 could have been the day Mattingly got fired. Instead, it was the day the Dodgers hit the rocket booster on their season. From that game that Greinke won in San Diego to the gem Kershaw pitched in Philadelphia on August 17, the Dodgers went a mind-boggling 42-8, the best fifty-game stretch for any team in over seventy years. They had gone seven weeks without losing two consecutive games. On June 21 the club was 30-42, tied for the fourth-worst record in MLB. On August 17 the Dodgers were 72-50 and tied for the second best. "Anything less than a World Series championship at this point would be a disappointment," said Ethier that week. His teammates began calling Ethier "Joke," due to the frequency of his repeating the phrase "we're so good we're a joke." And the club's bullpen began calling itself the "Dot 'Em Up" pen, in reference to the laser-like accuracy they were using to locate pitches.

They had a point. During that incredible fifty-game run, the Dodgers' pitching staff posted the following ERAs:

Kershaw	1.40
Greinke	2.25
Ryu	2.84
Nolasco	2.97
Rodriguez	0.47
Howell	0.52
Belisario	0.90
Jansen	1.35

Over fifty-three games, Hanley Ramirez hit thirteen home runs, stole nine bases, and tallied an OPS of over 1.000. The Dodgers were pitching, they were hitting, and when they got a lead, their bullpen did not blow it. In thirty-one innings since Mattingly's D-Day, Jansen had given up just four runs while striking out forty-nine. The rest of the staff was nearly as good: the Dodgers combined to pitch eight shutouts in August, and finished the season with an MLB-leading twenty-two. The Reds and the Rays each threw the next most, with seventeen. The Phillies staff tossed just three. While impressive, these raw statistics didn't tell the whole story. It wasn't as though the club clobbered the competition every night. During their historic fifty-game stretch, twenty-two of their forty-two wins were decided by two runs or fewer. The team that couldn't stand each other weeks earlier when they were losing now seemed to be one of destiny, and found ways to pick each other up and win games they trailed night after night. Winning, it seemed, healed all rifts.

On August 9, the Dodgers trailed the Rays 6–0 in the seventh inning and rallied to win 7–6. That tied the largest deficit they'd overcome since moving to Los Angeles. The next week, the Mets came to town for a three-game set and started three talented young pitchers, including phenom Matt Harvey. The Dodgers fell behind early each night, only to rally late with the help of a different hero. In the first game, Puig hit a sacrifice fly to break the tie in the sixth, and little Nick Punto clubbed just the seventeenth home run of his thirteen-year career to pad the Dodgers' lead in the seventh. In game two, A. J. Ellis collected a two-out, two-run single off Harvey that made the difference. And in a wild game three, Ethier came off the bench after sitting out with a calf injury to smack a pinch-hit, opposite-field two-run home run to tie the game in the bottom of the ninth. Adrian Gonzalez won it with a walk-off double that plated Puig in the twelfth. The wins were so improbable that Vin Scully began referring to Dodger Stadium as the Magic Castle.

Not everything around the stadium was magical, however. When Tim Bravo left, he took with him any hope of keeping the riffraff away from Puig. "Oh to be twenty-two and a Dodger," Scully said of Puig, and he was right. Puig lapped up the Hollywood nightlife, becoming a constant presence on the club scene and chronicling his run-ins with other celebrities via his social media accounts. While his escapades were, for the most part, innocuous, his presence in these venues made it easier for grifters and snake oil salesmen to approach and befriend him. Soon he had an entourage of new buddies, including a guy whom Puig began referring to as his best friend despite having known him only for days. Puig's new crew began showing up at Dodger Stadium hours before each game, every day, and stood on the field during batting practice as his guests. The ringleader seemed to know everyone, though nobody really knew how or what he did. Hanley Ramirez knew him from Miami. When the Yankees came to town, Cano walked over and hugged him. Even Cristiano Ronaldo seemed familiar with him. Another member of Puig's entourage carried a binder with pictures of shoes and other swag he claimed to have access to, and approached Dodger players during batting practice.

These men roamed between the locker room and the field with guest passes from Puig hanging from their necks every day from around 4:30 until the time the game started. And when they got kicked out of the clubhouse between the end of batting practice and game time, they'd go hang in the dugout, to the chagrin of stadium security, who had a hard time getting them to leave. If a guard tried to kick Puig's entourage out of the dugout minutes before, say, Kershaw arrived for his pregame ritual, one of the guys would simply call Puig, who would then leave the locker room and come to the dugout to hang with them. And then the guards could do nothing. Players tended to see the locker room as their sacred space; most thought the media's pregame window was too long and were relieved when writers left. When the locker room was closed to everyone but players and staff, they were free to be themselves without worrying about saying or doing something that would be shared with the world. While Puig's friends weren't media, their presence in the locker room and dugout annoyed his teammates who did not appreciate the violation of personal space. And because nobody in a position of authority wanted to say no to Puig, it continued for the rest of the season.

A week after the Miami incident, Puig put another foot wrong. In an afternoon game against the Cubs, he struck out in the bottom of the third, then took his time walking to his position in right between the third and fourth innings. He often was the last Dodger onto the field after their side was retired, only this time he was so late getting to his spot that he wasn't fully facing the batter's box when Ricky Nolasco delivered the inning's first pitch. Between pitches, outfielders demonstrate their attentiveness by slapping their gloves, bending their knees, or bouncing in place. The best outfielders move their feet in preparation with every pitch. Puig annoyed coaches and teammates by standing flat-footed with his hands on his hips. He thought the other stuff was a waste of time, because he believed he could catch with one hand any ball that was hit to him. The first batter of the inning, Anthony Rizzo, lined a ball to Puig, which he caught. He snagged the third out as well. After Nolasco finished the inning and the Dodgers retreated back to the dugout, Mattingly asked Puig if anything was wrong. Puig told him he was tired. So Mattingly pulled him from the game and subbed Schumaker. When Mattingly told Puig he was benched, Puig begged Mattingly, through Adrian Gonzalez, to stay in the game. But the skipper had made up his mind. Puig stomped into the tunnel in a rage. Nick Punto stopped him from redecorating the locker room. After the game, a cryptic Mattingly told the media he made the change because he felt Schumaker gave the club the best chance to win. Nolasco was a bit more forthright. Though he didn't divulge what happened, he said simply, "Puig knows what he did." As other players left the stadium, Puig met with Mattingly and Colletti for a half hour and apologized. "I always give my best but honestly today there was some fatigue and I wasn't prepared," he said to reporters through a translator after the game. He was back in the lineup the next day, and stole two bases and collected four hits, lifting his batting average to .354.

There was one more move Colletti wanted to make before the Dodgers began their stretch run. Though Jansen had been brilliant, Colletti wasn't comfortable entering the last legs of the season with a first-year closer and no real insurance if he got hurt or flamed out. Plus, the kid had never finished a game in October before. So Colletti signed the eccentric former Giants closer Brian Wilson to the roster for depth. Wilson was coming off his second Tommy John surgery and had not pitched in a game in sixteen months. Dodgers officials watched him throw a bullpen session at UCLA in secret and were impressed by the mid-90s velocity on his fastball. Hoping to keep the potential deal under wraps, Colletti set up a clandestine meeting with Wilson at a hotel near the campus. His cover was blown when the hotel valet took his keys, smiled, and asked if he was there to sign Wilson. With Wilson it seemed nothing could be clandestine.

When he took the mound for the Dodgers for his debut outing on August 22, there was no question his stuff was electric. The first batter he faced was the Marlins' superstar power hitter Giancarlo Stanton. He struck him out looking. Wilson would go on to appear in eighteen games in August and September for the Dodgers, usually in front of Jansen as the eighth-inning man. He gave up just one earned run. But Wilson was known as much for his peculiarities as he was for his talent. He looked normal enough during his first few seasons with the Giants, then he decided to grow an unruly beard down to his chest and dye it jet black, like a disguise. No one knew what he was hiding from. Wilson developed a new persona as well. He gave clipped, bizarre answers to questions about baseball, and often walked around the clubhouse with a plate full of unidentifiable purple and gray food he referred to as whale puke.

Wilson had won two World Series rings with San Francisco in the last three years, but his time with the Giants did not end well. When the Dodgers visited San Francisco in mid-September, Wilson walked across the field after a game to confront Giants CEO Larry Baer about why he hadn't yet received his latest World Series ring. Though San Francisco said they had invited Wilson to their on-field team ceremony earlier in the season and the pitcher hadn't responded, Wilson was irate, and screamed at Baer for keeping the ring from him, while stunned fans and former teammates looked on. Colletti knew Wilson well from his time with the Giants and was aware of the pitcher's erratic behavior. Still, he had signed him only to a one-year deal worth a million bucks. If things got too weird he could always cut him.

During the second week of September, when the Dodgers were a few victories away from clinching the division, something strange happened: they started losing. The Giants took three of four in Los

Angeles, including a 19–3 drubbing. Then they traveled to Arizona on September 16 and dropped the first of a three-game set. At that point, the Diamondbacks were the only team that could catch them in the division, as they trailed the Dodgers by nine and a half games with twelve to play. Los Angeles needed two wins to clinch.

Before the second game of the series, Mattingly addressed the team. He told his men they were playing to clinch instead of playing to win, and that it was making them tight. All they had to do, Mattingly said, was put the division title out of their heads and just play for the day. Those in the room said it was an effective speech. When he was finished, Zack Greinke stood up. "I've got something to say," Greinke told the room. This was unusual, not just because Greinke wasn't prone to public speaking, but also because he was pitching that day, and most pitchers don't even like to make eye contact with other humans in the hours leading up to their starts.

"I've been noticing something," Greinke said. His teammates leaned in. Greinke was generally thought to be the smartest, most observant guy on the roster. The room became silent. This was going to be good.

"Some of you guys have been doing the number two and not washing your hands," said Greinke. "It's not good. I noticed it even happened earlier today."

More silence.

"So if you guys could just be better about it that would be great," he said, and then he sat back down.

His teammates looked around the room at each other, stunned. They were expecting an insight into why they were losing, some kind of brilliant observation that would help them bounce off the schneid. But Greinke wanted to talk proper bathroom hygiene. At first the players weren't sure if he was kidding. But as the meeting broke up and they began heading out to the field and they realized he was serious, they laughed hard and long enough to shake off their tightness. When Puig's translator told him what Greinke had said, Puig didn't believe him. He asked Adrian Gonzalez if it was true, and Gonzalez confirmed that it was. Of Greinke, Puig said, *Man, that guy is crazy,* and laughed. One player said later that Greinke's public service announcement was just what the team needed to relax. The Dodgers went out and thumped Diamondbacks ace Patrick Corbin for four runs on five hits in the first inning, and won the game 9–3. Two days later they won the division.

After knocking Arizona out of the race on their own turf, the Dodgers decided they wanted to go swimming. Arizona's Chase Field has a swimming pool behind the right-field fence that fans and companies can rent for parties. Dodger players took it over. They jumped, they danced, they cannonballed into the water. The Diamondbacks were not amused. While some thought it was just an impromptu celebration, in fact, veteran players planned to jump into the pool after they clinched and hold a chicken fight tournament. A few had even practiced on the shoulders of teammates in the locker room the day before. Finally, some drama happened that Puig wasn't responsible for.

After the players traipsed out of the water and wandered back to the clubhouse, they continued their celebration with hoots and hollers and champagne spray. Matt Kemp had just returned from the disabled list three games earlier after a two-month absence. During the festivities, a reporter thought he heard Kemp bragging about a celebratory piss in the Diamondbacks' pool. Kemp had said it as a joke. It didn't matter. A blogger picked up the story that the Dodgers had peed in the Chase Field pool, and it went viral. The Diamondbacks' front office raged. "I could call it disrespectful and classless, but they don't have a beautiful pool at their old park and must have really wanted to see what one was like," said Diamondbacks president and CEO Derrick Hall. Even Senator John McCain weighed in. "No-class act by a bunch of overpaid, immature, arrogant, spoiled brats!" the Diamondbacks fan wrote on Twitter. "The Dodgers are idiots." In response, Magic Johnson offered his thoughts. "That wasn't nothing!" he said. "We got a lot of things happening in the NBA on other people's court, guys jumping on tables. I've seen it all. We apologized, but I'm happy for my players." Johnson later told Jay Leno that even though he couldn't swim, he would strip down to a Speedo in solidarity if the Dodgers won the World Series.

The pool headache wasn't as big of a nuisance as the Dodgers' crowded outfield, however. Even though they entered the season with three highly paid outfielders in Crawford, Kemp, and Ethier, and added Puig along the way, finding room for all four was never an issue because they were never healthy for a full nine innings at the same time. Until now. When Kemp returned from the disabled list, Kasten met with Mattingly to ask what he intended to do with four guys for three positions. Mattingly told Kasten about how he planned to play matchups and platoon the men, as two were right-handed and two were lefties. A person with knowledge of the chat said Kasten told Mattingly that a rotation was fine, but if Puig wasn't in the starting lineup they would have a problem.

Later, Mattingly summoned all four men into his office and told them that with the division sewn up, he would work out a rotation to keep all four outfielders fresh for the playoffs. Puig and Crawford shrugged. Ethier told Mattingly he would do whatever was best for the team. Kemp fought for playing time. "I'm a starter," he said to his skipper, in front of the other three. If Mattingly and Kemp had once been close, their relationship now seemed over.

But Mattingly didn't need to worry about juggling his four outfielders after all. Days after the platoon conversation, Kemp's slow-healing ankle was reevaluated and team doctors discovered that the injury was much more significant than previously thought. One of the bones in Kemp's foot was so swollen that if he continued to put any weight on it he risked snapping it and ending his career. Kemp was told he'd need surgery on the final day of the season. It was the second time in as many years that he had played through a freak injury that had been missed. Another disastrous season, complete.

The Dodgers had invited their fans to stay in the stadium after that game for a playoff pep rally. Players gathered on the field and some spoke to the jubilant crowd. After starting the season with a 30-42 record, the Dodgers had finished the season at 92-70, winning the National League West by eleven games. A division title wasn't really what the Dodgers were after, however. They wanted a world championship. And as the players looked around at each other, they believed they had the talent and the momentum to do it.

8

THE BEST TEAM
MONEY CAN BUY

The Dodgers entered the 2013 playoffs on an auspicious note. Only four teams in history had ever won forty-two of fifty games during the regular season. Each went on to make the World Series.

Earning a spot in the Fall Classic was not going to be easy, however. To get there, Los Angeles would have to beat two very good National League teams, and they'd have to do it without home-field advantage. Because they were the first team to clinch their division and had injury issues all year, the club's brain trust chose to rest many starters during the season's final week. With backups on the field, the Dodgers dropped four of their last five contests, and slipped down to the third seed in the National League behind St. Louis and Atlanta.

First, they had to face the NL East champion Braves in a best-of-five series. Though the Dodgers sent Kershaw to the mound for Game 1 of the division series, victory was no guarantee. The Braves countered with their own ace, Kris Medlen, who had been named the NL's pitcher of the month for September. Medlen had faced the

Dodgers twice earlier in the year and flummoxed Los Angeles hitters both times, allowing zero earned runs in 13.2 innings pitched. But both of those games came early in the season, when the Dodgers weren't any good.

During batting practice before Game 1, Stan Kasten stood on the dirt near the visiting on-deck circle and greeted old friends. It had been ten years since he had left the organization he helped turn into an annual contender, and a lot had changed. Atlanta had won its division in twelve of Kasten's last thirteen years as team president, but they'd captured that crown just three times in the decade since. The biggest reason for that drop-off, of course, was the loss of Hall of Famers Greg Maddux, Tom Glavine, and John Smoltz to free agency and middle age. In some ways, the nineties Braves had set the standard for what the Dodgers were trying to do. Los Angeles could control winning the NL West most years by outspending everyone else. And since the playoffs were a crapshoot, the best way to win a World Series title was to buy a ticket to the postseason every year and hope for the best. The Braves had been very good under Kasten but they had also been unlucky. The club's twelve division titles had produced five trips to the World Series but only one championship. Maybe it was because Atlanta hadn't won a playoff series since 2001, or perhaps so many first- and second-round flameouts in the nineties had numbed fan excitement, but enthusiasm for the 2013 Braves squad around the city was tepid. The day before Game 1, Dodger officials were told that Turner Field still had eighteen thousand unsold tickets.

While Kasten pressed Atlanta flesh, Matt Kemp ambled his way up the dugout steps toward his teammates who were waiting to hit. As Kemp rested on his crutches, a cameraman circled him for a shot, and he became annoyed. "I think you got enough," he said, as he stared out into space. Puig approached him, and Kemp said something awkward to him about steak and eggs, the meal Puig credited for giving him his power, and forced a laugh. It was not a coincidence that these two fan favorites were so uneasy around each other. Imagining the two of them playing in the outfield together for a championship team was difficult; they were like the same sides of a magnet, so fundamentally similar that they repelled each other. Puig was an alpha male in a group of alpha males, and did little to hide it. In a game in St. Louis in early August, Gonzalez was on first base when Puig doubled off the wall. After Gonzalez held at third rather than trying to score on the hit, a visibly angry Puig threw his hands in the air in disgust. Confused, Gonzalez turned to him and yelled "What?" across the diamond. After they both eventually came in to score, Puig screamed at Gonzalez in the dugout. Cameras captured the incident. Knowing viewers at home had seen his outburst, Puig waited until the camera was on him later in the game, and then went over to Gonzalez, smiled, put his arm around the first baseman's shoulder, and patted his head as if he were a child. That sort of thing would never have flown with Matt Kemp. These Dodgers had won the West, but they played very few games with both Kemp and Puig in the lineup. The two men were contracted to play some combination of right and center field together in Dodger blue through the 2018 season. That seemed unlikely. And since Puig was much cheaper and younger, Kemp was more likely to be traded. He knew it.

Before he took his hacks in the cage, Puig removed his cap to put on his batting helmet and revealed a freshly shaved playoff Mohawk. In his first three months in the big leagues the rookie outfielder was exceptional at the plate, hitting .349 with an on-base percentage of greater than 40 percent. But he sputtered in September, posting a .214 batting average and a .333 OBP. "They found the hole in his swing," said one Dodger staff member as he watched him take batting practice that evening. "It's not where you would look at first, but they found it." While Puig feasted on low fastballs thrown near his shoe tops, he struggled to hit heaters in the upper third of the strike zone—which was the wheelhouse of most players.

If Puig did have some kind of glitch it was understandable. Most ballplayers take years to perfect their swings in the minors. Puig was forced to make his adjustments at the highest level. Because the mechanics of his swing were otherwise almost perfect, opposing pitchers knew they had to beat him between the ears. The Dodgers' coaching staff expected Puig's emotions to be amplified in the playoffs, the time of year when the ability to slow the game down is most crucial. They worried that the more he tried to do, the less effective he would be.

To accommodate playoff television programming, Game 1 started at 8:07 in Atlanta—some fifty-seven minutes later than night games typically kicked off at Dodger Stadium. Kershaw did the math and wrote down the adjusted times for his pregame rituals. But it was clear from the first inning that the Dodgers' ace did not have his best stuff. Though he struck out two hitters in the opening frame, he struggled to throw his fastball where he wanted and had to use nineteen pitches to get the first three outs. The big southpaw liked to paint the corners of the strike zone with four-seamers to get ahead of batters early in counts and then mix in his off-speed pitches to put them away. When he got ahead by two strikes, he was lethal. In 0-2 counts versus Kershaw, batters struck out more than 50 percent of the time, and were five times more likely to whiff than collect a hit. He gained such an advantage because he didn't have to throw strikes in these counts; hitters often flailed at pitches in the dirt.

In the fourth inning, Kershaw threw first-pitch fastballs to each of the six Braves he faced. But they caught too much of the plate. Atlanta hitters capitalized on his lack of command, collecting two hits and a walk. And even though they managed only one run against him, they had made him throw seventy-seven pitches to get twelve outs—no minor victory. The best way to win a game Clayton Kershaw pitched was to somehow get him off the mound. Knowing this, in the fifth inning Kershaw decided to turn his fastball into a secondary pitch. It worked. Of the eight pitches he threw to B. J. Upton and Jason Heyward in the fifth, seven were sliders, the other was a curve. He struck them both out. He fanned the Braves' best hitter, Freddie Freeman, the next inning without throwing him a fastball, either. After the game, some of the Braves said his slider was one of the best they'd seen all year. As a matter of fact, it was so good they hadn't seen it at all. Kershaw struck out nine of the last eleven hitters he faced, and finished the game giving up one run on three hits—all singles—while striking out twelve in seven innings. His dozen strikeouts were the most by a Dodger in a postseason game since Sandy Koufax had struck out fifteen in Game 1 of the 1963 World Series. The Dodgers rolled over Medlen and the relievers brought in to back him up, scoring six runs on eleven hits, including three doubles and a home run.

Los Angeles took a 1–0 series lead but the win came with a cost: Kershaw had thrown 124 pitches, which made it unlikely that he'd be able to come back and pitch Game 4 on short rest. Zack Greinke and Hyun-Jin Ryu were scheduled to pitch Games 2 and 3, with Ricky Nolasco on track for Game 4. Though Nolasco had pitched well for the Dodgers in the regular season, he had never taken the mound in the playoffs in his eight-year career, and those around the team said he looked terrified. If the Dodgers dropped the next two games of the series, Nolasco would have to pitch an elimination game unless Kershaw could work on three days' rest. Because of this, Mattingly was criticized for leaving Kershaw in to toss more pitches than he'd thrown in five months in a game the Dodgers appeared to have well in hand. But Mattingly knew how much his ace wanted to stay on the mound and said afterward that he felt he owed Kershaw the opportunity to try to get twenty-one outs.

Of course, there would be no need for Game 4 if Los Angeles could beat Atlanta in Games 2 and 3 and sweep the series. With Greinke on the bump for Game 2, the Dodgers liked their chances of heading back to L.A. needing one more victory to advance. They jumped out to a quick lead in the first inning, after Mark Ellis walked and Hanley Ramirez doubled him home. It was Ramirez's first postseason appearance as well, but he seemed to the coaching staff to be as relaxed and confident as Nolasco was nervous. Greinke looked like the pitcher the Dodgers envisioned when they signed him in the off-season, giving up two earned runs in six efficient innings. Though he had thrown only eighty-three pitches and might have had another inning left in him, with the Dodgers trailing 2–1 and Skip Schumaker on second with one out, Mattingly opted to pinch-hit for Greinke in the top of the seventh with a new player on the team, the veteran infielder Michael Young. Young collected an infield single, setting up runners at the corners. But Carl Crawford grounded into an inning-ending double play.

The top of the seventh wasn't Mattingly's fault. Though Greinke hit well—he would go on to win the NL Silver Slugger award as the league's best-hitting pitcher—Young was a .300 career hitter, and two years removed from finishing with the most hits in the AL. The bottom of the seventh threatened to cost Mattingly his job. He sent rookie flamethrower Chris Withrow to the mound to relieve Greinke. The trouble with being blessed with a fastball that travels 98 mph is that the man throwing it often has no idea where it's going. Withrow walked the first batter he faced, then allowed a single. The Braves gave the Dodgers a gift out by asking shortstop Andrelton Simmons to bunt the runners up a base. Then Withrow bounced back, striking out Elliot Johnson looking on three pitches. With runners on second and third and two out, the pitcher was due up in the order. Atlanta sent light-hitting Jose Constanza to the plate to pinch-hit.

The left-handed Constanza had collected just eight hits on the year, all singles. Nevertheless, Mattingly was uncomfortable with the fact that all eight of those hits had come off right-handed pitchers, such as Withrow. So he replaced Withrow with lefty Paco Rodriguez. Braves manager Fredi Gonzalez countered by substituting right-handed pinch-hitter Reed Johnson for Constanza to get the matchup that he wanted. Rather than pitch to the veteran journeyman Johnson, who had hit just .244 with one home run on the year, Mattingly had Rodriguez intentionally walk him to load the bases for Jason Heyward, one of Atlanta's best hitters. Heyward was a lefty, and the average left-handed hitter has a much more difficult time hitting left-handed pitchers, because the ball tails away from him. But Heyward was no ordinary player. In 2013 his batting average and on-base plus slugging percentage were both higher against lefties than righties. His numbers against southpaws were significantly better than Johnson's, too. Knowing those numbers, giving Johnson a free pass to pitch to Heyward seemed like a mistake. It was. Heyward singled in two runs, and the Braves took a 4–1 lead. Mattingly's gaffe was made even more painful when Hanley Ramirez hit a two-run home run the next inning that would have given the Dodgers the lead. Instead they lost 4–3. The club flew back to L.A. with the series tied at a game apiece, and two guys lined up to start Games 3 and 4 who had never thrown a pitch in a playoff game in their lives.

There was another reason the outcome was especially devastating to Mattingly's hold on his job. Since the Dodgers had played .800 baseball for most of the summer, no one outside Los Angeles seemed to notice the manager's in-game strategy decisions. But during the playoffs everyone was watching. National columnists eviscerated him. Some within the organization wondered if he would follow in the footsteps of Grady Little, the man who led the Red Sox to the 2003 American League Championship Series but was fired after the season because he left a tiring Pedro Martinez in the decisive Game 7 too long. Fredi Gonzalez was not considered a master tactician, so being outmaneuvered by him hurt worse. Because of this perception, players wondered if they would have to win the World Series for Mattingly's job to be safe.

Game 3 of the NLDS was the Dodgers' first playoff home game under the Guggenheim regime. Puig led the team onto the field, sprinting to his spot in right. Hyun-Jin Ryu took the mound and struggled from the start. Though he had pitched well in his first year in Los Angeles, Ryu was typically mediocre in the opening frame: he gave up seventeen runs in thirty first innings for a 5.10 earned run average. Like a marathon runner, he seemed to gain strength the longer the game went. While Ryu's ERA in innings one through three was 3.50, he improved to 2.58 in innings four through six, and to 2.45 from the seventh to the ninth. It may have been his first time pitching in the playoffs, but Ryu was no stranger to big stages. He started the gold medal game in the 2008 Olympics for his native South Korea and pitched brilliantly in victory over Team Cuba, allowing just two runs in eight and a third innings.

Whether he was nervous or just melting in the ninety-degree heat, Ryu was sweating so much on the mound that it appeared he had difficulty gripping the ball. The Braves capitalized on his tentativeness right away, scoring two quick first-inning runs. But the Dodgers got four runs back in the bottom of the second off a sacrifice fly from Ryu and a three-run home run from Carl Crawford. The Braves evened the score in the top of the third, before the Dodgers exploded for six in the next two innings to take a 10–4 lead. Ryu admitted later that he was hurt by his failure to adjust his strategy for the playoffs. Because bullpens risked being burned out during the regular season, it was more valuable for a starting pitcher to go seven innings and give up three runs than go five innings and give up none. In the postseason it was the opposite. Relievers were no longer being stashed away for rainy days, and the best were often called upon to work more than one inning. A manager's job was to try to get twenty-seven outs from his staff by any means necessary, while giving up as few runs as possible. Instead of throwing 91 mph fastballs so that he might conserve energy to go deeper in the game, Ryu would have been better served throwing 95 until he tired, because tomorrow wasn't guaranteed. He gave up four runs in just three innings of work, but on that day the Dodgers didn't need him to be great. Chris Capuano pitched a scoreless fourth, fifth, and sixth, and Los Angeles pounded the Braves 13–6 to take a 2–1 series lead.

Before Game 3, Mattingly insisted Nolasco would start Game 4. But the idea of losing and being forced to fly back to Atlanta for a winner-take-all Game 5 was too scary for the skipper and his staff to bear. So they summoned Kershaw on short rest to try to close out the series. Kershaw had never pitched on three days' rest in his career, and his catcher was nervous. It wasn't that A. J. Ellis didn't believe in Kershaw's ability. He was of the firm belief that his best friend was the best pitcher in baseball, and as mentally tough as anyone. But his talent didn't change the fact that firing a baseball overhand is not a natural motion for a human arm; knots of lactic acid form from the shoulder to the elbow as thick as meatballs during starts. Some starters are in so much discomfort they never sleep on the pitching-arm side of their body. Others have trouble finding feeling in their hands. The four days between starts are necessary to drain that acid from their arm muscles, so that blood can flow to the tips of their fingers unimpeded.

Kershaw's schedule in between starts was as regimented as his routine on game days. The day after a start he played catch. On day two he threw a bullpen session of forty or so pitches to stretch out his arm, a common practice many pitchers compare to an oil change. Day three was for long toss, and on day four he rested. Not only was Kershaw rushing that routine, but he was also coming off a game in which he had thrown 124 pitches and a season in which he'd tossed a career-high number of innings.

And there was something else: Kershaw still hadn't signed his contract extension. While it was true that a pitcher risked serious injury every time he threw a ball, catastrophe seemed more likely to happen when a player was tired. Because baseball contracts were guaranteed, if he signed a contract for hundreds of millions of dollars the night before Game 4 and then went out and hurt himself and was never able to start another game, he'd still collect all that money. But if he got injured before signing, Los Angeles could, in theory, significantly lower its off-season offer. Kershaw was still under the Dodgers' control for 2014, but after that he would hit a free agent market that didn't like to give injured pitchers long deals, regardless of pedigree.

C.C. Sabathia had been one of the best pitchers in the game when the Yankees rewarded him with a seven-year, $161 million contract before the 2009 season. Sabathia was coming off an extraordinary year during which he posted a 1.65 ERA in 130 innings for Milwaukee in the season's final two and a half months to help the team to its first playoff berth in twenty-six years. That workload came with a cost. Because they were in a tight race to the finish, the Brewers sent Sabathia to the mound on three days' rest three outings in a row to close the season. Some wondered if the decision to risk his arm health was perhaps made easier by the fact that the Brewers knew they could not afford to re-sign him once he became a free agent. An exhausted Sabathia pitched poorly in his only playoff start for Milwaukee, allowing five earned runs and getting just eleven outs with ninety-eight pitches. Sabathia pitched well in his first four seasons with the Yankees before injuries from overuse compromised him at age thirty-two.

Kershaw was just as competitive as Sabathia. Regardless of the money at stake, he wanted the ball with the chance to clinch. Facing elimination, the Braves countered with Freddy Garcia, a thirty-seven-year-old journeyman pitcher who had been on their roster for a month after spending most of the summer in the Orioles' minor-league system. On paper it didn't seem to be a fair fight. But the game began on an ominous note, with Adrian Gonzalez, a Gold Glove Award winner, booting a grounder hit to him on the first play of the contest. Kershaw got the next three outs without the ball leaving the infield. It looked as though the Dodgers might beat up Garcia from the start after Carl Crawford greeted him with a leadoff home run in the bottom of the first. But aside from another solo shot from Crawford in the third, Garcia gutted through a stellar performance, allowing just those two runs in six innings—which was more than the Braves could have hoped for.

Kershaw was his usual self, striking out four and allowing just one hit through the first three innings. Then Freddie Freeman led off the fourth with a single, and Evan Gattis grounded an easy double-play ball to Gonzalez. But Gonzalez threw the ball away. So instead of two out and the bases empty Kershaw was forced to face the Braves' star catcher, Brian McCann, with no out and runners on first and second. He struck McCann out. But Chris Johnson singled in a run, and a ground-out from Andrelton Simmons tied the game. The score stayed even at two through six, and both managers pulled their starting pitchers.

Kershaw became the first pitcher to go six innings and give up no earned runs on three days' rest since his teammate Josh Beckett did it in the 2003 World Series ten years earlier with the Marlins. But because of Gonzalez's fluke errors, it didn't look as though it would be enough. Ronald Belisario came in to pitch the seventh inning for the Dodgers and surrendered a triple and a single to give the Braves a 3–2 lead. Gonzalez had a chance to atone for his earlier mistakes in the bottom of the seventh, when he came up with two on and two out. He flied out to right. Despite Kershaw's efforts, he couldn't will the team to victory by himself. And when the Dodgers went to bat in the bottom of the eighth inning, it felt as if their season was on the line as well. The Braves were three outs from giving the ball to Craig Kimbrel, their excellent closer. If Los Angeles did not score in the eighth, the club would almost certainly have to fly back to Atlanta for a winner-take-all elimination game on the road.

Puig led off with a double. When he reached second base he slapped his hands together and threw his fist at the sky. Juan Uribe was up next. After staggering through his first two miserable years with the Dodgers, Uribe had worked hard to prepare for his final season under contract, and came into 2013 looking to somehow salvage his time in blue. "If you don't play good people don't remember you," he said a month earlier. So the free-swinging Uribe stepped up to the plate looking to do something people would not forget. But Mattingly asked him to bunt. It was a strange call. The Dodgers needed only a run to tie the game, and Puig was fast enough to score from second on a single. Perhaps a better plan would have been to let the three men behind Puig try to get a hit to drive him in, rather than give the Braves an automatic out to advance him ninety feet. It was also head-scratching because Uribe had sacrificed only three times that season and once the year before. But Mattingly preferred Puig on third with one out to his being on second with no out, reasoning that a fly ball from Skip Schumaker could sacrifice him home. Uribe tried twice to get the bunt down and failed.

After taking the next two pitches to work the count to 2-and-2, Uribe waited for the next offering from Braves reliever David Carpenter. Kimbrel stood in the bullpen, furious. He had told his manager that since the club would be eliminated if they lost, he wanted to get the last six outs. Gonzalez's decision to let Carpenter start the inning was defensible. The third-year man had been excellent for Atlanta in sixty-five innings that season, striking out seventy-four hitters with a 1.78 ERA. But once Puig made it to second base with no outs, Kimbrel wanted in the game. Brian McCann flashed a signal for Carpenter to bury a slider in the dirt, while Uribe stared out at the reliever, flicking his bat back and forth over his right shoulder. It was the worst possible moment in David Carpenter's young life to hang one, but that's what he did. The ball floated straight down the center of the plate parallel to the blue lettering on Uribe's white jersey. Uribe unloaded, crushing the ball high into the Los Angeles night toward the Dodgers' bullpen. When it landed just inside the left-field foul pole to give Los Angeles a 4–3 lead, the fifty-four thousand people who were in attendance that night all seemed to scream and bounce in unison. Uribe rounded the bases, touched home, and ran back to the dugout, where he was mobbed by teammates. Los Angeles faithful remained on their feet. It was the biggest hit by any Dodger since Kirk Gibson's homer that won Game 1 of the 1988 World Series. Kimbrel stood in the bullpen with his hands on his hips and cursed. Kenley Jansen then struck out Jordan Schafer, Jason Heyward, and Justin Upton to end the game and send the Dodgers to the National League Championship Series.

After the game Kershaw returned to the locker room to find Sandy Koufax waiting for him. While his teammates hollered and sprayed champagne and beer around him, Kershaw embraced his idol. Uribe was the last Dodger to leave. Hours after his home run he was still in uniform, drenched in liquor, standing on the soaked carpet in his soggy socks, as if the moment he changed back into his street clothes the night would no longer be real. In a roller-coaster season when so many of these players struggled to exist in the same clubhouse, it was fitting that the team's most popular player got the hit that put them in the National League Championship Series. "Juan has been, I think consensus, he's probably been the most liked teammate we have," Kershaw said after the game. "He's always the same no matter what. You couldn't tell if he's one-for-thirty or thirty-for-thirty. The way he plays, I couldn't be happier for him. I just love him to death."

When Jansen recorded the final out, a relieved Mattingly hugged his coaches. What no one outside the coaching staff and front office knew was that when the Dodgers advanced to the National League Championship Series, Mattingly's contract automatically vested for 2014. But there was no celebratory press conference. His players didn't even know he would be back. The club made no announcement.

Mattingly assumed that silence meant he was out. In that way, whatever the Dodgers did versus the Cardinals wouldn't matter to his future. Even though the Dodgers' trip to the NLCS triggered a clause in his contract, all that meant was that the club would have to pay him for the 2014 season. They could give him that money and fire him. Yes, it would be harder for them to let go of the man who took them to their first World Series in twenty-five years if he accomplished that, but the lack of acknowledgment that his contract had vested stung him. After all, this was an organization that sent out regular press releases about national anthem singers and garden gnome giveaways. When the Dodgers flew to St. Louis to take on the Cardinals for the first two games of the NLCS, they did so with a manager who did not feel wanted.

For National League teams, the road to the World Series always seemed to go through St. Louis. In the past fourteen seasons, the Cardinals had made it to the NLCS eight times, and won World Series titles in 2006 and 2011. Their eleven world championships were most in the NL and second only to the Yankees. That the Cardinals were able to field championship-caliber teams year in and year out was re-markable, given their market size. The Dodgers had bullied their way to the National League Championship Series by spending well over $200 million on player salaries. The Cardinals paid their players about half what Los Angeles did. What the St. Louis starting nine lacked in talent they made up for in depth. They were so good at drafting and developing young players that they seemed invulnerable to injury. If a guy got hurt, the organization suffered minimally because it had no shortage of viable replacements. Magic Johnson stood on the cut of the Busch Stadium grass before Game 1, visibly anxious. "I'm nervous and I'm crazy and I've gotta sit in the stands and be more nervous and crazier," said Johnson. "The Cardinals are the model. We want to build the same thing back in L.A."

When Vin Scully described the inside of Busch Stadium as looking like an internal hemorrhage, he meant it with great affection. Scully deeply admired the Cardinals' winning ways and loved to talk about how the organization had both the first female owner and the first in-fielder who wore glasses. Since Kershaw had pitched the final game of the NLDS and needed to rest, the Dodgers sent Greinke to the mound for Game 1. St. Louis countered with young Joe Kelly, who had pitched fewer innings in his career than Kershaw had that season. But Cardinal youth weren't wired with the same tremors as young players on other teams. They seemed bred from birth not only to expect to play in maxi-mum pressure situations, but to thrive.

After the public address announcer said Carl Crawford's name, Kelly stood on the mound holding the ball with both hands and breathed in the weight of the moment. Then he fired strikes one, two, and three. Crawford walked back to the dugout. Mark Ellis stepped into the batter's box next to polite applause from St. Louis fans. Quiet and midwestern nice, Ellis did not have much in common with most of the better-known Dodgers. Whether or not they were arrogant, there was no denying that Los Angeles played with a panache that bothered op-ponents. The Cardinals preferred the kind of hard-nosed, head-down, aw-shucks baseball that had long been glorified as the "right way" to play the game. They were like the Diamondbacks, but better. The 2013 NLCS was more than just a battle for a spot in the World Series: it was a culture war.

Ellis singled.

Since the Cardinals had home-field advantage, the Dodgers would have to win at least one game on foreign soil to take the seven-game series. Swiping Game 1 with Kershaw on deck to pitch Game 2 would be ideal, and doing it by drawing blood in the first inning to knock the optimism out of the home crowd would be even better. Hanley Ramirez walked up to the plate looking to drive in Ellis. Ramirez had scorched the ball during the NLDS, going 8-for-16 with four doubles, a triple, and a home run. His six extra-base hits tied a playoff record for most ever in a National League Division Series. To say he had enjoyed a great year at the plate was an understatement. Ramirez's 1.040 OPS was the best in major-league history for a shortstop with at least 300 at-bats. It was also tops in the NL, and second-best overall, behind only Detroit's Miguel Cabrera (1.078). Had he played in enough games, he might have been the National League's MVP. And unlike Puig, Ramirez didn't rattle. Cardinal pitchers knew it.

Teams in the NL Central had developed a reputation for pitching inside to brush hitters off the plate. In 2013, the four NL teams that hit opposing batters the most were in the league's Central Division, with Pittsburgh, Cincinnati, and St. Louis going 1-2-3, and the Cubs taking fourth. It wasn't that they were necessarily trying to hit opponents on purpose. A good way to gain an advantage over a hitter was to buzz him with an inside fastball to move him off the plate. If that player got hit, well, so be it. The free base was annoying, but it was the cost of the strategy. Plus, many of the hit batsmen were dangerous sluggers that opposing teams wanted to pitch around anyway. The approach was economical, too: hitting a guy cost only one pitch, but walking him required four.

It's not often that the most important pitch of a seven-game series is thrown in the first inning of the first game. But that's what happened. After getting ahead of Ramirez in the count 1-2, Kelly drilled him in the left flank with a 95 mph fastball that ricocheted off his body so hard it sounded as though it had hit his bat and cracked it. Ramirez reeled away in agony, and after talking with Dodgers trainer Sue Falsone, walked to first base. At first it was difficult to tell how badly Ramirez was injured. He had been so brittle during the season—playing in just eighty-six games—that every time he ran or threw or swung he seemed to wince. Each trip around the bases was an adventure. With Ellis and Ramirez on first and second with one out, Gonzalez and Puig both struck out to end the threat. Ramirez remained in the game, hopeful he had just sustained a bone bruise. But as the innings wore on, the sharp pain near his skin radiated deeper, through his bones and into his lung. Each breath he took felt like a mistake.

Greinke mowed down the first six Cardinal hitters he faced, allowing only one ball to leave the infield. Carl Crawford doubled to lead off the third inning for the Dodgers, and Ramirez came to bat again after Ellis grounded out. This time Kelly walked him. And then, unable to locate the strike zone, he walked Adrian Gonzalez to load the bases for Puig. With the count 2-1, Puig grounded into a force-out at home. Then Uribe came up with two out and slapped a first-pitch sinker-ball up the middle to drive in Ramirez and Gonzalez. Those two runs looked like they might be enough for Greinke, who took the mound in the bottom of the third and struck out Cardinals third baseman David Freese and shortstop Pete Kozma to start the inning. But Kelly worked a two-out hit, and leadoff hitter Matt Carpenter walked, bringing up the dangerous Carlos Beltran with two on and two out. Beltran whacked a changeup from Grienke toward the deepest part of center field. Andre Ethier sprinted back to the fence, jumped, and missed it. Two runs scored. Ethier was playing out of position, but the Dodgers had had little choice but to put him in center with Matt Kemp injured and unable to play. By October, even the players who weren't on the disabled list were battling some kind of nagging injury. For Ethier it was shin splints. Perhaps the most amazing thing about these Dodgers was that they were playing for the National League title without a true center fielder on their roster. An excellent defender would have caught Beltran's fly ball. The game was tied 2–2.

It stayed that way for ten more innings.

Greinke went eight full frames, giving up two runs and striking out ten. He became the first pitcher to strike out double-digit Cardinal hitters in a playoff game since 1944—an extraordinary feat considering St. Louis had participated in more postseason games in the last sixty-nine years than any other team in the National League. In his two playoff appearances with the Dodgers so far, Greinke had given the club fourteen innings while surrendering just four runs, debunking any lingering concerns about his anxiety disorder.

With the contest tied at two in the eighth, Adrian Gonzalez led off with a walk. Because Gonzalez represented the potential winning run and also possessed the slowest feet of any Dodger player, Mattingly opted to have the speedy Dee Gordon run for him and substituted Gonzalez out of the game. It was a questionable move: Ramirez had struck out to end the previous inning, and the shortstop was in obvious pain. Removing Gonzalez from a tie game meant that if the contest went to extra innings, the Dodgers' lineup would be without its cleanup hitter on an evening when its number-three hitter could hardly swing a bat. Gordon was fast, but the Cardinals' catcher, Yadier Molina, was the toughest backstop to run on in the league. While it was possible that Gordon could successfully steal second off him, Mattingly didn't send him, which all but negated the value of subbing him for Gonzalez.

Some Dodger players could not believe Gonzalez was being removed from a tie game. It didn't help their frustration when Gordon was erased a batter later after Puig grounded into a fielder's choice. Mattingly put Michael Young into the game for Gonzalez at first base, and it was clear he was quickly becoming the skipper's favorite bat off the bench. The Dodgers had claimed the veteran Young off waivers from the Phillies in late August, and he had fit in well with his team-mates right away. Young had never won a championship during his fourteen seasons in the big leagues, though he did finish as a runner-up on the Texas Rangers team that had their hearts broken by these Cardinals in the 2011 World Series. Texas had been one strike away in back-to-back innings from its first-ever title in Game 6, only to lose to furious comebacks by St. Louis.

Young was dealt to Philadelphia before the 2013 season. As he was nearing the end of his career, the thirty-six-year-old infielder told the Phillies he didn't want to be traded again. But when the Dodgers gauged his interest, the situation was too good to pass up. Young had been born and raised in Los Angeles County, and grew up a Dodger fan. What could be better than winning a ring with his hometown team? Beating the Cardinals to do it, perhaps. Heading into the series with St. Louis, Young was perhaps the most outwardly animated Dodger; he sent many inspirational expletive-laden messages to a group-text chain of eight or so teammates in hopes of firing them up.

Batting in Gonzalez's spot, Young got his chance to be the hero in the top of the tenth inning. After Carl Crawford flied out to right, Mark Ellis tripled, becoming the first Dodger to make it to third base since the third inning. The Cardinals then walked Ramirez intentionally again to set up a potential double play but also because whether he was injured or not, they didn't want any part of him. With one out and runners on first and third, all Young had to do to give Los Angeles a lead was hit a fly ball deep enough to score Ellis. With that in mind, he got under a pitch from Cardinals closer Trevor Rosenthal—who was in his second inning of work—and drove it to right field. Carlos Beltran caught the ball, and Ellis broke toward home. Dodgers third-base coach Tim Wallach knew Beltran had a strong arm in right, but he also knew that Puig, who was due up next, had failed to hit the ball out of the infield in four earlier attempts that night, so this might be the Dodgers' best chance to score. Ellis sprinted for home. Beltran threw him out by an eyelash.

Young got another chance in the top of the twelfth. Crawford led off the inning with a single and Ellis bunted him over to second. The sacrifice opened up a free base to put Ramirez on at first, which is what the Cardinals did, avoiding the Dodgers' best hitter again. With runners at first and second and one out, Young grounded into a double play. Then in the bottom of the thirteenth, Beltran singled home the winning run. The Cardinals took a 1–0 series lead.

"That was probably one that got away," Mattingly said afterward. And who knows how it would have turned out had Gonzalez remained in the lineup? Gonzalez led the Dodgers in runs batted in, which usually didn't say much about a hitter, except that in Gonzalez's case it did because he was much better at hitting with runners on base than with nobody on. Batting in his place, Young had stranded four runners. That hurt. But what hurt worse was the sight of Hanley Ramirez sitting at his locker after the game, doubled over his knees with his forehead resting in his hands. For almost ten minutes, he did not move or speak. This was not good: as Ramirez went, so went the Dodgers. They had suffered countless calamities during this crazy season and they had survived. After everything they had overcome, would their dream year end on a hit-by-pitch? No one knew whether Ramirez would play again. And no one knew whether Puig would start hitting. The only certain thing was Kershaw. He got the ball for Game 2.

The day began with Ramirez penciled in the Dodgers lineup. But minutes before Game 2 started, the ailing shortstop was scratched. Though X-rays came back negative, he was unable to swing a bat because of the pain in his side. The training staff offered to give him a Toradol injection, but Ramirez was terrified of needles. A powerful anti-inflammatory painkiller, Toradol had a reputation for keeping broken athletes on the field when there was no time to rest. Dallas Cowboys quarterback Tony Romo—who often dealt with rib and back fractures—had relied on a weekly shot of the drug to save his career. During Game 3 of the NLDS, Carl Crawford had crashed into the stands to catch a foul ball and landed on his shoulder with his feet over his head. He received a shot after the game. The following day, he homered in his first two at-bats. Afterward, when he was asked about the pain he laughed and said he didn't feel much of anything.

Ramirez did not win any friends in the locker room by nixing the painkilling shot. He was the best hitter on the team and the Dodgers' offense had gone limp without him; the same hitters who hung thirteen runs on the Braves in a playoff game had failed to score one run in the previous ten innings. Whether it was fair to expect Ramirez to swing a bat through pain, this was the playoffs, and it was difficult to imagine champions like Tom Brady, Kobe Bryant, or Michael Jordan asking out of a postseason lineup unless they were facing limb amputation. Dodger players weren't happy with Ethier, either. After he said he couldn't go in Game 2 because his shin hurt, his replacement in center field, Skip Schumaker, took him aside and chewed him out. When Ramirez was scratched, the club still believed his rib was merely bruised. A later MRI would show a hairline fracture.

Opposing Kershaw was Michael Wacha, a twenty-two-year-old rookie with a nifty changeup who had made just nine regular-season starts in the major leagues. Wacha stood on the mound and wiggled his limbs to stretch all six foot six of himself with a detached calmness, as if he had no idea he was pitching the biggest game of his life. What he lacked in experience he made up for in confidence. During his final start of the regular season, he came within one out of no-hitting the Nationals. In his next start, in Game 4 of the NLDS versus the Pirates, he saved the Cardinals from elimination by pitching seven-and-a-third innings of one-run ball, striking out nine. Still, no one thought Wacha would best Kershaw, except maybe Wacha himself.

Wacha flummoxed Dodger hitters from the start. Figuring Kershaw would throw him a first-pitch fastball, the Cardinals' leadoff hitter, Matt Carpenter, ambushed him by swinging hard at his first offering of the game. He tripled. But Kershaw stranded Carpenter at third by not allowing the next three St. Louis batters to hit the ball out of the infield. He retired the side in order in the second, third, and fourth, too. The pitcher's duel was on.

Wacha was just as dominant. He set Los Angeles down in order in the second, third, and fourth; the Dodgers had managed to hit only a few lazy fly balls. When Puig struck out for the second time to end the fourth inning, it was clear Yadier Molina was in his head. Molina had been playing Puig like a marionette in the series. When Puig looked for a ball up, Molina called for one down. When Puig looked outside, Molina went in. The Cardinals' catcher had company in Puig's psyche. The drug cartel that helped smuggle Puig to the United States was always around and asking for more money. It was unclear how much they would need to be paid to go away forever, but those close to Puig felt the extortion might never end. What could he do? If he didn't pay them what they wanted, they threatened to kill him and his family. His mother worried constantly. Opposing fans hated Puig for being a cocky, rich punk—but in reality he was nearly broke. Puig had signed a seven-year contract worth $42 million in the summer of 2012, and received $12 million up front as a bonus. After taxes, most of that money had gone toward paying off the people who had orchestrated his escape from Cuba, as well as agents, lawyers, and managers. Plus he was being sued by one of the men he defected with.

And then there were the new friends who were ripping him off. One of them asked to borrow his Lincoln, and Puig said sure, because he always did. Unbeknownst to Puig, his friend took the car to get expensive work done to it to make it flashier, then slapped Puig with the bill. Puig may have been naïve but he wasn't stupid: the figure sounded too high. His security team got rid of the friend after that. Puig's financial troubles were not uncommon among young ballplayers. But his recklessness, and the fact that he went from an unknown kid to a superstar overnight in the country's second-biggest market, amplified the tension. Everyone wanted a piece of him. It weighed on all he did.

The Cardinals scored an unearned run in the bottom of the fifth off a double, a passed ball, and a sacrifice fly to take a 1–0 lead.

Kershaw led off the top of the sixth with a single to left and clapped toward the dugout after he reached first base. Crawford followed with a ground ball that took forever to skid into the glove of Cardinals second baseman Matt Carpenter. Because he had to rush to catch the speedy Crawford at first, Carpenter chucked the ball into a camera well. Kershaw took third and Crawford trotted over to second. With nobody out, runners at second and third, and the meat of the Dodgers' order coming up, it looked as if the club might score its first run in its last sixteen playoff innings. Some in the Cardinals organization noted that the Dodgers had an advantage going into the series because Mark McGwire, the club's former hitting coach, was intimately acquainted with the strengths and weaknesses of St. Louis hitters. But McGwire's intel didn't matter if the Dodgers couldn't score. Through the first nineteen innings of the NLCS, L.A.'s potent offense had managed just two runs. "Two and a half billion dollars," a team executive said later. "And two fucking runs."

The Cardinals drew their infield toward the grass for a possible play at the plate. Mark Ellis stepped into the box just needing to hit a fly ball deep enough for Kershaw to tag up and tie the game. He took a ball from Wacha, then popped up the second pitch he saw to Carpenter. One out. Adrian Gonzalez was up next. With one out and first base open, Molina called for Wacha to issue the first intentional walk of his career, loading the bases for Puig. Although the Dodgers' right fielder had pummeled Atlanta pitching in the Divisional Series, going 8-for-17 and accounting for more runs (5) than strikeouts (4), the Championship Series had been a disaster for him. Puig had gone a miserable 0-for-6 in Game 1, leaving a game-high seven runners on base. He had struck out in his first two at-bats in Game 2. But with the bases loaded and the Dodgers down 1–0, the young Cuban could give his club the lead and change the momentum of the series with one swing.

Wacha surprised Puig with a first-pitch 95 mph fastball down the middle of the plate. Puig was late and swung through it so violently that he fell down to one knee. Wacha threw another fastball that nicked the bottom of the zone for a called strike two. Puig thought that pitch was low, and he turned around and glared at home-plate umpire Mark Carlson. The crowd got even louder. Puig took the next pitch, and the next and the next to work the count full. With the bases loaded and nowhere to put Puig, Wacha threw a fastball in the dirt. Puig started to swing, then tried to stop himself. It was too late. He struck out with a feeble stab at the ball, then began the slow walk back to the dugout with his head down. He descended the steps past Mattingly, turned right down the tunnel that led to the batting cages, collapsed against the wall, and sobbed. His new translator, Roman Barinas, found him huddled against the wall just as Michael Young passed him on his way back to the dugout from the indoor batting cages. Young, who had been preparing to pinch-hit if necessary, leaned in to console Puig. "It's not over yet, we need you," Young said. Barinas translated. "You're gonna get another chance." The Dodgers trailed by only a run but it didn't matter. Puig had come to St. Louis to show the people who wanted to see him fail that he could lead the Dodgers to the World Series. And now he was humiliated.

While this was going on, Uribe came up to bat with the bases loaded and two out. He struck out. Puig dried his tears and jogged back out to his position in right. The next nine Dodger hitters went down in order, save for a Nick Punto single. Puig struck out looking in the ninth. Kershaw had been brilliant again, allowing two hits and no earned runs in six innings. Desperate to generate offense, Mattingly had pulled him for a pinch hitter in the top of the seventh after he'd thrown just seventy-two pitches. Kershaw removed his cap and stood alone with his hands on his hips and watched as Young hit for him. He flied out to end the inning. In nineteen playoff innings in 2013, Kershaw had given up one earned run. Despite managing only two hits in Game 2, the Cardinals won to take a commanding 2–0 NLCS lead. The series headed back to Los Angeles for Games 3, 4, and 5.

If the Dodgers could win at least two of those games, the clubs would be forced to return to St. Louis for Games 6 and 7. But after the brutal Game 2 loss, even pushing the series to five games seemed like a tall order. The Dodgers had already burned Greinke and Kershaw, while St. Louis had held on to its ace. In Game 3, Hyun-Jin Ryu would face off against the superb Adam Wainwright, the only pitcher in the National League who had thrown more innings than Kershaw that season. After Game 2, Hanley Ramirez sat quietly at his locker with his shirt off and two large bandages covering his left side. A large contingent of media gathered around Puig's locker, waiting for him to appear from the showers. Of the sixty or so people in the room, the only person making any noise was Matt Kemp, who was riding around on a scooter chirping "meep meep." Puig emerged ten minutes later to face reporters with wet, red eyes.

If Don Mattingly was worried about being fired, at least he knew he had one powerful ally in his corner. Before Game 3 in Los Angeles, Mark Walter and his daughter, Samantha, approached him on the field during batting practice at Dodger Stadium and threw their arms around him. If the front office wanted to get rid of Mattingly, they would have to come up with reasons compelling enough to trump Walter's obvious affection for the man. Though he valued the opinion of others in the organization, Walter was the self-described decider-in-chief. He would ultimately make the call.

Hyun-Jin Ryu had played it safe against Atlanta in the NLDS, and his conservative approach led to his removal after three innings. He arrived at Dodger Stadium before Game 3 of the NLCS vowing not to make the same mistake. Rather than conserve energy so he could stick in the game longer, Ryu signaled the sense of urgency the entire team felt by pumping a 95 mph fastball to Carlos Beltran in the first inning. It was the hardest pitch he'd thrown all season. Ryu cruised through the first four innings and did not give up a hit until the fifth. The life on his fastball caught the Cardinals flat-footed; in the seven innings Ryu pitched, St. Louis was able to muster only three singles and a walk. Nobody made it to third base.

As Cardinal bats remained cold, Dodger bats heated up. Ramirez returned to the lineup without the Toradol injection, and it sparked the club. Despite his broken rib, the shortstop singled in the first, hit a fly ball deep enough to advance Mark Ellis to third in his next at-bat, and beat out an infield single that plated a run in the eighth. Puig snapped out of his funk, too. After striking out looking in the second inning, he tripled in a run in the fourth. When the ball left his bat he assumed he had hit it out of the park, so he flipped his bat, raised his arms in celebration, and stopped to watch it fly. Upon realizing it bounced short of the fence and remained in play, Puig sprinted to third and celebrated again. This did not sit well with those who thought he was a hot dog. Puig didn't care. He had been mortified to tears during the previous game and probably would have executed a front flip on third base now if it had occurred to him. Brian Wilson and Kenley Jansen closed out Ryu's gem, and the Dodgers took Game 3 to crawl back into the series, besting Adam Wainwright 3–0.

The Dodgers' coaching staff thought about moving Greinke and Kershaw up a day to pitch on short rest for Games 4 and 5 but quickly nixed that idea, in part because they didn't want to push Greinke, but also because they didn't want to find themselves in a situation where Ricky Nolasco had to pitch an elimination game on the road. So Nolasco took the mound in Game 4, and it marked the first time he had pitched in more than two weeks. Nolasco looked as uncomfortable as Ryu had appeared confident the day before. He got through the Cardinals lineup the first time just fine, but fell apart the second time through the order, giving up a single, a double, and then a mammoth home run to Cardinals left fielder Matt Holliday that gave St. Louis a 3–0 lead. The Dodgers battled back in the bottom of the fourth, with RBI singles from Puig and A. J. Ellis. With two on and one out, Mattingly pinch-hit Schumaker for Nolasco. Schumaker grounded into a double play. The Dodgers never got another good chance after that and dropped the contest 4–2, pushing them to a loss away from elimination. After the game, Ramirez said he was in way more pain than he was the day before. His discomfort was obvious; after fouling a pitch off in the first inning he grabbed his side and bent down in agony in the batter's box. He struck out three times.

The mood in the Dodger locker room was glum, but Mattingly told reporters he wasn't nervous. "I've got one of the best pitchers in the world going tomorrow," he said of Greinke. But Greinke was antsy. He had never pitched twice against a team in the same series in his career, and his restless mind worked through all the possibilities of how Cardinal hitters might try to attack him. "They're going to make an adjustment," he said before Game 5. "And you've got to be faster than them at it." But being quick with countermoves was going to be difficult. Of all the teams Greinke had faced in his ten-year career, he felt the Twins and the Cardinals adjusted the fastest.

Ramirez still hadn't taken the Toradol shot and his status for Game 5 remained in question. Even though the Dodgers had Greinke and Kershaw lined up to potentially even the series, the players seemed nervous before Game 5 and barely spoke to each other. Ramirez sat in the dugout and a media scrum formed around him. "I owe it to the city and to the fans to play today," he said. It seemed to make people feel better, as if having an injured Ramirez in the lineup was better than no Ramirez at all. But by the seventh inning he would be pulled from the game and replaced by Nick Punto because he could no longer move. When Greinke took the mound in the first inning he had the same uneasy look in his eye as Nolasco the day before. His discomfort was made even more obvious by the amount of time he took between pitches, which was much longer than usual. The Cardinals jumped on him, loading the bases with a single, a walk, and another single before many fans had made their way in from the parking lot. Their big power-hitting lefty Matt Adams came up to the plate in a dream scenario: with no out and the bases loaded. Greinke outsmarted him and employed the strategy Kershaw used in Game 1 of the NLDS to wiggle out of the jam. Of the nine pitches the first three St. Louis hitters saw, eight were fastballs. Greinke started Adams with a fastball, and Adams took it for a called strike. It was the only heater he would get. With Adams looking fastball all the way because there was nowhere to put him, Greinke used three curveballs and a changeup to fool him, striking him out on a pitch in the dirt. He then got Molina to ground into an inning-ending double play with another curveball. As Greinke settled down, Dodger hitters stayed hot. Crawford and A. J. Ellis each homered, and Gonzalez homered twice. Greinke went seven and allowed two runs, and Los Angeles won 6–4 to push the series back to St. Louis.

The Dodgers had never overcome a 3–2 game deficit in a postseason series in club history. But based on the way the guys were goofing around on the field before Game 6, one might have assumed they were up 3–2. After the Dodgers won Game 3, Adam Wainwright described some of the club's on-field celebration antics as "Mickey Mouse." A Cardinal fan Photoshopped a picture of Gonzalez wearing Mickey Mouse ears on Dumbo the elephant ride and called it Dumbo and Dumber. He turned the picture into a poster and made another poster comparing Puig to a squirrel. Gonzalez and Puig saw the posters during batting practice and loved them. They ran over to the fan, signed the artwork, and happily posed for pictures. Gonzalez had worn a Mickey Mouse T-shirt the first day he showed up to Dodger Stadium after being traded from Boston. He had come full circle. It was an odd scene, but the Dodgers felt good for a few reasons. First, they had Kershaw taking the mound. Second, the Cardinals had coughed up a 3–1 NLCS lead to the Giants the year before and San Francisco went on to win the World Series. The possibility of history repeating itself weighed on St. Louis heavily. "We got Kersh going tonight, then in Game Sevens anything goes," Dodger players said to reporters and to each other. And they believed it. With Kershaw on the hill there was no doubt in anyone's mind that the series was going seven. And then it would be all hands on deck.

The Dodgers were facing Michael Wacha again, but they felt they had a better shot at getting to him this time with Ethier and Ramirez back in the lineup. Ramirez thought the off day between Games 5 and 6 would help his rib cage feel better, but it had the opposite effect. When Game 6 started the temperature in St. Louis was fifty-two degrees—thirty degrees colder than it had been at first pitch for Game 5 in L.A. The chill made his ribs hurt worse. The Dodgers' training staff had tried everything to ease Ramirez's pain and gift him some mobility: ice, steam, ultrasound—to no avail. Ramirez finally acquiesced to the needle.

It was fitting that the Dodgers were entrusting their season to Kershaw. At just two wins away from a National League pennant, Los Angeles was the closest it had been to a World Series berth in twenty-five years. When the Dodgers made the NLCS in 2008 and 2009 the Phillies needed only five games to eliminate them. Game 6 started out on a promising note, with Crawford beating out an infield single. But Mark Ellis grounded into a double play, and after getting ahead in the count 3-0 Gonzalez tapped out to third. If Cardinal fans were worried about a redo of the previous year's collapse, it was perhaps a blessing that Wacha was a rookie and those ghosts didn't occupy his psyche.

Puig came up to bat with the bases empty and two out in the top of the second. He lowered his bat, carved a cross into the dirt just outside the batter's box, and took a deep breath. With the game still scoreless and no men to drive in, he was looking to untie the contest with one swing. Puig had posted one of the best rookie seasons ever and was now one of the most famous players in the game. He knew that. He also knew that his brazen style of play inspired his detractors to hate him as much as his fans loved him. He was the most polarizing player since Barry Bonds. But unlike Bonds, who grew up in MLB locker rooms when his father played and learned how to isolate himself in a bubble of indifference, Puig had not mastered the art of self-protection. He believed that he could win Game 6 by himself. But Wacha had found the hole in Puig's swing. After falling behind 2-0 Wacha threw Puig a high fastball that he swung at and missed. Then, he threw him another high fastball that he fouled off. With the fifth pitch of the at-bat he struck him out looking with yet another fastball. Puig stepped back over the cross and walked back to the dugout.

The only Dodger who could will the team to Game 7 was perhaps Kershaw himself, and he wouldn't have had it any other way. Two hundred days earlier he had taken the mound on the opening day of this wild season, and he had shut the Giants out and hit a home run. He had won the National League's ERA crown for the third consecutive year by posting a minuscule 1.83 ERA, the best mark for any pitcher in either league since Pedro Martinez finished the 2000 season with a 1.74 ERA for the Red Sox. He was weeks away from winning his second Cy Young Award before his twenty-sixth birthday. He possessed the best slider in the game, and a top-three curveball. His stuff was as good as his karma. For all those reasons, what happened next was shocking.

Kershaw collapsed.

The first sign that Kershaw was fighting an unusual battle came in the bottom of the second when, after getting the first two hitters to pop up, he gave up a single to Shane Robinson and then threw two wild pitches to advance Robinson to third. In the Division Series, he salvaged a night when his fastball sailed on him by sticking his curveball and slider for strikes. But he seemed to have trouble spinning the curve in the cold, and it failed him. He watched, helpless, as one of his most potent weapons abandoned him when he needed it most. With Robinson on third, he went back to his fastball and struck out Cardinals shortstop Pete Kozma to end the inning.

Cardinals second baseman Matt Carpenter would go 1-for-4 in Game 6. No one would remember the three times he made an out. With one out in the third, Carpenter took ball one, then fouled off seven straight pitches. Left-handed batters had hit .165 against Kershaw that season, with a .253 slugging percentage. He had faced 171 lefties, and struck out 71 of them. Because of these numbers, opposing managers went out of their way to stack their lineups with righties against him (though their odds were just slightly improved). With each hack Carpenter took, it became more and more evident that something was wrong with Kershaw. He simply could not put Carpenter away. On the eleventh pitch of the at-bat, Carpenter doubled. Carlos Beltran followed that up with an RBI single. Kershaw rebounded to strike out Matt Holliday, but then gave up singles to Molina and David Freese. With the score 2–0 and two runners on, Kershaw walked Matt Adams on a 3-2 pitch that probably should have been called strike three. Then, with the bases loaded, Shane Robinson smacked a single to right, which Puig threw away. The Cardinals became the first team to bat around on Kershaw in an inning in four years.

It was only four runs, and L.A.'s potent lineup had eighteen outs left to match that total. But after watching their ace get knocked around, Dodger hitters looked as if they'd just walked away from a bus wreck. Michael Wacha didn't worry about them anyway. The rookie starter was brilliant, scattering just two hits and a walk over seven shutout innings. It was the line many expected Kershaw to post, and it demonstrated the beauty and the agony of the game. Kershaw remained on the mound after his torturous third inning but was pulled after giving up hits to the first three batters he faced in the fifth. It was his shortest start not related to the flu in over three seasons. When it was all over, he was charged with seven runs on ten hits. In a season of improbable highs and lows, the impossible had happened. The Dodgers went out with a whimper, losing 9–0.

After the game, Kershaw stood at his locker with his arms folded in front of him and his eyes fixed straight ahead. He maintained his composure when he spoke, but when he paused to consider a question his lips constricted into an upside-down horseshoe. He made no excuses. He had pitched poorly when his team needed him most, and there was nothing left to say. He had failed, for the first time in his professional career. And he had done so in the biggest game of his life. He would blame himself, but he was not the only Dodger who had failed. With their season on the line, their vaunted offense had mustered two hits against a pitcher who had spent most of his season in the minors. As players dressed in silence, Mark Ellis stood in front of his locker and shook his head. "This team is too good to be done," he said. "There's way too much talent in this room for it to be over." The Cardinals were headed to the World Series. The best team money could buy was headed home.

When the Dodgers sent out a press release announcing a year-end media session the Monday after the club was eliminated from the play-offs, reporters arrived at Dodger Stadium expecting nothing more than clichéd sound bites to sum up a disappointing end to a championship run. It had been a surreal season, but one of the reasons Mattingly had hung on to his job when the team flailed was that he was a man who chose his words carefully. He toed the company line even better than his mentor, Joe Torre, and for the most part resisted saying anything that would draw attention to the club's personality clashes. When he and his coaching staff disagreed with the front office over how to dis-cipline Yasiel Puig, he said nothing about it to the press. When the Dodgers didn't announce that his contract for 2014 had automatically vested he kept his mouth shut. But perhaps trotting out Mattingly to answer questions about his future with the team when he still had no idea whether he would be back was the final insult.

Three days after the Dodgers were eliminated, Mattingly took his seat on a dais next to Ned Colletti. The interview room was jammed with so many media members that many were forced to lean against walls. Though Mattingly and Colletti sat in identical chairs behind the same table, there was an awkward distance between the men, as if a third person had been invited to sit between them but failed to show up. Mattingly sat with his arms crossed and his back turned slightly away from Colletti. It was unusual to see the skipper field questions in jeans and reading glasses. Baseball is the only of America's big four sports where the club's coaches wear uniforms like the players. Per-haps wearing clothes without the word DODGERS across his chest gave Mattingly the psychological distance he needed to speak out.

Colletti opened the session by giving a positive review of the season. "This team went from at one point being nine and a half games out and twelve games under .500 to win the West by eleven," he said. "We beat Atlanta in the first round—a very good team—and came two wins from going to the World Series. I think it was quite a remarkable season."

When it was Mattingly's turn to talk, a reporter asked him about his job status.

"My option vested once we beat Atlanta," Mattingly revealed to a room of reporters who had no idea. "That doesn't mean I'll be back." He continued: "I love it here. But I don't want to be anywhere where you're not wanted."

His words stunned the room. The new ownership group had, for the most part, been pitch-perfect in its two seasons running the team. But it had made its first major misstep: underestimating Don Mattingly.

Regardless of his perceived tactical deficiencies, Mattingly had taken a room full of pernicious egos that sat in last place at the season's midway point to within two wins of the World Series. Had Hanley Ramirez not been neutralized by a fastball to the ribs the Dodgers might have won the whole thing. He kept his cool when the habitually tardy Puig turned a deaf ear to him. Another manager might have leaked stories about how impossible the kid was to coach to make himself look better. But when Mattingly had the chance to criticize Puig, he pointed out, time and again, everything his right fielder had been through even to get to Los Angeles. He called Puig a good kid. And he had done all of this as a lame-duck manager, knowing he was hiding the team's inner turmoil from the public when he wasn't sure if management had his back. Even if ownership agreed to let him return to manage for one more season, Mattingly told friends he would rather leave than work on a one-year contract again and have to answer questions after every two-game losing streak about whether he thought he would get fired. "This has been a frustrating, tough year, honestly," he said.

Colletti sat and listened while Mattingly spoke and appeared nervous that Mattingly was lumping him in with the people who perhaps did not want him back. "I hired Donnie, and I've been supportive of him all the way through," said Colletti. "Even in April, May, and June."

So if Colletti wanted Mattingly back, as he claimed, and Mark Walter was obviously a fan, then who wanted Mattingly gone? Stan Kasten was not present for Mattingly's press conference, but he couldn't have been happy with what was said. What Kasten valued most was control, and his soldier had gone rogue. The rest of the Dodgers' coaching staff was also at Dodger Stadium that day for organizational meetings. They watched Mattingly's press conference on a television in a room just down the hall. When it was over, Mattingly left the stage and joined them. They took turns high-fiving him.

The next day, Mattingly flew home to Indiana without resolving whether he would be back in 2014. Kasten flew to Chicago to meet with Walter. Mattingly's calculated risk turned out to be smart. Even if the front office wanted him gone, Mark Walter, king of common sense, would require someone to come up with the name of a man who could do a better job under the same circumstances. It was easy to second-guess Mattingly's game management, but far more difficult to find someone else who could handle that locker room. Puig wasn't going anywhere. Matt Kemp probably wasn't, either, at least not before the 2014 season began. Next year, the Dodgers figured to enter camp with the same four outfielders, each expecting to start. It was not easy to manage these personalities and there were no obvious outside candidates to take Mattingly's place.

So Mattingly went home and waited for a phone call. The day after his press conference, the Dodgers announced the firing of his bench coach, Trey Hillman. Two weeks later, with his job status still up in the air, Mattingly was named runner-up for National League Manager of the Year.

The following day, Clayton Kershaw earned his second Cy Young Award, collecting twenty-nine of the thirty first-place votes.

•   •   •

That blockbuster trade between Los Angeles and Boston a year earlier did propel one team to glory—but not the Dodgers. Thanks to L.A.'s willingness to take on hundreds of millions in salary commitment, the Red Sox used their newfound financial freedom to build a team that won the American League pennant in 2013. Then they beat the Cardinals to win the World Series.

Just before the Red Sox hoisted that trophy, Dodger players packed up their lockers ahead of a long off-season. Yasiel Puig was one of the last to leave the stadium. On his way to the elevator, a reporter asked him through a translator if, now that it was over, he would like to talk about all the crazy things that had happened during his incredible rookie season, to separate fact from fiction once and for all. He smiled. "In twenty years we can sit down and I'll tell you everything," he said in perfect English.

9

NO NEW FRIENDS

The 2014 season did not start out well for Yasiel Puig.

After splitting time between Los Angeles and Miami in the off-season, the young right fielder reported to spring training weighing twenty-five pounds more than at the end of the 2013 season. But unlike the muscle that seemed perfectly concentrated in his arms and upper back the year before, these new pounds hung like Christmas garlands from his belly and backside. He looked like the chubby kid who had auditioned for major-league scouts in Mexico.

Portly Puig collected just eight hits in forty-eight chances during spring training, with no home runs or stolen bases. It was a small sample size, to be sure, but the Dodgers' coaching staff wasn't happy. How could a twenty-three-year-old baseball player whose game relied on his legs already weigh over 250 pounds? What did that say about his commitment to his career? Puig wanted to be the best player in the game, but he also hated working out. Could he ever achieve the former without the latter?

His off-season had not been as quiet as his bosses had hoped, either. With a reckless driving charge from the summer already on his record, a few days after Christmas Puig was pulled over by a Florida Highway Patrol officer for doing 110 on Alligator Alley through Naples at nine thirty on a Saturday morning. He was contrite, but when the officer noticed he was speeding with three passengers including his mother, he went ballistic.

"This is your mom? Oh, you're going to jail. You are putting your mom in danger, oh hell no," the trooper said to Puig in Spanish, in audio captured by a police recording of the incident. "Why were you driving that fast? You don't care about anyone's life in the car?"

"Yes, I do care. I'm sorry," Puig responded. "Please forgive me." But the officer was unmoved.

"Officer, I'm sorry. I'm begging you, sir," Puig said. "I'll do anything. I'll never drive again. Please don't take me to jail."

After placing Puig in his squad car, the officer returned to Puig's vehicle to explain to his mother, his cousin, and another passenger why he was being arrested.

"The reason why we're in this situation is because he didn't care about his mother's life, or your lives, and he's going to jail," the cop said over Puig's mother sobs.

In the backseat of the squad car, Puig berated himself. "Why do you have to drive so fast, Puig?" he said. "You have to learn." This marked Puig's second arrest for reckless driving in eight months. He subsequently promised the Dodgers he would hire a driver.

By the time the regular season started, Puig had dropped most of the off-season weight. The Dodgers opened the 2014 season in late March with a two-game series against the Diamondbacks in Sydney, Australia. The trip was supposed to help spread baseball fever to Oceania. But it was such a long haul to take on the eve of a grueling 160-game season that Dodger players didn't want to go. Puig rebounded from his dismal spring, going three-for-ten with a couple of RBIs in two games to help the Dodgers sweep Arizona. His antics also returned to midseason form. After he struck out in the late innings of the second contest he grabbed his back and asked to come out of the game. When reporters inquired about his injury, Mattingly chuckled. He had protected Puig throughout his rookie campaign, but the young slugger's flair for the dramatic was exhausting his manager's patience. During the off-season the club had awarded Mattingly a three-year contract extension. He was now free to talk without worrying he'd get fired. "He grabs something every time he takes a swing and misses," Mattingly said of Puig. "Shoulder yesterday, back today. I'm not quite sure what we'll do. We may not do anything."

Puig's baserunning blunders had also reappeared in game two. He tried to stretch a single into a double in the third inning and was easily thrown out. And when a pitch in the dirt rolled away from Diamondbacks catcher Miguel Montero in the sixth, Puig tried to steal third and was nailed again. After the game, reporters heard Puig and Adrian Gonzalez shouting at each other through the clubhouse walls. The chatter of Puig's imminent implosion got louder, as beat writers began reporting on the rift between Mattingly and management on how to handle their young star. It became clear that Mattingly was ready to rein in his wild horse. But after a year of Puig doing as he pleased without consequences, was it too late?

Two days after they returned from Australia the Dodgers held their first workout of the season at Dodger Stadium. It was scheduled to begin at 10:30 a.m. Puig walked into the locker room in street clothes at 10:27. Most of his teammates had been there for hours. He muttered something about his back and disappeared into Mattingly's office with the team's vice president of medical services, Stan Conte. After Mattingly and Puig discussed Puig's tardiness, the two men walked into the clubhouse together. Mattingly told Dodger players that Puig wanted to address them. The men fell silent. Puig walked to the center of the room. "Okay," he said to his teammates, through a translator. "You guys tell me how you want me to play."

Juan Uribe went first. He told Puig to just show up on time. Then it was Hanley Ramirez's turn. He shook his head. "I just don't want your career to go the way my career went," he said, of his time with the Marlins. "All my teammates hated me because of the way I played." It was a profound admission from Ramirez, who despite his superstar status was still hurt by the way things had ended in Miami. Ramirez had spent his time in Los Angeles trying to undo his reputation as an aloof player who hustled only when it suited him and challenged teammates to dugout fistfights when they called him out on it. "I got a fresh start here. I got a chance to make things right," he said. "This is a great place to play. This is a great place for you to start over."

New Dodger Chone Figgins was the next and final person to speak. He told Puig the season was long and that he couldn't get too high or too low or he'd burn himself out and take his teammates down with him. When Figgins finished, and nobody else spoke up, Puig walked back to his locker. Then Mattingly grabbed him by the arm and said, "We're all proud of you." A few Dodgers said it was the strangest team meeting they'd ever been in. It seemed to other players that Mattingly had put Puig up to it, that the fourth-year skipper was trying to get his embattled young star to be more accountable to his teammates so none of them wound up punching him. But did Puig really care what the rest of the locker room thought of him? Some Dodgers talked it over afterward, and though they agreed the summit was awkward, they were optimistic that good could come from it. Many of them had wanted to talk to Puig about how to behave during his rookie season, but they were afraid of how he'd receive it. They hoped that Mattingly's ploy had at least opened that dialogue.

Skip Schumaker and Nick Punto had been two of Puig's teammates most willing to get in his face when he acted like an ass during his first year, but they had both signed with other teams. Though Puig often rolled his eyes at them when they told him to clean it up, his friends said he secretly admired Punto and Schumaker a great deal. They had stood up to him and he respected them for it. Like Punto and Schumaker, Mark Ellis had been one of the most popular players in the clubhouse in 2013, and he too was gone. In exit interviews, the Dodgers' coaching staff had told the front office how valuable those men were to keeping the locker room from combusting during the first three awful months of the 2013 season, and that they hoped at least two of them were re-signed. The front office let all three walk. That loss was felt deeply by the players.

There is a running joke among baseball writers that every player shows up to spring training proclaiming to be in the best shape of his life, every year. But for many of the 2014 Dodgers it was actually true; the bitter taste of a devastating playoff exit fueled long off-season hours of work. Kershaw spent the winter at home in Dallas adding muscle mass to his shoulders in hopes that the extra strength would give him more endurance in October. Knowing he'd be in a four-man fight for three outfield spots, Andre Ethier showed up as lean as he had been in years. Adrian Gonzalez and Hyun-Jin Ryu shed weight, too. With the end of his Dodger contract nearing and free agency on the horizon, Hanley Ramirez spent the winter months running and hitting and lifting more than usual. He showed up to camp trimmer in the waist and broader in the shoulders, motivated by the knowledge that a monster season could earn him a new nine-figure contract, and optimistic that Los Angeles would be the team to give it to him.

The Dodgers were in a tough spot with Ramirez. After his turbulent time in Miami, the talented shortstop had found his footing in Los Angeles. He had been a brilliant player and a good teammate in the year and a half he'd been a Dodger, and he was a favorite of Mark Walter, which was no small detail. Walter had locked up his other favorite player, Clayton Kershaw, to a $215 million deal weeks before spring training began. Ramirez made no secret of his wanting to play out the remainder of his career in Los Angeles. But he had just turned thirty, and his recent injury history was as frightening in its length as it was in its diversity: shoulder, thumb, back, hamstring, ribs. He'd missed seventy games in 2011 and seventy-six more in 2013. At the end of the previous season, he avoided telling reporters what hurt because everything did. Ramirez was seeking a six- or seven-year contract extension. The Dodgers preferred to overpay him for three or so years to save themselves risk on the back end. The two sides began the season at an impasse.

Clayton Kershaw's 2014 started out better than Puig's. On the day he finalized that seven-year deal with an opt-out after five for $215 million, Kershaw explained his thinking. "Five years is the max for me that I could see myself competing at the highest possible level that I'm comfortable with," he said. "Anything else I don't think I could've—I think it would have been too overwhelming to know—oh my gosh I've gotta do it for this much longer. This helps me by knowing that it's not a sprint by any means but it's not a marathon, either. It's probably a win for the Dodgers to some extent because they don't have to worry about paying for ten-plus years. I think it worked out perfectly for both and I'm really excited about it."

Though the trip to Sydney messed with everyone's biorhythms, Kershaw took the mound on opening day at 2 a.m. Los Angeles time and showed no ill effects, pitching into the seventh inning while allowing one run and striking out seven. But the following day, he felt pain in his upper back that he couldn't shake. The Dodgers kept his injury quiet. With only two games in Australia and then a week off until their regular season resumed back in the States, club officials hoped Kershaw would heal before anyone found out.

He didn't.

Even if Kershaw had not just signed the richest contract for a pitcher in baseball history, he would still have hated to start the season on the disabled list. The money just made it worse. Two days before the Dodgers' stateside opener, Kershaw told Mattingly he was pain-free and wanted the ball. Mattingly was skeptical. The last thing he or anyone in the Dodgers' front office wanted was for Kershaw to hurry back and hurt himself worse. The training staff had come under fire the year before for missing the severity of Matt Kemp's ankle injury, and for letting him rush back too soon after shoulder and hamstring woes. The team's poor physical health had sent it spiraling into last place and caused hurt feelings among training staff that lingered. Keeping a roster healthy over a 162-game season was a tall task. Preventing injury to a room full of veterans with dicey medical histories was damn near impossible. At the end of the 2013 season, the Dodgers fired their strength coach, and their beloved trainer, Sue Falsone, resigned.

The Dodgers' 2014 opening day roster cost $240 million to field, ending the Yankees' fifteen-year streak of having the highest payroll in baseball. L.A.'s starting lineup was packed with talent again, and the principal cast remained the same. The only major change the club made was replacing sure-handed second baseman Mark Ellis with the speedy youngster Dee Gordon. Originally, that spot was supposed to go to power-hitting Cuban refugee Alex Guerrero, whom the Dodgers signed to a four-year, $28 million contract in the off-season. But the coaching staff was surprised to find during spring training that the club's international scouting department had overlooked a key detail: Guerrero couldn't field the position. So they called on the diminutive Gordon to take over second base full-time. Even though Gordon had struggled to hit major-league pitching in his brief stints with the club, the Dodgers had little choice as the organization's depth remained shallow. It would still take years before the new ownership group could replenish the farm system depleted by the McCourt regime; their new-found cash infusion could provide only a Band-Aid. After Ricky Nolasco left L.A. to sign a multiyear deal with Minnesota, Josh Beckett returned from his injury-plagued 2013 season to replace him as the Dodgers' number-four starter behind Kershaw, Greinke, and Ryu. The club also signed veteran starter Dan Haren to fill out its rotation. But if any of their starting pitchers got hurt, the list of potential minor-league replacements offered them very little in the way of a safety net.

The day before the stateside opener, Kershaw played catch in the outfield at Petco Park in San Diego with head trainer Stan Conte, taking a few steps back after each throw so that he'd have to hurl the ball harder and farther each time. After toss number twenty-seven Kershaw felt a twinge in his back and stopped. The next day, a week after his twenty-sixth birthday, Clayton Kershaw was placed on the disabled list for the first time in his career.

He fought the decision, but the Dodgers were right to be cautious. The left upper back muscle he strained was responsible for holding his rotator cuff in place. If he pitched with a weakened upper body and it allowed muscle or tendon to tear in his shoulder, the injury could jeopardize his career. Spring training lasts about six weeks. The Dodgers had been forced to cut their camp two weeks short to go to Australia. Some wondered if the abrupt spring coupled with the fourteen-hour flight to Sydney contributed to Kershaw's injury, which made them even more bitter about the trip. The morning Kershaw was placed on the DL, he was the first Dodger to arrive at the ballpark. He jogged to the outfield grass by himself armed with a stopwatch. He couldn't pitch, but he could time his sprints. It wasn't much, but it was something. He was anxious to avenge the end of his previous season. To sit and do nothing but wait to heal was torture.

For Matt Kemp, the wait had been long enough. Having to watch his team go on that record run the previous summer without him only to be eliminated by the Cardinals just two wins from the World Series (again without him) had been a nightmare. Feeling himself slip from being one of the stars of baseball to a mere afterthought on his own team had been worse. If there was one good thing that came out of his freak ankle injury it was that it gave his shoulder the rest it needed to heal fully. As the 2014 season approached, Kemp could finally swing the bat with his arms at full extension with no pain. Baseballs he hit once again screamed toward the outfield fence and over it. He was back.

The same teammates who months before had pointed out that the Dodgers played .800 ball without Kemp were now buzzing about how great he looked at the plate in batting practice. To be extra cautious, the Dodgers held him out of their first five games of the season, but told him he would be back in the lineup for the home opener against the Giants. But when Kemp arrived at Dodger Stadium that morning for the one o'clock start, Mattingly summoned him into his office. He had Conte break the news: Kemp wouldn't be starting after all. They blamed it on his ankle, and told him they wanted to work him back into the mix slowly to protect him from getting hurt again. Kemp would get a chance to pinch-hit that day, but the club's medical team wasn't yet comfortable with him running around in the outfield.

Kemp was furious. He was convinced he was healthy and that the coaches and trainers knew it, too. He felt they were feigning concern over his ankle as a way to deal with the uncomfortable fact that they still had four starting outfielders. Some of his teammates wondered if he was right. The Dodgers were 4-1 so far without Kemp, and perhaps Mattingly didn't want to tinker with the lineup that was working. Many of his teammates felt bad for him: after Kemp had waited months to play again, they didn't think it was fair that Mattingly waited until that morning to tell him he wouldn't be in the lineup. Kemp sat at his locker with his head down and thumbed through text messages on his phone. Ramirez saw him slumped down in his chair by himself and yelled: "Matt Kemp! Matt Kemp! Why you no talk today? In San Diego you wouldn't shut up!" But Kemp ignored him. "What's wrong with him?" Ramirez wondered aloud. Then Mitch Poole posted the lineup card next to Ramirez's locker. The shortstop ran his index finger down the list of names, and saw Kemp's wasn't one of them. "Oh," he said. "So that's why he's so sad."

As the team took the field to stretch at 9:40, Kemp sat by himself in the dugout for a few minutes to watch. The last two years had been filled with disastrous injuries. Now he was living a different kind of hell. The idea of watching the Dodgers' home opener from the bench as a healthy bystander made him sick to his stomach. But the club had bigger problems than Kemp's hurt feelings.

Yasiel Puig had gone missing.

When twenty-five players and a dozen coaches and trainers take the field to stretch before every game, it's difficult to notice who isn't there if you're not looking for him. Puig usually hit in the first group with four of the other best hitters in the Dodgers' lineup. Group One came and went. He was nowhere to be found, and he wasn't answering his phone. Uribe pulled Kemp aside and told him that even if Puig did show up, Kemp would be starting in his place, so he had better get his head right.

While all of this was going on, Mattingly—who had no idea that Puig wasn't at Dodger Stadium—was busy describing to the media why Kemp was benched. Tim Wallach, the new Dodgers bench coach, jogged back into the clubhouse to find Mattingly. It had been only a week since Puig had stood in the center of the Dodgers' locker room and asked his teammates to tell him how they wanted him to behave, and now he was late to opening day.

At 10:30, Puig finally emerged from the dugout and jogged onto the field, some fifty minutes after batting practice had started. He apologized to his teammates as they shagged fly balls and asked Adrian Gonzalez what he thought. "I think," Gonzalez said, "that you need to get your ass here on time." Puig told Mattingly that he'd been confused about what time he was supposed to arrive at the field, as he thought the game started at 5 p.m. The Dodgers' traveling secretary, Scott Akasaki, had texted players with game-time information, as he always did. But Puig had changed his phone number after the Australia series and didn't tell anyone. And even though it was his first home opener as a big leaguer, he hadn't bothered to check what time the game started. Some of Puig's teammates who worried about his safety had already wondered if this was the day the cartel got him. After he showed up in one piece, the coaching staff debated what to do with him. Mattingly yanked Puig from the lineup and replaced him with Kemp.

It was an unnecessary headache for the Dodgers' skipper. He'd angered Kemp by benching him earlier under the premise that the training staff didn't think his ankle was strong enough to patrol the outfield. And now that Puig was grounded, Kemp's ankle was fine? Kemp was upset with Mattingly, Mattingly was mad at Puig, and it was only open-ing day. If Mattingly couldn't get Puig to change, he was determined to change the way he managed him. A year earlier Puig had shown up late for stretch before that game in Miami and Mattingly benched him only to sub him into the late innings and watch him hit the game-tying home run. Because the incident obviously hadn't taught Puig anything, Mattingly told his coaching staff that this time he intended to keep the young right fielder on ice the entire game to send a mes-sage. If management got mad at him for holding Puig out on opening day, Mattingly didn't care. The kid was still the prize signing of the new ownership's group tenure, and a symbol of how smart they had been to sign him when other teams balked. They had built a market-ing campaign around Puig, and millions of dollars were at stake. But management supported Mattingly's decision to bench him. At some point, regardless of his talent, he was going to have to learn to abide by the rules. The next day, Puig apologized to Mark Walter on the field during batting practice.

The Giants jumped out to an 8–0 lead. Kemp misplayed a ball hit to him in center in the first inning, allowing a run to score. An inning later, he attempted to make a running catch, but the ball jarred loose as he crashed into the wall. Fans in the left-field bleachers began chant-ing "We Want Puig." But Mattingly kept Puig on the pine. It was the first time ever that all four outfielders were healthy for a whole nine innings, and Puig didn't figure to be the odd man out for long. After the game, Kemp affirmed his stance. "I want to play every day," he said.

Two games later, Kemp clubbed two home runs off Giants starter Matt Cain during a nationally televised Sunday night game. After the game he didn't mince words. "I know I can hit," he said. "Opposing pitchers know it, too." Uribe chimed in with his textbook ribbing: "Hallelujah, Matt! Hallelujah! It was time for you to do something for this team."

With four healthy outfielders, Mattingly was now juggler-in-chief. He told the media that he believed the best three players would eventually distinguish themselves, and he was right. With Puig entrenched in right field and not going anywhere, and Matt Kemp hitting well enough to nail down the job in center, Crawford and Ethier began sharing time in left. It was an expensive platoon. The two men were paid $36 million combined in 2014, which was more than any single player in the league earned. Their time-share might have worked if they could spell each other against left-handers and righties. Unfortunately for the Dodgers, neither of them hit lefties. The coaching staff settled on Crawford as the starting left fielder because he was faster and more dynamic, and they thought he put together tougher at-bats. To Mattingly's relief, Ethier showed exceptional class in handling his new bench role, telling reporters he wanted to do whatever he could to help the team win, and in not undermining the clubhouse with a sour attitude.

Then, on May 22, with Zack Greinke on the mound in Queens versus the Mets, Kemp let two balls sail over his head in center and misplayed a third into a triple. The coaching staff knew that after devastating injuries to his ankle and both hamstrings, Kemp had nowhere near the speed he used to possess in center field. They didn't expect Willie Mays—but they did hope he would put in the work to improve. The previous year when Hanley Ramirez was coming back from his right thumb injury he took dozens of extra ground balls at shortstop every day with his good hand to stay sharp. Kemp had often struggled to read the ball's trajectory off the bat, but in the past he had enjoyed the luxury of speed to compensate when he was slow reacting. With bum wheels he was a different player.

After the game, Mattingly called Kemp into a closed-door meeting and informed him he was no longer the team's center fielder, and asked him to start shagging balls in left. Kemp was angry. Mattingly stressed to him that this change wasn't permanent, that he'd have the opportunity to earn back his job, but Kemp didn't take any solace in those words. Had the compromised bone in his ankle been found right when he injured it he could have had surgery in July instead of October and already be back at full strength. He had sacrificed his body by smashing into walls for this team and this is how they were repaying him? He felt stranded on his own little island again; he didn't want to play in left.

The standoff began. Los Angeles played three games in Philadelphia and then headed home to take on the Reds on May 26. Kemp stayed on the bench. After he entered his second series in the doghouse his agent, Dave Stewart, aired his frustrations to the press. "In my opinion, not playing for four straight days is a little harsh," he said. "Two years ago this guy ran into a wall, literally, for the ball club. He came back and injured his hamstrings, then his ankle. They feel he's missing a step. When I played if you gave one-hundred percent and got hurt you have the right to come back and play your position." At that point in the season, the Dodgers weren't terrible, but they weren't great, either. They had posted a 28-24 record and sat in second place behind San Francisco, five games out.

Kemp might have remained on the bench even longer had Carl Crawford not sprained his ankle. But on May 28, Kemp was back in the lineup in left field. He had faced many watershed moments during his nine-year career, but perhaps none was as critical to his future with the club. "It could be his last chance to prove us right or wrong," one Dodger staff member said before the game. "If he doesn't step up, I guess it'll be time to move on."

When Kemp shifted over to left field he was stuck in an 0-for-20 slump. The Dodgers lost three in a row and the Giants kept winning. San Francisco had cruised out to a 36-19 record, the best in baseball. And unlike the Diamondbacks team that the Dodgers overtook the previous year, this Giants squad didn't appear to be smoke and mirrors. After all, they had won two World Series championships in the last four years. The Dodgers would need vintage Kemp to catch them.

They would need Kershaw, too.

He had returned from the disabled list on May 6 and appeared healthy, shutting out a very good Nationals team over seven innings and striking out nine. Though he downplayed the damage his NLCS collapse inflicted on his psyche, that failure seemed to change his demeanor on the mound. Before, he was content to best hitters with his creativity. Now he pitched mad. In his third start back from the disabled list on May 17, he tossed the worst game of his career, giving up seven earned runs in an inning and two-thirds of work against the Diamondbacks. He was so irritated afterward that he vowed to A. J. Ellis that he would never hang another breaking ball again. In the first 75 innings he pitched in 2014 he struck out 100 batters and walked just 9. It was the fewest walks issued against 100 strikeouts in franchise history. (The previous record was 19, set by Sandy Koufax in 1965.)

On July 4, Kershaw's ERA dipped below two and would remain there for the rest of the season. Only eight pitchers in history had won three or more Cy Young Awards. Kershaw was hoping to become the ninth. At one point, he had a streak of forty-one consecutive scoreless innings. Ellis described how Kershaw had gotten even better. "He used to throw maybe ten pitches or so a game that a hitter could actually do something with," he said. "Now he maybe throws three." The left-hander did not load the bases until August 27, his twenty-second start of the season. He escaped the one-out jam without giving up a run.

On June 18, an otherwise unremarkable summer evening at Dodger Stadium, Kershaw nicked the corners of the strike zone with fastball after fastball, and used his slider and curve to knock the legs out from under Colorado hitters. Despite everything he had achieved in his young career, Kershaw had never come close to throwing a no-hitter. He took one into the ninth that night, and Ellis called the pitches behind home plate with tears in his eyes. When Kershaw struck out Corey Dickerson to end the game, he stood on the mound with his arms raised to the sky. His final line read nine innings, no runs, no hits, no walks, and fifteen strikeouts. It was the second-best nine-inning game score from a pitcher in major-league history, trailing only Kerry Wood's twenty-strikeout one-hitter in 1998. Kershaw had needed only 107 pitches.

It would have been a perfect game, too, had Hanley Ramirez made a play on a ground ball hit to him in the seventh. Ramirez fielded the tough hop in plenty of time but threw the ball away, which drew an error. It wasn't an easy play, but it was one most major-league short-stops would have made. By many statistical measures, Ramirez was the weakest defensive shortstop in the game, and the myriad injuries he had sustained during his first two seasons with the Dodgers did not help his fielding range. To his credit, Ramirez told club officials he was willing to move off the position and over to third base as long as he didn't have to keep shifting back and forth. But the Dodgers still had Uribe at the hot corner, and the veteran infielder was quietly excel-ling at the position and hitting well. "I just want to get my four at-bats every day," Ramirez said before the season. The Dodgers wanted that, too. They needed Ramirez's bat in the lineup, but in reality he was probably best stashed in left field or at designated hitter. And since the Dodgers didn't get the benefit of a DH in the National League and were already trying to cram four outfielders into three spots most of the time, they were forced to keep Ramirez at short.

Ramirez's defensive deficiencies would perhaps not have been as bad if he were the only weak link in the field. But the Dodgers were paying their five outfielders (including backup Scott Van Slyke) a com-bined $62 million for 2014—and they still didn't have a true center fielder. The bottleneck would have been best solved by an off-season trade of one of the outfielders, but the big contracts of Kemp, Ethier, and Crawford scared off potential suitors. Because of this mess, the team ranked last in fielding in center, too, which meant their defense up the middle was horrendous. It was especially frustrating because Los Angeles was paying its starting pitchers $64 million in 2014 and fielded a weak defense behind them.

Hanley Ramirez, it was becoming clear, was a shadow of his for-mer self. The Dodgers had shelled out hundreds of millions of dollars since Ramirez was traded to the team in the summer of 2012, and now that his contract was expiring, they had suddenly tightened their purse strings. When it became obvious the Dodgers didn't want him back,

Ramirez sulked and often refused to speak to the media. He isolated himself from teammates, too, preferring to shuffle between the training room and sitting alone at his locker. Gone were the inspirational "Attitude is everything" quotes he had posted all over his social media accounts the year before. "I wish I could play one day without pain," he said in a rare revealing moment. Sometimes he would smile and joke before games like the Hanley of 2013. Other times a person might say hello and ask how he was doing and get snapped at. Ramirez's mood swings exhausted teammates and staff, and Mattingly admitted his contract uncertainty had created a distraction in the clubhouse.

Because of the knock on him that he couldn't stay healthy, Ramirez vowed that in his last season before free agency he would try to play in as many games as possible. While on the surface it was an admirable endeavor, it wound up hurting the team. Ramirez kept getting injured almost as often as he had the year before, but he balked at going on the disabled list, in hopes that whatever ailed him wouldn't take the full fifteen days to heal. If Ramirez was unavailable but not on the DL, that left Mattingly with one less able body on the bench—sometimes for up to a week. When Ramirez did play, many around the club didn't think he gave maximum effort in the field, since diving for a baseball might result in injury that might hurt him in free agency. Skip Schumaker had signed with the Reds in the off-season, and when his new club played the Dodgers he gave a Cincinnati paper a telling quote. "That lineup is very good," Schumaker said. "When certain guys want to play it's even better."

Schumaker wasn't wrong. It was obvious Ramirez was playing hurt or with hurt feelings, and he just wasn't the same guy he had been the year before. Through the first two months of the 2014 season, Ramirez's on-base plus slugging was .772, some 270 points lower than his 2013 output. An unhappy Ramirez had hit .240 in his final two seasons with the Marlins. Some wondered if his good mood during 2013 was just an act, and if his Miami malaise was who he really was.

On June 3, a year to the day after his call-up, Puig was named the

National League's Player of the Month. During the month of May, he had led the league in batting average, home runs, RBI, on-base percentage, and slugging. Dee Gordon excelled, too. Though he wasn't even expected to make the opening day roster when he first showed up to spring training, Gordon seized the opportunity when the job became open and flourished. Batting leadoff, he posted a .360 on-base percentage during the first six weeks of the season and terrorized opposing pitchers on the base paths. He was named to the NL all-star team and would finish the season with a major-league-leading sixty-four stolen bases and twelve triples. Puig was named to his first all-star team, too. He had a star shaved into the side of his head to mark the occasion.

The day after Puig won player of the month, the Dodgers trailed the Giants in the NL West by eight and a half games, despite their rotation and their lineup being better than San Francisco's. Mattingly was angry. "I'm sick of talking about individual players," he said before the game. "It seems like we keep talking about one guy or two guys instead of how we can win the game as a team. Last year when we got rolling it felt like we had a true team focus. Like we were a collective group."

He continued: "The focus needs to just be on winning, and we haven't felt that. I can't pinpoint what it is, but the feeling just isn't here," he said. "I want guys to have a great season. I tell them that. There's nothing wrong or selfish about wanting to have a great season because it helps everyone. Just take a walk. Swing at strikes. No matter who gets the game-winning hit it doesn't matter."

When asked for his thoughts on why the Dodgers had already fallen so far behind the Giants, Mattingly was blunt: "It's just being basically shitty," he said. "We're just not that good."

With Kemp moved to left, Mattingly inserted Ethier into center field and hoped for the best. But Ethier didn't belong there, either. And after a particularly rough day in the field in Detroit, Mattingly fired Ethier from the position as well. The coaching staff wanted the front office to call up Joc Pederson, the organization's top prospect, to play center.

Pederson was not only the best defensive center fielder in the Dodgers' organization, he was also tearing through Triple-A. In 2014, the twenty-two-year-old lefty would become the first player in the Pacific Coast League in eighty years to hit thirty home runs and steal thirty bases.

But Pederson still struck out too much. Also, there was a general sense among the Dodgers' coaching staff that Colletti remained terrified of youth even though Puig had helped save their season the year before. Mattingly had tried to force the front office into calling Pederson up by starting the club's fifth outfielder, Scott Van Slyke, in center even though he wasn't used to the position, either. The coaching staff thought about playing Puig in center, too, but they worried that if they made him captain of the outfield he would run over teammates. They were especially concerned for the survival of Gordon, who weighed ninety pounds less than Puig. But when the front office stalled in calling up Pederson, Mattingly moved Puig to center, Kemp to right, and Crawford back to left.

Then, some luck.

The Giants went into free fall, thanks to a couple of key injuries and some atrocious play. The Dodgers caught them by mid-July and went into the all-star break with the best record in the National League. "It doesn't feel that way, though, does it?" Stan Kasten said of his team's place at the top of the NL at the time. He was right. While the 2013 team had rolled off a 42-8 stretch of baseball where they had seemed invincible, this club had quietly worked its way to the top, never losing more than three games in a row but never winning more than three in a row, either. Kemp was still unhappy, and Dave Stewart said his client would prefer to be traded to a team that played him in center. But Kemp eventually settled into his new position, and began mashing the ball as he did before his injuries. In the sixty-four games after the all-star break, Kemp hit .309 with an on-base percentage of .365 and slugging clip of .606. His seventeen home runs over that span would have put him on pace for forty-three over a full season—four more than he had hit during his runner-up MVP campaign in 2011. "He would never admit it, but I think he's comfortable in right," said one teammate.

But to recapture his form at the plate Kemp had to swallow his pride. During the first half of the season, he was still having trouble driving the ball with any consistency because of the bad habits he had developed to overcompensate for his injuries. So when the Dodgers returned from the all-star break with a series in St. Louis on July 18, Kemp went to the team's hitting coaches and asked for help. Mark McGwire and John Valentin had noticed that back when Kemp was one of the most feared hitters in the National League his batting stance was much more upright. His leaning over the plate made it difficult for him to hit inside pitches, and also forced him to yank his elbow back farther than optimal when he swung, which sapped his power. McGwire and Valentin urged him to widen the distance between his feet and change the line from his head to his feet from eleven o'clock to five o'clock back to 12/6. It worked. In a way, Kemp looked as if he had unclenched his stance; his more relaxed approach helped him wait on the ball, which put him in a better position to drive it. On August 4, Kemp was named the National League's player of the week. On August 6, he hit his sixth home run in nine games.

When Kemp's power returned his good mood followed close behind. Gone was the brooding outfielder who announced he would rather play every day for a last-place team than sit on the bench for a championship contender. After two-plus years of ups and downs, Kemp was back on track at the plate and in the clubhouse. He was hitting even better than Puig, and seemed much more equipped emotionally to lead the Dodgers in October.

Kemp and Puig were never close, and their relationship became further strained in September during a game in Colorado. With Kemp on deck and Puig on first, Adrian Gonzalez singled to right and Puig trotted to second. Kemp then struck out. Puig came home a batter later on a Hanley Ramirez double. As Puig high-fived his teammates after scoring the run, Kemp chased him the length of the dugout and screamed at him. After being separated by Mattingly, an enraged Kemp stormed down the tunnel toward the clubhouse. It was an odd time for a quarrel. The Dodgers were in the middle of an eight-run inning, and would go on to win the game 11–3. Afterward, both Kemp and Puig declined to talk about what led to the incident, but the best explanation seemed to be that Kemp was angry that Puig, one of the team's fastest runners, had failed to go from first to third on Gonzalez's hit. Ironically, it was the same thing Puig had screamed at Gonzalez for the year before.

When asked about his relationship with Kemp months later, Puig told CBS Sports, "He stated he's the best outfielder in the league. I think there are better outfielders."

But at the time, Mattingly downplayed the incident. "Oh, just talking in the dugout, same old things," said Mattingly. "We're like the '72 A's." He may have been trying to gloss over what happened, but in doing so Mattingly compared his squad to a club whose members hated each other so much that one locker room fight led to its starting catcher suffering a crushed disk in his neck.

Forty-eight hours later, Puig was involved in another altercation with his teammates. After the Denver series, the Dodgers flew to Chicago to play the Cubs. The club opted to do its annual rookie hazing on the trip. Veterans wanted rookies to come to the front of the bus to sing on the way from O'Hare to their downtown hotel, but Puig and others were playing dominoes, blocking the aisle. When some players asked to stop for pizza, the rest told the driver to continue to the hotel and circle back for the guys getting food. But Puig had opened the door to the luggage bay on the bus so he could retrieve his bag, and the driver couldn't move until the door was shut. Greinke got out and threw Puig's bag into the street. Puig responded by pushing Greinke, but J. P. Howell intervened to stop Puig.

The Dodgers had a more pressing issue than Puig not getting along with his teammates, however: their bullpen was melting down. Going into the 2014 season, Colletti had filled the Dodgers bullpen with expensive former closers way past their prime. He inked former Indians closer Chris Perez to a multimillion-dollar deal, and re-signed Brian Wilson to a one-year, $10 million contract for 2014 with a $9.5 million player option for 2015. At first blush the Wilson deal was seen as a steal. Since he had pitched so well for the Dodgers in September and October 2013, the club had hoped it could count on Wilson to set up for Jansen in 2014 as well. But he wasn't the same player. Wilson gave up eight earned runs in his first six innings in 2014, and when Mattingly demoted him from the eighth-inning job, he pouted. Some of his teammates believed he threw his fastball in the mid-80s in protest and that he wouldn't bother throwing hard and risking injury until the 2015 season, when he was pitching for another contract. Wilson's kooky clubhouse behavior hadn't bugged teammates as much the year before when he dominated on the mound. But now that he struggled, his oddball persona started to grate. He would finish the season with a 4.66 ERA and minimal life on his fastball.

Chris Perez was just as ineffective, striking out only thirty-nine batters against twenty-five walks and posting a 4.27 ERA. But unlike Wilson, who had pitched brilliantly the year before, Perez's numbers were no surprise: they were almost identical to what he did in his final year in Cleveland. Because they were veterans, Perez and Wilson could not be demoted, and they were owed too much money to cut. As if that weren't bad enough, the bullpen's hardest thrower, Chris Withrow, suffered a season-ending injury early in the year, which left J. P. Howell and Jansen as the club's only two reliable relievers. The Dodgers' starting rotation would be brilliant in 2014, notching a 3.20 ERA—second-best in baseball. But their relief core posted a 3.80 ERA, which was twenty-second out of thirty teams. With stellar starting pitching but poor defense and relief pitching, the 2014 Dodgers roster seemed built to cannibalize itself. What good was getting out to a lead if you couldn't protect it?

The club's poorly constructed roster didn't seem to matter much during the regular season, however, since talent usually wins out over the course of 162 games. The Dodgers streaked past the Giants in September and captured their second-straight NL West crown by six games. Despite the club not being nearly as exciting as it was the season before, the Dodgers' ninety-four wins were two better than what they posted during their 2013 campaign.

But as the club was soon reminded, playoff baseball is a different game altogether. In October the best offense is often defense. Pitchers throw harder and fielders tighten screws. Scoring runs becomes much more difficult. The best way to survive and advance is to give up as few runs as possible.

The Dodgers weren't built that way. With the exception of Adrian Gonzalez at first and Juan Uribe at third, every Dodger fielder was below average, which made it unlikely that the club's pitchers would be bailed out by an incredible play that prevented runs from scoring. (Puig was an above-average right fielder, but he was playing out of position in center.) Compounding that problem: Dodger starting pitchers didn't have the luxury of just getting through five scoreless frames and then turning the ball over to the bullpen to close out the game—the formula the Kansas City Royals used to make an improbable run to the World Series—because their relief corps was such a mess. J. P. Howell had been excellent for the Dodgers for the first five months of the season, but he broke down in September. He gave up just six earned runs in his first forty-six innings of 2014. In his final three innings before the playoffs began he gave up seven.

Clayton Kershaw was aware of the Dodgers' bullpen struggles when he took the mound in Game 1 of the NLDS. The Dodgers drew the Cardinals in the first round, giving them a chance to avenge their 2013 exit. On the surface, they appeared to have more of an advantage. Matt Kemp was healthy. Michael Wacha—the St. Louis pitcher who shut them out twice in the 2013 NLCS—was not. And the Dodgers had home-field advantage in a short series, so Kershaw and Greinke could each pitch perhaps twice. Los Angeles was experiencing an unforgiving October heat wave, and when Game 1 started it was ninety-six degrees. Dodger Stadium is a pitchers' park except on hot days before sunset, when the ball flies off the bat much farther than usual. The Cardinals' seldom-used outfielder Randal Grichuk took advantage of the conditions and clubbed a first-inning home run off Kershaw just inside the left-field foul pole. Kershaw retired the next sixteen batters in order before giving up another solo home run to Matt Carpenter. But the Dodgers were cruising. They scored six runs to knock Adam Wainwright out of the game in the fifth, and Kershaw took a 6–2 lead into the seventh.

That should have been more than enough. Matt Holliday started the Cardinals' seventh inning innocently enough with a single to center. Jhonny Peralta then singled Holliday to second. Yadier Molina singled on the first pitch he saw to load the bases for Matt Adams, who then singled Holliday home. With the bases loaded and no out, Kershaw struck out Pete Kozma on three pitches. But Jon Jay singled in Peralta to cut the Dodgers' lead to 6–4. The Cardinals' subbed talented rookie Oscar Taveras in as a pinch hitter, and Kershaw struck him out on three pitches, too. Then, Matt Carpenter stepped into the box.

It was Carpenter who had homered off him in his last at-bat. And it was Carpenter who had put together the interminable at-bat that derailed Kershaw—and the Dodgers' season—in Game 6 of the 2013 NLCS. This was Kershaw's shot at redemption.

Carpenter fouled off the first three pitches, which were Kershaw's 103rd, 104th, and 105th offerings of the day. Dodger fans unstuck themselves from their sweaty seats and rose to cheer him on. Carpenter took pitch number 106 in the dirt, and watched number 107 sail high for ball two. He fouled off 108 and 109, a fastball then a slider. The Dodger Stadium crowd began to chant "MVP! MVP!" at Kershaw, in equal parts appreciation and encouragement. With the bases loaded, two out, the count 2-2, and nowhere to put Carpenter, Kershaw grooved a 95 mph fastball toward A. J. Ellis's mitt. Carpenter hammered it. As the ball sailed through the air and toward the fence, the packed stadium became so quiet that it was possible to hear screams from the Cardinals' bench. The ball didn't clear the wall, but it may as well have. It clanked off the blue fence in the deepest part of center for a bases-clearing double. After all three Cardinals scored, St. Louis led 7–6.

This was not supposed to happen to Kershaw, not again. Not against the same team—the same batter!—as last year's collapse. It was as if the thing he feared most was willed into being after it became a thought in his brain. And this fresh hell was playing out in front of fifty-five thousand people and millions more on television. Kershaw had been beaten when it mattered most the year before, and he had done everything within his power to make sure it would not happen again. He had failed. "Every time he wound up to make a pitch I was thinking, Okay, this is where it ends," Ellis said about the Cardinals' seventh-inning hit parade. But Kershaw couldn't stop it. No matter how hard he worked or how closely he followed his routine to give himself some semblance of control, the devastating reality was he had very little.

The Dodgers mounted a rally, but lost the wild game 10–9.

It was such a shocking turn of events that afterward teammates and coaches struggled to find an explanation. It had to be the heat, right? Or maybe the Cardinals, who were known as some of the best sign stealers in the game, had seen the pitches Ellis called from second base and relayed that information to the hitter? Or maybe Kershaw was tipping what he was about to throw? "I know I'm going to stay up until three a.m. and second-guess every pitch I called," Ellis said after the game. Kershaw stood in the hallway outside the Dodgers' clubhouse to answer questions from a crowd of media looking for answers. He had none. "It's a terrible feeling," he said. "As a starting pitcher, it's your game to lose. I did that."

The Dodgers tried to rebound the next day by sending Greinke to the mound for Game 2. Greinke was terrific, allowing no runs on just two hits over seven innings. The Dodgers took a 2–0 lead into the eighth and needed just three outs to get the ball to Jansen. Since Greinke was at 103 pitches and would be facing the Cardinals' lineup a fourth time, Mattingly called on J. P. Howell. The lefty reliever gave up a single to Oscar Taveras and then a first-pitch home run to Matt Carpenter—who else—to tie the game. Brandon League relieved Howell and got the Dodgers out of the inning with the score still knotted at two, but Greinke's brilliant effort was wasted. Matt Kemp led off the eighth for the Dodgers and turned on a slider, homering down the left-field line. The Dodgers won the game 3–2 to even the series at a game apiece. Then they boarded a flight back to St. Louis for Games 3 and 4.

After sitting out for three weeks to nurse his tender throwing shoulder, Hyun-Jin Ryu turned in a gutsy performance in Game 3, giving up one run over six innings. Mattingly was prepared to let Jansen get the final six outs of the game, but someone still had to pitch the seventh. With no better ideas and the game tied at one, he turned to Scott Elbert, a seldom-used reliever who had just been recalled three weeks earlier after missing two years to recover from multiple arm surgeries. Elbert gave up a double to Yadier Molina and a home run to second baseman Kolten Wong. The Dodgers couldn't solve Cardinals starter John Lackey and lost the game 3–1.

Kershaw got another shot in Game 4. Pitching on three days' rest, he struck out the side to begin the game, then cruised through the first six innings, allowing just one hit and no runs while striking out nine. He took a 2–0 lead into the seventh. Had the Dodgers' bullpen been solvent, Mattingly probably would have ended Kershaw's night after six innings, as he had done in Game 4 of the Division Series against the Braves the year before—the last time his young lefty pitched on short rest. But Mattingly didn't have any arms. He could bring Jansen in for the eighth and ninth, but he still needed those three outs in the seventh. So Kershaw went out to pitch the same inning that had caused him so much trouble in Game 1 and gave up a single to Matt Holliday, just as he had four days earlier. Then he gave up a single to Jhonny Peralta, following the script. The Cardinals' big first baseman, Matt Adams, stepped into the batter's box next. The left-handed Adams had hit .190 against southpaws during the regular season, with a .298 slugging percentage. Kershaw had not given up an RBI to a lefty in 2014 until the month of September. Those numbers didn't matter. Ahead in the count 0-1, Kershaw hung a breaking ball to Adams, who hit it into the Cardinals' bullpen. St. Louis took a 3–2 lead, which became final two innings later. The Cardinals advanced to the NLCS to face the San Francisco Giants. The Dodgers went home.

10

THE BEST FRONT OFFICE MONEY CAN BUY

The Guggenheim group had spent more than $250 million on all the players who graced the Dodgers' roster in 2014. It bought them one playoff win.

On the flight home from St. Louis, Ned Colletti was angry. He knew the press was roasting him over the Dodgers' failure to add relievers at the trading deadline when it was already obvious the club's bullpen was a disaster. He wanted people to know it wasn't his fault. Colletti had come so close to trading for Padres reliever Joaquin Benoit back in July that San Diego's front office thought it had a deal. A veteran in his thirteenth season, Benoit had staggered through his first eight years with Texas, bouncing between being a starter and a reliever and posting a 4.79 earned run average. Then, in 2009 he blew out his throwing shoulder and had to have surgery to fix a torn rotator cuff. He sat out a year to recover from the injury. Many thought his career was finished.

But the small-market Tampa Bay Rays liked what they saw in

Benoit. Because their limited finances prevented them from paying a premium for established stars, their shrewd front office began stockpiling broken relievers with excellent changeups, figuring their pitching coaches could help the player sharpen it and turn it into a devastating weapon. With no better offers, Benoit accepted Tampa's invitation to minor-league camp in 2010. The Rays called him up to the big leagues at the end of April and he dominated the rest of the way, striking out 75 batters in 60 innings with a 1.34 ERA. Benoit's success was bittersweet for Tampa. They had taught him that throwing more strikes early in the count would make his changeup even harder to hit when batters fell behind, and he had flourished. And because they had helped him so much, they could no longer afford him. Detroit signed Benoit to a three-year deal worth $16.5 million before the 2011 season. He pitched very well for the Tigers, too, striking out ten batters per nine over 199 innings with a 2.89 ERA. In his final season in Detroit, he was promoted to closer.

Benoit had been one of the best relievers on the market before the 2014 season when the Padres signed him to a two-year deal worth a guaranteed $15.5 million to pitch the eighth inning ahead of their closer, Huston Street. As a guy who had proven he had the psychological mettle to handle the ninth inning, Benoit remained on Colletti's radar. And when the Chris Perez and Brian Wilson signings blew up in his face and he knew the Dodgers' bullpen would be a liability in October, he tried to deal for Benoit at the trading deadline.

But the Dodgers' analytics department thought it was a bad idea. The thirty-seven-year-old Benoit's shoulder was on the verge of exploding, they argued: it was just a matter of time. And Colletti had gotten the Dodgers' bullpen into this mess by overpaying for former closers. If Benoit did get injured, Los Angeles would still be on the hook for over $10 million, plus whatever prospects they gave San Diego to get him. Had they learned nothing from recent history? Colletti disagreed with their assessment of Benoit, perhaps because he knew he would be blamed for failing to trade for reinforcements who could shore up the bullpen. Stan Kasten may have been in the game for a long time, but he had shown a willingness to listen to the opinions of the new-school stat-heads and embraced the idea that there was no such thing as too much information. Kasten sided with the geeks. The deal was nixed. Padre officials were left with the impression that Colletti couldn't pull the trigger because he didn't have room in a bullpen already crowded with veteran relievers he couldn't cut. So the embattled Dodgers GM made no moves at the deadline and told reporters that he felt good about his club. The Dodgers' analytics department was proven right immediately: Benoit reported shoulder soreness two weeks after Colletti had tried to trade for him. He pitched just five innings in the last seven weeks of the season.

That didn't stop Colletti from laying into one of the employees who he believed blocked the trade, on the flight back to Los Angeles from St. Louis. "Thanks for having my fucking back on Benoit," he was overheard saying to the man. The nerds had been right about Benoit and had saved the Dodgers millions of dollars and prospects. But in that moment it didn't matter much to Colletti. Had he traded for Benoit and watched the righty's arm fall off as a Dodger, at least he could say he had done *something* to try to help the bullpen and could blame the failure on the club's bad injury luck.

The Dodgers flew home on a Tuesday. By Friday, rumors swirled within the organization that Colletti had been fired. The club denied it. But on the following Tuesday the Dodgers announced they had hired the whip-smart architect of Tampa Bay's improbable success, Andrew Friedman, as their new president of baseball operations, with the expectation that he would hire a new general manager. But Kasten still hated firing people, and it seemed he had a soft spot for Colletti. Ever magnanimous, he reassigned Colletti to the ceremonial position of senior advisor. For the 2015 season Colletti would move into the broadcast booth.

Friedman and his sabermetric-inclined front office had picked a thirty-two-year-old Benoit off the scrap heap, signed him for little money, and watched him develop into one of the best relievers in the game. Colletti, in his desperation, sought to trade at least one decent prospect for the thirty-seven-year-old, on-the-verge-of-major-injury version of Benoit, in addition to paying the remaining three-quarters of his $15.5 million contract. Colletti had survived the McCourt regime and the Guggenheim takeover because he excelled politically with those he worked for. But the game was changing: information was now king. And in his two and a half years owning the Dodgers, Mark Walter had learned that money couldn't buy championships. Being the richest team wasn't as important as being the smartest.

The Friedman hire caught everyone by surprise because many teams had tried, and failed, to lure him away from Tampa. The Los Angeles Angels came calling, and Friedman turned them down. He had also said no to Theo Epstein and the Cubs, and to his hometown Houston Astros. Like Colletti with the Dodgers, the thirty-seven-year-old former Bear Stearns analyst had been the Rays' general manager for the past nine seasons. When he took over in late 2005, the seven-year-old club had never experienced a winning season. Despite their limited payroll, he led them to the World Series three years later, powered by an approach steeped in advanced statistics. During his time as GM the Rays were always in the bottom half in MLB payroll. But they made the playoffs four times. The problem, of course, was that whenever his talented young players were about to hit free agency, Friedman was forced to trade them for prospects, one by one, to rich teams like the Dodgers because the Rays could never afford to keep them. Given the nature of the team's finances, everything would have to break right for Tampa to win one world championship. A dynasty wasn't possible.

But Friedman liked the challenge of playing poker with the short stack. He had joined the Rays' organization with his close friend Matthew Silverman, who became the club's president. And he enjoyed a close relationship with the team's owner, Stuart Sternberg, and manager, Joe Maddon. By most accounts, he had the freedom to do

whatever he wanted, and he treasured his comfortable working relationships. Because of this, the rest of the industry thought he might stay
in Tampa forever. When the Dodgers lured Friedman away it stunned
baseball. No one should have been that surprised. Mark Walter had
proven, time and again, that he was a man who got what he wanted.
From buying the Dodgers the night before they were to go to auction,
to taking on hundreds of millions in dead money from the Red Sox to
land Adrian Gonzalez, to overpaying to snap up Yasiel Puig, Walter
had shown he wasn't someone who liked to hear the word *no* when his
sights were fixed. In his introductory press conference, Friedman said
that while he loved his time in Tampa, he couldn't pass up a chance to
run such a storied franchise, but the Cubs were pretty storied, too. The
amount of money the Dodgers offered Friedman to leave Tampa was
not disclosed but he was rumored now to be baseball's highest-paid
executive. He convinced one of Billy Beane's lieutenants, Farhan Zaidi,
to leave the Oakland A's to become the Dodgers' new GM.

Friedman sat at a table next to Kasten to greet the pack of local
reporters crammed into the same press-conference room that was the
site of Mattingly and Colletti's awkward year-end session the season
before. He appeared nervous as he read from several pages of prepared
remarks, as if he were giving a speech to fellow high school classmates
in hopes that they would elect him student body president. He had
good reason to be anxious. In Tampa, he never had to deal with the
weight of championship expectations. He and his team had made their
bones taking chances on misfits and previously injured (or incarcer-
ated) players with tremendous upside who, if they failed to pan out,
would not lead to his being ridiculed or fired. And for every frog he
was able to turn into a prince, he'd be hailed as a genius. There was
very little risk. For these Dodgers, anything less than World Series appearances would be viewed as failure. And unlike in Tampa, where
he called most of the shots, the Dodgers would still be Stan Kasten's
team.

Friedman stressed the importance of "sticking to the process" and gathering as much information as possible before making decisions. He promised he wasn't just some myopic stat-head and said he valued the opinions of scouting reports on a player's character as much as data any computer could spit out. "The goal," he said, "is synthesizing this information." He said he put a premium on player personality and team chemistry. To become a more functional group, the Dodgers would have to get rid of players who divided the locker room and follow the adage of addition by subtraction. A reporter asked Friedman if he knew that Kasten would never allow him to trade Puig, and whether his experience working for Bear Stearns made him uniquely qualified to dump overvalued assets. Friedman just chuckled and deflected the question. He was not in Tampa anymore.

Kasten denied that he had told Friedman that he wasn't allowed to trade Puig, but as team president and CEO he was well within his rights to issue that edict. Whatever Puig's issues were, he was one of the best players in the game, he sold tickets, and he was relatively cheap.

The questions would not stop coming for Friedman, Kasten, and the rest of the Dodgers, not until they hoisted a championship banner. After depressing playoff defeats at the hands of the Cardinals two years in a row, the Dodgers entered the 2015 season having not won a title in twenty-seven years. Even worse: the 2014 Giants won another one, their third championship in the past five years. The Dodgers were better on paper. But the Giants had better pitching and defense and seemed to like each other more. Did chemistry matter that much? The Dodgers were about to find out.

After Friedman was hired, he called Clayton Kershaw to introduce himself, and the two men talked about the state of the team. Kershaw hung up the phone impressed by Friedman's acumen and confident the Dodgers had hired the right man for the job. Other Dodger players on shakier footing tried to get an audience with Friedman, but Friedman declined, saying he didn't want to speak with any of the guys on the team before baseball's annual winter meetings. Friedman knew he would have to make several tough moves to heal a sick roster, and he didn't want to meet a guy, develop a personal affinity for him, and have that affect his thoughts on trading him.

Friedman and Zaidi began nibbling at the roster's edges right away, adding bench players and backups for much-needed depth. They offered Hanley Ramirez a one-year deal for $15.3 million—a hollow pittance that would allow them to recoup a high draft pick as compensation from the team that signed him if he left. When he rejected it, as expected, they watched him leave for Boston for four years and $88 million. The Red Sox knew he was no longer a shortstop, so they planned to play him in left field. The Dodgers would miss Ramirez's bat, but they would not miss his moods. In continuing their mission to rid the locker room of distractions, they released Brian Wilson even though they would still have to pay him $9.5 million in 2015.

After letting Ramirez walk, the Dodgers' front office capitalized on second baseman Dee Gordon's breakout year, trading him and pitcher Dan Haren to the Marlins for a package of prospects. Then, they flipped one of those prospects to the Angels for second baseman Howie Kendrick, whom Colletti had tried to trade for a year earlier. To replace Haren and the retiring Josh Beckett, Friedman signed sabermetric-friendly starting pitchers Brandon McCarthy and Brett Anderson to round out the rotation. Those moves were lauded.

But all these transactions the new Dodgers' brass made didn't solve their biggest problem: they still had four outfielders for three spots—five if super-prospect Joc Pederson was included. Yasiel Puig wasn't going anywhere. Even though he was a source of constant stress for the Dodgers' coaching staff, he would make only $4.5 million in 2015, when a player of his caliber was probably worth over $20 million on the open market. So that narrowed their options to moving Crawford, Ethier, or Kemp.

The Dodgers would have preferred to keep Kemp and trade Crawford or Ethier, but the latter two had significant contracts that were viewed across the industry as gross overpays. It was unlikely the club could move either man without eating most of the money they were owed, and since they were both still good players, it was unappealing to pick up big chunks of their salaries and pay for them to play on other teams. Given how well Matt Kemp had performed in the second half, he seemed to be the most likely trade candidate because he could fetch the most value in return. Still, would this new group have the guts to finally trade the player Colletti couldn't bring himself to ship out again and again?

The answer came in early December when the Dodgers struck a deal to send Kemp and backup catcher Tim Federowicz to San Diego for catcher Yasmani Grandal and two prospects. After the season ended, the Dodgers' farm director, De Jon Watson, had left for Arizona. Logan White, the man who had drafted Kemp more than a decade earlier, had also moved on from the Dodgers and taken a job with the Padres in a similar capacity. White had long been one of Kemp's biggest fans, and championed the deal.

The Dodgers flipped one of the prospects they got for Kemp to Philadelphia for shortstop Jimmy Rollins to replace Ramirez for a year while they waited for their top prospect, twenty-year-old Corey Seager, to take over the position in 2016. With Ramirez and Kemp gone, the Dodgers' lineup figured to lose some power in 2015, especially from the right side. But Rollins and Kendrick offered significant defensive upgrades at short and second, and it became clear the new front office valued run prevention as much as or more than offense. The coaching staff rejoiced. The Kemp trade meant that Puig could shift back to his natural position in right, and Joc Pederson would finally get his shot in center field. This new Dodger team, with an emphasis on pitching and defense, would be built much more like the Royals and Giants, the two teams that had just played in the World Series. While the two previous Dodgers rosters were flush with star power, they weren't designed for October. This new front office would not make that mistake.

There was a hang-up in the Kemp trade, however. After word of the rumored deal leaked, days passed before either team confirmed or denied it. This was strange. Adding Matt Kemp was one of the most significant moves in Padres franchise history. Their previous record for a contract was the $52 million they gave starting pitcher Jake Peavy in 2007. Kemp was still owed more than twice that. The deal was good for Kemp. Though it was strange and awkward and sad for him to leave the only organization he'd ever known, there always seemed to be drama in Los Angeles, and sometimes he had no idea where he stood. In San Diego he would be treated like a god. The lackluster 2014 Padres had posted some of the worst offensive numbers in National League history, finishing the season with a .226 batting average and just 535 runs scored—38 fewer than the next most anemic offense and 183 fewer than the Dodgers. So when San Diego traded for Kemp, fans were thrilled. But after the thirty-year-old took his physical, word leaked that his body was more broken than previously thought. While the Padres knew about Kemp's surgically repaired ankle and shoulder, according to the report they were stunned to find the slugger had severe arthritis in his hips. The trade, which was thought to be a done deal, was now in jeopardy.

Los Angeles had already agreed to send San Diego $32 million to help offset the $107 million Kemp was still owed. The Padres asked for $18 million more to make the results of Kemp's physical look more palatable. The Dodgers were furious. They knew that if a deal fell apart and Kemp was forced to remain on the team, it would be a toxic situation for both the player and the club. The leak of Kemp's medical information to the public was a gross violation of privacy, and probably even against the law.

Had the Padres exposed his medicals on purpose to extort more money out of Los Angeles? No one knew for sure. But the Dodgers called the Padres' bluff, and San Diego agreed to the original terms of the trade.

Matt Kemp was gone.

EPILOGUE

Ten days after Andrew Friedman left Tampa Bay for the Dodgers, news leaked that the Rays' brilliant manager, Joe Maddon, was also leaving the organization. Because of the timing, the baseball press assumed Maddon was following his former boss to Los Angeles to replace Don Mattingly. Mattingly's job status was very much in doubt when the 2013 season ended, and that was after the Dodgers won a playoff series. The 2014 Dodgers were better, and they hadn't made it out of the first round.

But unlike the year before, when the front office let Mattingly twist in the wind post–playoff exit, Kasten immediately quashed the rumor, telling a reporter that Mattingly would be the Dodgers' manager in 2015. The minute Friedman heard about Maddon, he got in touch with Mattingly to reassure him the Dodgers would stick by him. "He called me and he was like, 'Hey, don't even worry about it,' " Mattingly said. "It's nice when somebody does that. That's the way I deal with a player. If something pops up, I'll call him or text him and be like, 'Hey, bro, don't even buy in to that.' It's quick, and it doesn't let anything go forward."

That Mattingly had embraced the uber-analytical approach of Friedman and the Dodgers' new general manager, Farhan Zaidi, became evident when he began using the term *spin rate* when talking about his pitchers. Spin rate was a relatively new metric that quantified something that knowledgeable observers of the game had long understood: the way a pitch moved was more important than how fast it was traveling. A pitcher throwing 90 with a high spin rate probably got more swings and misses than one who threw 95 with average movement. Mattingly used the term to describe why the Dodgers had overlooked reliever Yimi Garcia and his 91 mph fastball when he was in the minors, despite his strikeout rate of 29.2 percent. "He was one of those guys in the minor leagues that had success all the way through. His velocities aren't like the velocities that you'd think get the punchouts he does," Mattingly said of Garcia. "But he's got a real action to his ball. It's one of the things Andrew [Friedman] and the guys will talk about. We talk about spin rates and things like that." When the new front office noticed that Garcia's spin rate was much higher than average, he earned a spot on the major-league roster to start the 2015 season. The Dodgers had invited many veteran free agent relievers to spring training to compete for bullpen jobs. None made the team. By the end of April, Garcia emerged as one of the best relief pitchers in baseball, striking out an average of 14.9 batters per nine innings. The rookie even began closing games in place of the injured Kenley Jansen. It was hard to imagine the twenty-four-year-old getting such an opportunity under Colletti's regime, but it was clear Friedman and Zaidi preferred young, live arms to veteran experience; they valued spin rates over save totals.

Friends said Mattingly entered the 2015 season happier in his job than ever before. His opening day lineup was the same around the edges, but unrecognizable up the middle. Adrian Gonzalez took his familiar spot at first base, and rolled a ground ball over to Juan Uribe at third. Carl Crawford ran out to left field as Puig made his way to right. During spring training, the new front office decided to form a leadership council of sorts among the players, and to bring Puig into that group—the idea being that if the young right fielder helped set team rules, he would be less likely to break them. Most Dodger team charter flights are for players and staff only, but spouses and children are allowed to fly with the club back to Los Angeles at the end of a road trip. As one of a handful of single players on the team, Puig wanted to be able to bring friends on the plane, and took the idea to the leadership committee. Then he presented his rule change to the rest of the team. Veteran players who had been in the league for a decade or more had never taken team flights with somebody's entourage. They weren't interested in trying it out, and told him so. An angry Puig stormed out of the clubhouse.

By the start of the 2015 season, Puig seemed to realize that most of his teammates—and all of his critics—were exhausted by his antics. A week into the season, he showed contrition, telling the *LA Times* that he had decided to, among other things, tone down his bat flips. "I want to show American baseball that I'm not disrespecting the game," Puig said.

As harmless as it seemed, the Dodgers had been trying to get Puig to do that since before they called him up to the big leagues. Maybe if Puig had spent all of 2013 in the minors he would have learned how to behave better on the field and in the clubhouse. Maybe not. Puig was the ultimate Hollywood child star, thrown into the trap of too much money, too much fame, too much pressure, too young. And everyone around him—from teammates to coaches to ownership to the front office—had been complicit in his uneven upbringing. Getting Puig to quiet his emotional outbursts while holding on to the intensity that made him great would not be easy for him or for the Dodgers. But Puig's future with the team seemed to depend on it.

• • •

On opening day, Jimmy Rollins took Hanley Ramirez's old spot at shortstop and tossed the ball over to Howie Kendrick at second. Young Joc Pederson ran out to his spot in center field behind them. This new Dodger lineup might not hit as many home runs as the one that trotted out Ramirez and Matt Kemp, but with its superior defense up the middle it might not have to.

A. J. Ellis squatted behind home plate, and Clayton Kershaw walked to the mound to thunderous applause. It had been a busy off-season for the Dodgers' ace. In addition to winning the Cy Young Award after the 2014 season ended, Kershaw had also been named the National League's Most Valuable Player. It marked the first time a pitcher had won the NL MVP since Bob Gibson in 1968. Kershaw accepted both awards at a banquet in New York the day after he became a father. The final acknowledgment in his MVP acceptance speech went to the St. Louis Cardinals. "Thank you for reminding me that you're never as good as you think you are," he said.

It didn't matter how many personal awards would fit into that glass case in his office back in Dallas. If he did not add a World Series ring to his list of accomplishments as a big leaguer, he would consider his career a disappointment. If the Dodgers made the playoffs again in 2015, as expected, he would get another shot at conquering those demons. But that wouldn't happen for six long months. First he had to face the Padres.

The last time Matt Kemp stepped into the batter's box at Dodger Stadium, he hit a home run to seal the Dodgers' only playoff victory in 2014. Now he was playing for the other side. Kemp had walked into the visiting locker room before the game with a Padres hoodie pulled tight over his head and a full beard on his chin. As he sat in the first-base dugout to talk to media before the game, he smiled and shook his head. "Man, it's weird being a visitor here," he said. "I thought I would be a Dodger forever." But if Kemp was battling mixed emotions, he hid it well. The outfielder seemed happier and more relaxed than he had been in years, and at peace with his time in blue. "I played my heart and soul out for the Dodgers," he said. "At least, I think I did."

In San Diego, Kemp got a chance to be the leader of an exciting team that the club's new general manager, A. J. Preller, was putting together. He also got to start over without any of the tension that had tainted his final years in Los Angeles. Kemp walked up to the plate to face Kershaw in the first inning, for the first time in his career. While they might not have realized it, the two men had much in common. Both had grown up as lonely only children raised by single mothers in bordering states in cowboy country. In all the years they were teammates, they had formed no real relationship. But that didn't stop Kershaw from stepping off the mound to give the crowd a chance to acknowledge Kemp. Dodger fans responded with a standing ovation.

Kershaw had hit the Padres' leadoff batter, Wil Myers, with an 0-2 pitch, and Myers had stolen second. During spring training, the new front office told Mattingly and his coaching staff that it wanted the Dodgers' defense to employ shifts more often, according to where each batter hit the ball. Since the data showed that Kemp was an extreme ground-ball pull hitter, Kendrick positioned himself behind second base when the new Padre came up to bat. Kemp responded by hitting the ball right to where a second baseman normally stands, and drove in the game's first run. While the new brainpower in the Dodgers front office gave the club a boost, it was not possible to outsmart the game in every at-bat. Friedman and Zaidi looked brilliant seven innings later, however. With the game tied 3–3 in the eighth, Rollins clubbed a three-run home run to give the Dodgers the lead for good.

But April didn't matter; October was all that did. The Dodgers had shattered their own record by taking the field on opening day with a payroll of $270 million. Though they had never made the playoffs three years in a row in franchise history, a third straight NL West title would not be enough to make them baseball's new superpower. The

Dodgers would have to capture their first World Series title since 1988 even to start that conversation.

No matter how much money they spent or how good they looked to stat heads or how well they got along in the clubhouse, winning a championship would not be easy.

It never was.

Notes

PROLOGUE

1: *I didn't think Clayton Kershaw:* Most of the information from the prologue comes from an interview I conducted with Clayton Kershaw at his Dallas home on January 15, 2014.

5: *Ellis, described Kershaw to me as:* Interview with A. J. Ellis on April 1, 2013.

6: *seventy-five cents per heartbeat:* Tweet from Buster Olney @Buster_ESPN, January 15, 2014.

CHAPTER 1: THE BILLIONAIRE BOYS' CLUB

14: *"It was just really, really weird":* Don Mattingly addressing media at the Dodgers' spring training in Glendale, Arizona, on February 18, 2013.

14: *"I wanted to do all these things":* Interview with Stan Kasten on July 15, 2014.

16: *Some seventy-eight thousand fans:* On April 18, 1958, the Dodgers played their first game in Los Angeles at the Coliseum in front of 78,672 fans. They beat the Giants 6–5. The previous record for the largest regular-season crowd was the 78,382 who saw the Chicago White Sox at Cleveland on August 20, 1948.

16: *For his efforts:* O'Malley was on the April 28, 1958, cover of *Time* magazine.

16: *In 1950 the state's population was just over ten million:* According to the U.S. Census Bureau, California had a population of 10,586,223 in 1950, and 29,760,021 by 1990 (www.census.gov).

16: *Jaime Jarrin:* referenced Neruda after the Dodgers beat the Braves to win the NLDS on October 7, 2013. According to an article in the *Los Angeles Times* written by Hector Becerra, Jarrin described Kershaw's curveball to listeners as "aristocratic" that night, and when Juan Uribe stepped into the batter's box just before hitting the series-clinching home run, the brilliant Jarrin said, "An interesting game is coming to an end, with two teams battling like dogs, faceup."

17: *O'Malley's son Peter was quoted:* From a January 7, 1997, article in the *New York Times* written by Murray Chass. O'Malley said: "I think family ownership of sports today is probably a dying breed. If you look at all sports, it's a high-risk business. Professional sports is as high risk as the oil business. You need a broader base than an individual family to carry you through the storms. Groups or corporations are probably the way of the future."

17: *Fox never wanted:* From many articles, including an August 18, 2002, piece in the *Los Angeles Times* by James Bates. "[Rupert] Murdoch realized the potential TV value of the Dodgers when he bought the team in 1998. Before he became owner, he never set foot inside Dodger Stadium. On his first opening day . . . he grilled executives on player contracts, expressing astonishment at baseball's rules on guaranteed contracts."

17: *But the idea of entering into a bidding war:* From many articles, including an August 5, 2007, *New York Times* piece by Jim Schachter. "The purchase [of the Dodgers] was part of Fox's rivalry with Disney, for dominance in sports broadcasting."

18: *the club was hemorrhaging tens of millions:* The Dodgers lost money from every year from 1994 to 2002, including an MLB-leading $54.5 million loss in 2001. *Los Angeles Times,* August 18, 2002, by James Bates.

18: *McCourt financed his $430 million purchase:* McCourt divorce filings and court testimony revealed the family put "not a penny" of their own money into buying the team.

18: *Fox wanted to get rid of the team:* According to court documents presented during the McCourt divorce trial, Fox lent McCourt $145 million to buy the Dodgers. He was to repay that loan in two years.

18: *His local claim to fame:* According to a November 5, 2003, *Los Angeles Times* article by Thomas S. Mulligan and Roger Vincent, "during the New Year's Eve 1980 closing on the [parking lot] in a plush Boston law office, a rival developer launched himself across a conference table at McCourt and threatened in colorful language to throw him out a window."

18: *"Stock smelling salts":* An email from McCourt Group COO Jeff Ingram to the McCourts in January 2001. Presented as evidence during McCourt divorce trial.

19: *his estranged wife described him:* According to the November 5, 2003, *Los Angeles Times* article (Mulligan and Vincent), McCourt's litigation opponents included Toronto's Reichmann family, owners of Olympia & York; Hartford, Connecticut, developer David T. Chase; and Chicago's Marshall Field family, owners of Cabot, Cabot & Forbes. Toward the end of his tenure with the Dodgers he was in litigation with both his wife and Major League Baseball.

19: *"He was more stubborn than an army of cockroaches":* Interview with a former Dodgers executive in June 2010.

20: Vanity Fair *magazine likened:* "A Major League Divorce," August 2011 issue, by Vanessa Grigoriadis.

20: *boycotted the wedding:* Interview with Jamie McCourt in her Beverly Hills office, June 22, 2010.

20: *"They were equally delusional but Jamie was better at parties":* From an interview with a former executive in June 2010.

22: *led the National League in attendance:* Figures under McCourt (Espn .com):

> 2004: 3,448,283 #1 in the NL, #2 in MLB
> 2005: 3,603,646 #1 in the NL, #2 in MLB
> 2006: 3,758,545 #1 in the NL, #2 in MLB
> 2007: 3,857,036 #1 in the NL, #2 in MLB
> 2008: 3,730,553 #2 in the NL, #3 in MLB
> 2009: 3,761,653 #1 in the NL, #1 in MLB
> 2010: 3,562,320 #2 in the NL, #3 in MLB

September 2010 McCourt divorce trial begins:

> 2011: 2,935,139 #6 in the NL, #11 in MLB

March 2012: McCourt forced to sell team to Guggenheim Baseball

> 2012: 3,324, 246 #3 in the NL, #5 in MLB
> 2013: 3,745,527 #1 in the NL, #1 in MLB
> 2014: 3,782,337 #1 in the NL, #1 in MLB

(Attendance across baseball fell after the recession began in 2008. It is just now returning to prerecession levels.)

22: *Despite promising fans that he would keep the team's payroll:* The Dodgers and Yankees play in the two largest markets in the country. In 2000, when the Dodgers were owned by Fox, L.A. ranked second in payroll behind New York, and the difference was $2.6 million. By the end of McCourt's tenure, the Yankees' payroll was more than double the Dodgers'. Within two years of owning the Dodgers, the Guggenheim group pushed the club's payroll past New York's (via *USA Today* and the Associated Press). Dodgers' opening day payroll under Fox:

> 2000: $90,375,953 2nd in MLB (Yankees #1 with $92,938,260)
> 2001: $109,105,953 3rd in MLB (Yankees #1 with $112,287,143)
> 2002: $94,850,953 5th in MLB (Yankees #1 with $125,928,583)
> 2003: $105,872,620 4th in MLB (Yankees #1 with $152,749,814)

McCourt buys the Dodgers:

> 2004: $92,902,001 6th in MLB (Yankees had highest payroll at
> $184,193,950)
> 2005: $83,039,000 11th in MLB (Yankees #1 again at
> $208,306,817)
> 2006: $98,447,187 6th in MLB (Yankees #1 at $194,663,079)
> 2007: $108,454,524 6th in MLB (Yankees #1 at $189,639,045)
> 2008: $118,588,536 7th (Yankees #1 at $209,081,577)
> 2009: $100,414,592 9th (Yankees #1 at $201,449,189)
> 2010: $95,358,016 11th (Yankees #1 at $206,333,389)
> 2011: $104,188,999 12th (Yankees #1 at $202,689,028)
> 2012: $95,143,575 12th (Yankees #1 at $197,962,289)

Guggenheim Partners buy the Dodgers during the 2012 season:

> 2013: $216,334,965 2nd (Yankees #1 at $228,344,965)
> 2014: $241,128,402 (Highest payroll of any team in American sports
> history)
> 2015: $270 million (First again, with nearly $44 million going to
> players no longer on the team)

22: *revealed McCourt's plan to cut:* Evidence submitted in the McCourt divorce court trial on September 1, 2010, called for cutting the Dodgers' payroll from $100 million in 2003 to $85 million in 2006. By the end of his ownership tenure McCourt had leveraged the Dodgers to the point that the team owed lenders $540 million. Court documents showed that most of the profit the Dodgers generated from ticket sales was going toward paying off interest on that debt.

22: *daily home salon sessions:* According to divorce court filings, the Mc-Courts spent $150,000 annually on a hairstylist who came to their home five days a week.

22: *Russian psychic:* His name was Vladimir Shpunt. According to a June 10, 2010, *Los Angeles Times* article by Bill Shaikin ("Dodgers Tap Into V Energy"), Shpunt, who lived most of his life in Russia, had three physics degrees and a letter of reference from a Nobel Prize winner. He would essentially close his eyes and visualize the Dodgers winning. He also held a healing session with Dodger right fielder Jayson Werth after Werth injured his wrist. Werth later said that Dodger doctors had misdiagnosed the injury and that he did not receive proper treatment until he went to the Mayo Clinic. Shpunt also "diagnosed the disconnects" between former manager Jim Tracy and general manager Paul DePodesta.

22: *a home on Charing Cross Road:* All home purchase information comes from McCourt divorce filings. It is also public record.

23: *"I never stopped worrying":* Jamie McCourt testified in her divorce trial. She also told me as much in an interview conducted in her office on June 22, 2010.

24: *"Frank and I practically raised each other":* Jamie McCourt testified in court on September 3, 2010, that she didn't know that in signing the marital property agreement, she essentially gave away her stake in the Dodgers. "Frank and I practically raised each other, and the notion that this was not something that we wanted to get together or that I would just give it up without remembering that and without worrying about what that would mean is preposterous."

25: *"Every day going to that stadium was like showing up to a funeral":* Interview with current Dodger executive.

25: *McCourt had been too cheap to pay for an increased security presence:* Bryan Stow emerged from his coma but sustained permanent brain damage in the attack. He later sued McCourt and the Dodgers for negligence. A jury awarded him $18 million in damages.

27: *It rejected Fox's loan to smoke him out:* In a statement, Bud Selig said the loan was "structured to facilitate a further diversion of Dodgers assets for the personal needs of Mr. McCourt." And that it would "have the effect of mortgaging the future of the franchise to the long-term detriment of the club and its fans."

27: *Players called their agents:* I was in the Dodgers' locker room that day and observed this.

27: *the winning bid isn't always the highest one:* In 2010 Mark Cuban and Jim Crane bid $390 million on the Texas Rangers at auction, which was more than the $385 million bid by a group lead by Chuck Greenberg and Nolan Ryan. But since Cuban and Crane still needed MLB's approval to buy the club, and that was likely to take weeks or months, Greenberg and Ryan's bid was valued to be worth more because it could close the following week. They subsequently bought the team.

28: *Bids for the Dodgers poured in from across the globe:* Peter O'Malley partnered with South Korean company retail conglomerate E-Land to submit a bid for the team.

28: *"But he turned me down, that son of a bitch":* Interview with Stan Kasten in his Dodger Stadium office on July 15, 2014.

29: *"It was like Earvin was going through the college recruitment process":* Interview with Lon Rosen at Dodger Stadium on July 15, 2014. Kasten had actually offered Magic Johnson the Atlanta Hawks GM job in Rosen's living room. Everything about Johnson joining up with Kasten came from the interview with Kasten on July 15, 2014.

32: *McCourt slid a piece of paper across the table toward Walter:* Conversation with Mark Walter on August 29, 2013.

32: *Walter told McCourt it was take-it-or-leave-it:* Ibid.

32: *The Guggenheim group worried McCourt would violate the handshake agreement:* From a Dodger executive with knowledge of the situation.

32: *"You know Frank went back to Stevie Cohen and said beat this":* From an executive with knowledge of the situation.

33: *"We might not have won":* Interview with Kasten on July 15, 2014.

33: *"The day the Dodgers deal closed":* From an executive with knowledge of the situation.

33: *Walter says he declined to set the record straight:* Conversation with Walter on August 29, 2013.

33: *"I have some bad news":* Conversation with Walter on August 29, 2013.

34: *When first determining the baseline value:* Conversation with Mark Walter on August 26, 2013.

35: *While McCourt hid from media:* During the two years McCourt was mired in divorce and bankruptcy proceedings he granted no interviews to journalists. In his desperation he did agree to go on a local sports radio station and take questions from Dodger fans. He was ripped to shreds.

35: *"I'm nothing special"*: Conversation with Mark Walter on August 26, 2013.

36: *MLB was as fiscally unregulated as the Wall Street*: As of March 2015, the largest contract ever signed by an NFL player was the eight-year, $132 million deal signed by Detroit wide receiver Calvin Johnson. Baseball teams have issued thirty-four contracts larger than that, including the record twelve-year, $325 million deal the Miami Marlins signed Giancarlo Stanton to after the 2014 season. Furthermore, all the money in MLB contracts is fully guaranteed, regardless of injury. NFL contracts do not offer the same luxury. Football players can break their necks and be cut the next day, and owed nothing. The NFL Players Association estimates that the average career lasts 3.3 years, which has led to the NFL being called "Not for Long."

36: *"We didn't have the dough"*: Conversation with Mark Walter on August 29, 2013.

CHAPTER 2: BURN THE SHIPS

39: *The Dodgers' then second baseman, Jeff Kent, made a suggestion:* Interview with a former executive in June 2010.

40: *McCourt was said to be particularly impressed when Colletti didn't ask how much money he would be given to spend:* From an interview with a former executive in June 2010.

40: *But the damage McCourt's tightfistedness:* According to Baseball America, the Dodgers spent the least amount of money of any team in baseball on international signings in both 2010 and 2011. In 2010, the Seattle Mariners led the majors with $6.47 million in international bonuses; the Dodgers paid $314,000 total. In 2011 the Rangers led the majors by spending $12.83 million on international prospects. The Dodgers spent just $177,000. The White Sox spent the next lowest in 2011, with $778,500.

40: *"I didn't think the problems"*: Interview with Stan Kasten on July 15, 2014.

41: *by his own estimation, Colletti grew up dirt poor:* He has mentioned this in many interviews, but most notably in a *Los Angeles Times* piece written by Bill Dwyre on March 10, 2013, "Colletti Is Writing a Different Story."

42: *letting young guys know they were fucking nobodies:* This was a common refrain among Dodger players, especially the fringe guys.

42: *Colletti worried that rookies didn't possess the guts required to succeed in October:* A common refrain from the coaching staff.

42: *J. D. Drew surprised him by opting out:* In a conference call with reporters after Drew opted out, Colletti said, "I know J.D. is a spiritual guy and a man of his word. I guess he changed his words." Drew said later that he was offended by the comments. According to a *New York Times* article written by Murray Chass on December 8, 2006, Colletti considered filing tampering charges against the Boston Red Sox, who signed Drew after he opted out of his Dodgers contract.

42: *"I care so much that I don't give a fuck":* A common joke among many players.

43: BURN THE SHIPS: I noticed the "Burn the Ships" shirts and asked a group of players what the phrase meant since I thought it was cool.

44: *"more psychotic than a psychologist":* From an April 27, 1988, article in the *Chicago Tribune*, "Bowa Handling It All: Hot Temper, Cold Club," by Jeff Lenihan.

45: *He finished second in the NL MVP award voting:* Kemp initially supported Braun after word leaked that Braun had tested positive for excessive testosterone levels. Braun was not suspended for his failed test after it was determined that the collector, Gino Laurenzi, failed to mail the Milwaukee Brewer's urine sample to be tested directly after he collected it. He held on to the specimen overnight, since it was a Sunday night and he wasn't aware that any FedEx shipping facilities were still open. Later, after it was determined that Braun was a client of Anthony Bosch, he was suspended for fifty games by MLB.

46: *He didn't:* Jason Schmidt pitched in ten total games for the Dodgers, and gave up 29 runs in 43.1 innings. In the end, he received more than one million dollars per inning. He won three games.

46: *the club was aware of Schmidt's partially torn rotator cuff:* When Jason Schmidt signed his three-year contract for $47 million, the Dodgers took out an insurance policy with ACE American Insurance to protect them if the pitcher got injured. Schmidt tore his labrum, and had an ineffective career in Los Angeles. The Dodgers sued ACE for $9.27 million to recoup some of the money they lost. During that trial, they had to disclose the fact that they knew Schmidt had a partially torn rotator cuff when they signed him, but that they did not believe that injury had anything to do with his torn labrum.

46: *Many Dodger fans were frustrated by Colletti's infatuation with former Giant players:* During his first three years in Los Angeles, Colletti gave contracts to many former Giants, including Jeff Kent, Brett Tomko, Bill Mueller, the infielder Ramon Martinez, Jose Cruz Jr., Kenny Lofton, Roberto Hernandez, Mark Sweeney, and Shea Hillenbrand. He would later award large, controversial contracts to Jason Schmidt, Juan Uribe, and Brian Wilson, who also all played for San Francisco.

46: *"I just don't like giving a lot of money to players":* Interview with Stan Kasten on July 15, 2014.

48: *At the top of that list:* Ibid.

49: *wasn't God's plan:* "Crawford, Gonzalez, and Two Different Takes on the End of the Red Sox Season," a September 29, 2011, article in the *Boston Globe* written by Peter Abraham. Gonzalez told Abraham, "We didn't do a better job with the lead. I'm a firm believer that God has a plan and it wasn't in his plan for us to move forward."

49: *Gonzalez blamed the club's schedule:* The Red Sox were featured regularly on ESPN's *Sunday Night Baseball.*

49: *"You go to the grocery store and you're getting hitting advice":* From an interview Nick Punto gave when the Red Sox came to Los Angeles to play the Dodgers, on August 23, 2013. Punto, who loved playing in Boston, was quoted as saying, "It's an unbelievable place to play. I loved the accountability factor."

49: *Colletti had called the Red Sox general manager, Ben Cherington:* "Sox-Dodgers Blockbuster Anatomy," by Gordon Edes for ESPN.com Boston.

50: *Colletti thought the Dodgers had struck:* Interview with Stan Kasten on July 15, 2014.

50: *Then, opportunity struck:* The story of how the Boston-Dodgers trade went down comes from my interview with Stan Kasten on July 15, 2014, and my conversation with Mark Walter on August 29, 2013.

51: *Terry Francona, and general manager, Theo Epstein, were both run out of town:* Francona took a year away from coaching to work as a broadcaster for ESPN before signing on to become the Indians manager in 2014. Epstein was traded to Chicago to become president of baseball operations for the Cubs.

51: *The players hated Valentine:* The problems started in spring training when he berated fringe utility infielder Mike Aviles during a drill. He made matters worse by going on a local sports radio show and questioning third baseman Kevin Youkilis's heart and commitment. All-star second baseman Dustin Pedroia fired back, "I know that Youk plays as hard as anybody I've ever seen in my life. I have his back, and his teammates have his back. . . . I don't really understand what Bobby's trying to do. But that's really not the way we go about our stuff here. I'm sure he'll figure that out soon." He was fired after one season.

52: *His coaches and teammates compared him to a clubhouse lawyer:* Every locker room has a clubhouse lawyer, or a guy who will argue every point to death. From players who had played with him in Boston.

53: *it took Kasten and Henry just fifteen minutes:* Interview with Stan Kasten on July 15, 2014.

53: *in exchange for James Loney and a package of minor leaguers:* All five players the Red Sox received in that August 2012 trade were on other teams by opening day 2015. Loney signed as a free agent with the Tampa Bay Rays before the 2013 season. DeJesus was traded three times before ending up with the Reds on a minor-league deal. Sands was traded to the Pirates, then went to the Rays before signing a minor-league contract with the Indians. And De La Rosa and Webster were traded to the Arizona Diamondbacks in late 2014 for pitcher Wade Miley.

55: *"I'm from an area where if":* From an ESPN.com article by Gordon Edes on February 23, 2011, "Red Sox 'Creeped Out' Carl Crawford."

55: *"We need to talk to you about the Navigator":* A story Crawford told me.

56: *He later told a teammate that he felt like the Rays:* A story told to me by that teammate.

56: *"That guy used to terrorize us with his bat and his speed":* A story told to me by that teammate.

57: *"For two years I was afraid to smile":* Interview with Carl Crawford on August 19, 2014.

57: *"I started growing grey hairs on my face from the stress":* USA Today sports article written by Paul White on April 24, 2013.

57: *"I was completely shocked":* Interview with Carl Crawford on August 19, 2014.

57: *"I broke it down into years":* Conversation with Mark Walter on August 29, 2013.

58: *Walter was so nervous that he let it sit unread:* Interview with Stan Kasten on July 15, 2014.

58: *forced to spray-paint Ramirez's navy blue glove:* Interview with Mitch Poole on August 31, 2012.

59: *The van's tire treads were worn so thin:* Ibid.

59: *Gonzalez found his locker:* From my observations that day at Dodger Stadium.

CHAPTER 3: THE ACE

61: *On the morning of April 1, 2013:* All details about Kershaw's routine in this chapter come from the many conversations with Kershaw about it, including specific interviews with him on August 12, 2013, and January 15, 2014.

61: *Go to work around one:* This is for games that begin at seven o'clock. Almost every weekday game at Dodger Stadium begins at 7:10. Saturday night games begin an hour earlier, and Sunday games start at 1:10.

62: *Kershaw had taken another girl to the homecoming dance:* Interview with Clayton Kershaw on January 15, 2014.

62: *Kershaw had been MLB's ERA champ at age twenty-three:* In 2011 he posted a 2.28 ERA; in 2012 he went 2.53.

63: *two of the nastiest pitches:* The opinion of most hitters in the National League.

63: *men who were paid millions of dollars a year:* The average MLB salary in 2013 was $3.3 million. It shot up to $3.8 million in 2014.

64: *public enemy number one:* During a spring training game against the Red Sox in March 2008, Kershaw threw a curveball to Sean Casey that froze him in the batter's box. Kershaw began walking off the mound toward the Dodgers' dugout before it even landed in the catcher's mitt for strike three to end the inning. That's when Scully nicknamed it.

64: *Before a game at Wrigley Field:* Conversations with Clayton Kershaw and A. J. Ellis.

65: *"You just don't see that pitch":* From a question I asked Kirk Gibson in a press conference at Chase Field in Arizona on August 27, 2014.

66: *"You watch tape":* Interview with Mark Trumbo after he faced Clayton Kershaw at Chase Field in Arizona on August 27, 2014.

67: *Close approached the Dodgers:* From a person with knowledge of the deal.

67: *when he tried to imagine his life beyond thirty:* Interview with Clayton Kershaw on January 15, 2014.

68: *traded a young Pedro Martinez:* What a mistake! As a twenty- and twenty-one-year-old he pitched 115 innings for the Dodgers and struck out 127 while posting a 2.58 ERA. He went on to become one of the greatest pitchers in baseball history.

69: *"We're like the pit crew":* Interview with A. J. Ellis on April 1, 2013.

70: *"I don't need the extra minute":* Interview with Clayton Kershaw on January 15, 2014.

71: *Clayton Kershaw was born:* Everything in this section that is not already common knowledge can be attributed to the interview I did with Clayton Kershaw on January 15, 2014.

75: *a consolation prize for their 2005 season:* The Dodgers went 71-91 in 2005. Dodger fans were so loyal that the club still led the NL in attendance that year, and the following year.

76: *"I totally thought I was going to the Tigers":* I asked both Clayton Kershaw and Logan White about this story, and they confirmed the facts. It was originally reported by Bill Shaikin on May 18, 2013, in the *Los Angeles Times,* "Clayton Kershaw Is a Dodgers Star Now but It Almost Didn't Happen."

76: *"She took on some pretty serious debt":* Interview with Clayton Kershaw on January 15, 2014.

77: *Lincecum helped the Giants win World Series:* They had last won the World Series in 1954.

77: *the Giants gave the opening day start to Matt Cain:* Matt Cain had been an all-star in 2011 and 2012, posting ERAs of 2.88 and 2.79, respectively. In 2011 he finished eighth in the NL in ERA; in 2012 he finished fourth in the NL in ERA.

77: *It seemed as though every opposing pitcher:* This is the opinion of many Dodger players who struggled to answer why the club gave him such lousy run support. In 2012 the Dodgers scored an average of 3.94 runs in games Kershaw started. The Cardinals' Lance Lynn, on the other hand, got the most support, with 5.90 runs a game that season. In 2013 the Dodgers' offense was even worse with Kershaw on the mound, scoring 3.79 runs a game. The same offense scored 4.11 runs on average for Zack Greinke and 4.70 runs for Hyun-Jin Ryu.

78: *"I went up there swinging at the first pitch":* Interview with Kershaw after the game on April 1, 2013.

79: *Johnson turned and high-fived Mark Walter:* This was shown on television.

79: *The next day, Kershaw was shagging balls on the warning track:* Story told to me by a person in the room.

CHAPTER 4: IT'S TIME FOR DONNIE BASEBALL

81: *The new owner's bunker had been open for two business days:* It was built in the off-season.

82: *Baseball was serious business for him:* An opposing catcher told me that whenever he tried to make small talk with Ellis in the batter's box, the second baseman would ignore him, annoyed that he had to retrain his focus. He could not have been more different off the field, and is described by teammates as one of the nicest men ever to put on a major-league uniform.

82: *Sellers was sent to the minors weeks later:* Ramirez returned on June 2. Sellers played his last game for the Dodgers on June 10.

83: *"He thanked him for being a professional":* Postgame interview with Ned Colletti on October 7, 2013.

83: *"Coming over here I was worried about making friends":* Postgame interview with Hyun-Jin Ryu on October 7, 2013.

84: *"I see the ball, I hit the ball":* Interview with Juan Uribe on September 24, 2013.

84: *"He's the best teammate I ever played with":* Interview with Matt Kemp on October 7, 2013.

85: *his wife, Cindy, had supported their family:* From a conversation with Cindy Ellis on July 1, 2014.

86: *"There's no worse feeling than taking a bad swing":* Interview with A. J. Ellis, September 5, 2014.

87: *everyone knew it was only a matter of time:* Beckett made eight starts for the Dodgers, before succumbing to injury on May 13. He had surgery to alleviate a pinched nerve in his neck, and didn't pitch again in 2013. He finished the season with a 5.19 ERA in 43.1 innings. He was paid $15.75 million.

87: *Hitters had no trouble:* Despite being a fly-ball pitcher, Ted Lilly enjoyed success during a fifteen-year career, until batters started hitting too many fly balls that weren't caught. He gave up four home runs in just twenty-three innings of work in 2013, with a 5.09 ERA.

87: *the time bomb in his arm ticked louder than most:* Rodriguez is known for having a funky arm delivery that hides the ball from hitters longer than usual. However, the low arm slot from which he throws has given him trouble in his young career. After an excellent 2012 rookie season he struggled in the second half of 2013 and made only nineteen appearances in 2014.

88: *visa issues:* Belisario had trouble gaining admittance into the United States for spring training, year after year, and would often report late. In February 2011 he disclosed that his visa problems stemmed from his testing positive for cocaine in the past.

88: *Only four of them were drafted by the Dodgers:* The four were Matt Kemp, Clayton Kershaw, Paco Rodriguez, and A. J. Ellis.

88: *signed as international prospects:* Hyun-Jin Ryu and Kenley Jansen.

88: *to paraphrase Dodger legend Don Drysdale:* After his Hall of Fame playing career, Drysdale went on to become a broadcaster for the Dodgers. His obituary noted that he had become critical of modern-day players. "You have to wonder when two players of different teams have the same agent," he said. "Who are these players really loyal to, the agent or their teams? You don't see 15 guys going out for a beer anymore. You see 24 guys living in 24 different single rooms on the road, and in some instances, taking 24 different cabs to the stadium." From "Don Drysdale, Hall of Fame Pitcher, Dies at 56," by Richard D. Lyons, *New York Times,* July 5, 1993.

88: " *'Getting along' is probably not the right way to say it":* Interview with Stan Kasten on July 15, 2014.

90: *"It's not the greatest working environment when Ned's around":* The opinion of multiple players, past and present.

91: *Only nineteen guys across both leagues:* A list of all MLB players who made at least $20 million in 2013 (*USA Today*):
    1. Alex Rodriguez, Yankees, $29 million
    2. Cliff Lee, Phillies, $25 million
    3. Johan Santana, Mets, $24.6 million
    4. Mark Teixeira, Yankees, $23.1 million
    5. Prince Fielder, Tigers, $23 million
    6. Joe Mauer, Twins, $23 million
    7. C.C. Sabathia, Yankees, $23 million
    8. Tim Lincecum, Giants, $22.25 million
    9. **Adrian Gonzalez, Dodgers, $21.85 million**
    10. **Zack Greinke, Dodgers, $21 million**

11. Vernon Wells, Yankees, $21 million

12. Miguel Cabrera, Tigers, $21 million

13. Matt Cain, Giants, $20.83 million

14. Cole Hamels, Phillies, $20.5 million

15. **Matt Kemp, Dodgers, $20.25 million**

16. Justin Verlander, Tigers, $20.1 million

17. Roy Halladay, Phillies, $20 million

18. Barry Zito, Giants, $20 million

19. **Carl Crawford, Dodgers, $20 million**

20. Ryan Howard, Phillies, $20 million

93: *"We had a lot of guys making less money"*: Interview with Don Mattingly on August 27, 2014, at Chase Field in Arizona.

93: *"They need to be self-motivated"*: Ibid.

96: *"He hardly ever gets mad"*: Interview with Preston Mattingly, August 1, 2014.

96: *"Everybody always thinks it was my back"*: From a story by Ramona Shelburne for ESPN.com Los Angeles, "Don Mattingly: The Manager, the Dad," on June 16, 2012.

97: *"Before he took the job he asked us"*: Interview with Preston Mattingly, August 16, 2014.

97: *"I liked helping guys"*: Interview with Don Mattingly on August 27, 2014.

98: *Zack Greinke believed:* Interview with Zack Greinke on August 31, 2013.

98: *Colletti signed so many broken former closers:* The 2014 bullpen featured Brandon League, Brian Wilson, and Chris Perez, among others. Each was given a multimillion-dollar contract years after being dropped from the closer role at his previous club.

100: *While minor on the surface:* When McGwire's Dodgers faced St. Louis in the NLCS, some within the Cardinals organization thought McGwire's knowledge of their hitters' strengths and weaknesses gave Los Angeles a distinct advantage.

101: *Hillman assumed:* I heard this from more than one player.

101: *a mean Excel sheet:* Hillman made gorgeous color-coded charts to show where and when hitters and pitchers were supposed to be during spring training, which were prominently displayed in the Dodgers' clubhouse.

102: *"I've never been around someone"*: Hillman said this at the Dodgers' Faith and Family Night on July 27, 2013, after a game at Dodger Stadium.

102: *Greinke had no energy for suffering fools:* From an article written by Tom Hardricourt in the *Milwaukee Journal Sentinel*, "Getting to Know Zack

Greinke," February 22, 2011. Greinke said this about speaking to reporters: "Every day I come to the park and want to get focused on my start, and then random people come and waste my time talking every day. It takes eight minutes to get a real question out because they're like buttering me up. Then they get to the question and it's a stupid question. So it's a waste of 10 minutes, and in that 10-minute time I don't get to do what I needed to do. The main reason is it gets rid of all the 'eyewash' comments from reporters and I actually get to focus on what needs to be focused on instead of wasting energy on other stuff."

102: *exchanged a few polite text messages:* Interview with A. J. Ellis on April, 1, 2013.

103: *"Well, the first thing I'd do is trade you":* Interview with A. J. Ellis on August 1, 2013.

103: *Ellis wondered what the hell he was talking about:* Interview with A. J. Ellis on July 29, 2014.

104: *"It was a changeup!":* Ibid.

105: *was named Gatorade's:* Greinke earned the award given to the nation's top prep baseball player in 2002; Kershaw earned it in 2006. Other players who have won the award include Gary Sheffield (1986), Alex Rodriguez (1993), and Justin Upton (2005).

105: *reminded Colletti of Greg Maddux:* Colletti said this on the Dodgers broadcast on September 2, 2013, talking to Charley Steiner and Rick Monday. He said it after Greinke stole the base, noting that Greinke was a thinking man, an excellent fielder, and swung a good bat. "He finds ways to help you win even without pitching," said Colletti.

106: *"They didn't tell me not to":* Spoken to reporters (including me) after a home game against the Padres on September 1, 2013.

106: *"I try too hard and it backfires":* Interview with Zack Greinke on August 31, 2013.

106: *On the mound, he was fine:* On February 15, 2013, Greinke addressed a pack of reporters at the Dodgers' spring training facility and said: "[My anxiety] never really bothered me on the mound . . . but I was raised to do what you enjoy doing, whether you are making several hundreds of thousands of dollars per year, or $30,000 per year. That was my thought, why am I putting myself through torture when I didn't really want to do it? I mean, I enjoyed playing but everything else that went with it I didn't."

106: *He devoured self-help books with little results:* "It hasn't been hard since I started taking the medicine. I don't know if I got lucky, or what,"

Greinke said. "I wish I knew about it before. I didn't know there was something for it. I used to read self-help books trying to make myself better." From a February 15, 2013, news conference with reporters.

107: *"I was pretty rude on my way out"*: From an article written on June 23, 2014, by Ken Gurnick for MLB.com, on the occasion of the Dodgers going to Kansas City to play the Royals.

108: *Kasten later called his meeting with Greinke:* Interview with Stan Kasten on July 15, 2014.

109: *Greinke thought he might be a general manager:* Interview with Zack Greinke on August 31, 2013. Greinke thought Ellis might make a good mouthpiece for him.

109: *"I could be in the lawn business"*: Interview with Zack Greinke on August 31, 2013.

110: *"Don't fucking touch me!"*: Matt Kemp was shown on television screaming at Bud Black.

112: *"He threw at him on purpose, okay?"*: This bizarre tirade by Tom Garfinkel was secretly recorded by a Padres season ticket holder and passed along to Jeff Passan, a reporter for Yahoo Sports. Passan published a story about the incident on April 18, 2013. Garfinkel apologized to Greinke and to Stan Kasten. Garfinkel would resign as president and CEO of the Padres three months later.

112: *"But just so you know"*: A person with knowledge of the call told me this.

CHAPTER 5: THE COLLAPSE

117: *Josh Beckett told Don Mattingly:* A person with knowledge of the exchange told me this.

118: *one even put on Gonzalez's neck brace:* Multiple teammates told me about this.

120: *he wondered if he would ever come back:* Interview with Matt Kemp at his Hollywood Hills home in April 2012.

121: *he was always the token black kid:* Ibid.

121: *But Kemp never wanted to be a professional baseball player:* Ibid.

122: *"It's only after you're rich"*: From an interview with Matt Kemp in March 2014 at the Dodgers' spring training complex in Glendale, Arizona.

123: *"So many nights I just went home and cried"*: Interview with Matt Kemp at his Hollywood Hills home in April 2012.

123: *he might notice a sick child:* Kemp is remarkable in his interactions with children, and has told me he prefers kids to adults. He visits hospitals unannounced and maintains lasting relationships with kids he meets. Once he met a child who couldn't watch Dodger games from her hospital bed, so he worked it out so she could get a login for MLB.com that bypassed the local blackout restrictions in L.A. and let her watch the games. He also noticed a sick child named Joshua Jones in the crowd at a game at AT&T Park in San Francisco in May 2013. After the game, he jogged over to the fan and gave him his autograph. Then he took the jersey off his back and handed it to Jones, and removed his cleats and gifted those to him as well. The incident was secretly recorded without Kemp's knowledge. It went viral the next day. Jones passed away three months later.

123: *"Trade me to the fucking Astros!":* He yelled this in the clubhouse in front of teammates and staff after arriving for a game early in the 2014 season and not finding his name in the lineup.

124: *stole forty bases, and:* Members of the 40/40 club:

    1988 Jose Canseco 42HR 40SB
    1996 Barry Bonds 42HR 40SB
    1998 Alex Rodriguez 42HR 46SB
    2006 Alfonso Soriano 46HR 41SB

124: *turned to a reporter:* The reporter Boras said this to was me.

125: *Jacoby Ellsbury:* Ellsbury later agreed to a seven-year contract with the Yankees worth $153 million.

125: *Kemp approached Gonzalez:* Gonzalez had the same surgery to repair a torn labrum, and told reporters afterward that he wasn't a power hitter anymore. Told to me by a person with knowledge of the conversation.

126: *A few of Kemp's teammates heard this and became enraged:* Told to me by multiple people who witnessed the incident.

126: *To amuse themselves, when Dodger pitchers watched game film:* Told to me by multiple team personnel.

126: *Dodgers front office dispatched a club executive:* Told to me by multiple people who witnessed it.

127: *a respected national columnist:* Ken Rosenthal of Fox Sports.

127: *transfixed by the double switch:* There is no known recording of the number of double switches a team executes in a season, though many with the Dodgers were convinced the 2013 club broke the all-time major-league record.

129: *Ethier had showed up to a Sunday matinee:* Told to me by a person with knowledge of the conversation.

131: *"That's not gonna help me in arbitration":* I heard this from a Dodger player the week it happened.

131: *"So at that number, you're looking at":* From an interview I did with Josh Collmenter at Dodger Stadium on June 15, 2014.

132: *Gonzalez loved to use RBIs as a measuring stick:* From many conversations I had with Gonzalez, but specifically on September 24, 2013 and on April 15, 2015. I consider Gonzalez to be a very thoughtful player, and I asked his opinion on who I should cast my NL MVP ballot for. (I voted for McCutchen.) At first I didn't agree with his citing RBI, but I'm glad he told me because it inspired me to look up his numbers with runners in scoring position—he is great.

133: *He began hustling out every ground ball:* The Dodgers' ranks were unanimous in their feelings about Andre Ethier being an unsung hero during their incredible run. The guys knew he was playing out of position, and they recognized he was busting his ass. His selflessness inspired many.

135: *Adam Wainwright, who convinced him:* From Skip Schumaker's testimony at the Dodgers' Faith and Family Night on July 27, 2013.

135: *"Believe it or not":* Schumaker told me this before the games versus the Cardinals on May 24, 2013. He could not believe how sore his body was from one inning of pitching.

136: *White was respected as one of the sharpest:* On one scouting trip to Mexico in 2012, White signed Yasiel Puig and Julio Urias, a fifteen-year-old pitcher who wound up being a top-five MLB prospect going into the 2015 season. This was perhaps the greatest scouting trip of all time.

136: *White took college athletes:*

     1st round Chris Anderson RHP JR Jacksonville University
     2nd round Tom Windle LHP JR University of Minnesota
     3rd round Brandon Dixon 3B JR University of Arizona

137: *an anxious Colletti emailed leadership surveys:* From players who received them.

CHAPTER 6: PUIGATORY

142: *White arrived alone in Mexico City:* All the information about Puig's tryout comes from an interview I conducted with White on October 23, 2014.

144: *So he called Kasten:* The details of this phone call were first mentioned to me by Stan Kasten in our July 15, 2014, interview. They were confirmed by White on October 23, 2014.

144: *"I thought it'd be funny":* Interview with Mitch Poole on August 13, 2013.

145: *"Papi":* Ibid.

146: *"You don't give them steak":* Don Mattingly made these remarks on April 6 to a pregame pack of reporters (including me).

146: *"Go to YouTube and type in 'Puig bat flip' ":* A Dodger executive told me this on April 2013.

149: *"What happened?":* I was at this game in Anaheim and asked Schumaker what happened after the game.

150: *"Please," said Kasten. "Do it for me":* Told to me by someone with knowledge of the conversation.

150: *Puig referred to himself as "El Secreto":* Told to me by a source close to Puig.

151: *ran through basic English with him:* I was standing near them and witnessed this.

154: *In 2012 he got so sick:* From a press conference Scully gave on August 23, 2013, announcing his return for the 2014 season.

156: *social media coordinator, Josh Tucker, not to hype Puig up too much:* Conversation with Josh Tucker the day Puig was called up.

156: *sticker still stuck:* One of my favorite pictures of Puig is a shot of him about to take the field for the first time. The sticker is visible.

158: *relied on a powerful Mexican drug cartel:* Most of the details of Puig's defection are supplied by the testimony of Yunior Despaigne, a boxer who left Cuba on a boat with Puig. Despaigne is suing Puig in federal court, and he filed his lawsuit under penalty of perjury. Sources around the Dodgers have confirmed the drug cartel's involvement in Puig landing in America. It has been widely reported, and Puig's camp has never denied it.

159: *"I don't really like the press":* Puig said this to *USA Today*'s Jorge L. Ortiz, as quoted in an article of July 8, 2013, "Puig Explains Himself: 'I'm a Ballplayer.' "

159: *Puig got down on his hands and knees:* I witnessed this on June 10, 2013.

159 *"He doesn't like all the attention":* Luis Cruz said this to a few of us reporters who were standing there before the game on June 10, 2013.

163: *"If you catch too much of the plate you're basically fucked":* National League West pitcher told me this.

163: *"But I don't really care because he rakes":* A Dodger pitcher told me this.

163: *"I always try to put on a show for the fans":* Puig said this to a pack of media reporters (including me) on July 12, 2013.

164: *"I don't think any of us were really thinking":* Interview of Don Mattingly on radio show *The Herd* with Colin Cowherd on July 3, 2013.

164: *"Oh na naaa":* I witnessed this often.

165: *"That's like you in San Diego!":* I witnessed this, too. It happened while reporters were in the room.

166: *One veteran infielder said he hoped a blogger:* The player who said this to me never did punch a member of the media.

167: *He wore number 74:* The number was significant to Kenley Jansen because when he was growing up the family constantly worried about being able to make the mortgage. During his first season in the big leagues he sent all of his paychecks home until it was paid off. From "No Man Is an Island," a column written by Bill Plaschke for the *Los Angeles Times*, September 11, 2013.

170: *"I'd never seen a pitcher throw at two different":* Interview with Skip Schumaker after the game on June 12, 2013.

170: *"He plays with a lot of arrogance":* Ian Kennedy said this to Arizona reporters after the club's game against the Dodgers on July 9, 2013.

170: *There was no doubt in Mattingly's mind it had come from Gibson:* I mean, this was obvious from his actions (running at Gibson and screaming at him). But a source close to Mattingly told me this.

171: *Kershaw was furious:* From multiple team sources.

172: *"I don't think anyone thought he was the problem":* Interview with Stan Kasten on July 15, 2014.

173: *to the ire of the coaching staff:* Every coach on that team wanted youth.

CHAPTER 7: THE RUN

175: *in the season's biggest moments:* Greinke was the starting pitcher in the brawl game against San Diego and the brawl game against Arizona.

175: *One popular theory:* This rumor wound up not being very far off base, as the Dodgers ultimately hired one of Hunsicker's old colleagues, Andrew Friedman, away from Tampa to take over baseball operations.

178: *"Winning does a lot":* Kershaw said this in his postgame interview with reporters after the game.

178: *Epstein was thought:* Epstein was also the guy some Dodger executives insinuated had tampered with J. D. Drew (encouraging him to opt out of his Dodgers contract by presenting his agent, Scott Boras, with an offer while he was still a Dodger, which is against the rules). According to a *New York Times* article written by Murray Chass on December 8, 2006, Epstein tried to call an angry Colletti to smooth things over, but Colletti refused to take his calls.

178: *Joe Torre's godson, Mike Borzello:* It had been widely reported that the Dodgers and Cubs were talking about trading Dempster. A team employee told me of Epstein's frustration later.

180: *"He's not a bad kid":* Mattingly said this to a group of reporters in the Chase Field dugout, including me.

180: *When Fernando Valenzuela was a rookie:* This story was told to me by Ken Gurnick, the prolific Dodger beat writer who has covered the team for decades and was there during Fernandomania.

181: *This became evident when a national television reporter:* This story was relayed to me by multiple players and staff members.

182: *Puig's friends say the incident:* From a source close to Puig.

182: *While Bravo was off working with Puig:* Bravo's sons illness had been widely reported.

183: *Puig, who had quietly:* Puig's son, Diego, was born in December 2013. Puig shares pictures of the boy on his social media accounts often.

184: *"I love him . . . But I can't fucking stand him":* Text from an NL East pitcher sent to a Dodger pitcher, who told me.

184: *if you wore Diamondback red you were his sworn enemy:* From a source close to Puig.

185: *Schumaker decided to watch:* Interview with Skip Schumaker after the game, July 16, 2013, in Phoenix, Arizona.

185: *"If the ball's away":* Postgame interview with A. J. Ellis on July 16, 2013.

187: *His mother had wanted to name him Juan Jose:* Interview with Hanley Ramirez on March 12, 2014.

189: *"Show me why you're the best hitter I've ever played with":* Postgame interview with A. J. Ellis on July 16, 2013.

192: *Angels for second baseman Howie Kendrick:* They would trade for Kendrick a year and a half later.

192: *the pregame festivities turned the dugout into a mess:* I witnessed all this.

193: *It was still possible to buy season tickets:* At the start of the 2015 season there was a wait list for season tickets. The cheapest season tickets, in the reserve level, cost five dollars a game.

194: *He arrived twenty minutes late for a team meeting:* Told to me by multiple people in the room.

194: *"I've seen guys that are in the Hall of Fame":* Interview with Don Mattingly on August 27, 2014.

198: *When the Yankees came to town:* I observed Robinson Cano greet Puig's friend on the field, and Puig's entourage's general presence in the dugout every day. Multiple players and employees complained to me about their presence in the locker room.

200: *His cover was blown:* Colletti told this story to a pack of reporters (including me) just outside the visiting clubhouse the night the Dodgers were eliminated in St. Louis, October 18, 2013.

200: *whale puke:* I asked Wilson what it was. He said whale puke.

201: *"I've got something to say":* I heard this from multiple players and staff who thought it was genius.

202: *chicken fight tournament:* I walked into the Dodgers' locker room the day before they clinched and saw players sitting on other players' shoulders. I asked what was going on. They told me they were planning on staging a chicken fight tournament in the pool. I gave the Dodgers' team photographer, Jon SooHoo, the heads-up.

202: *thought he heard Kemp bragging:* I didn't hear Kemp say this, but others did. Everyone I spoke with was adamant he was kidding. I tell this story as a way to demonstrate the ridiculous tension between the Dodgers and Diamondbacks. Even a senator weighed in on social media.

203: *"I'm a starter":* It was a phrase Kemp repeated often, in private and to reporters. When asked about it later, he explained that it was a no-win situation. If he accepted a platoon role then it would look like he didn't care enough to fight for his job. But if he bristled about having to share time it would look like he wasn't a team player. He was right.

CHAPTER 8: THE BEST TEAM MONEY CAN BUY

205: *injury issues all year:* The Dodgers were so banged up that head trainer Stan Conte (smartly) sat down with Mattingly to help plan out the line-ups after they clinched.

206: *Dodger officials were told:* A Dodger exec told me that before the game.

207: *They found the hole in his swing:* A Dodger staff member told me that before the game.

215: *"If you don't play good people don't remember you":* Interview with Juan Uribe at AT&T Park in San Francisco on September 24, 2013.

216: *Kimbrel wanted in the game:* TV cameras caught him cursing in the bull-pen. The footage is easily found on the Internet.

216: *all seemed to scream and bounce:* I have been to roughly five hundred Dodger home games in my life. This was the loudest I have ever heard that stadium, but I was not present for Gibson's home run, and sadly I was not old enough to remember watching it on television.

222: *Young was perhaps the most outwardly animated Dodger:* I heard this from multiple players on that text chain.

223: *but Ramirez was terrified of needles:* Multiple people with the team told me this.

225: *The drug cartel that helped smuggle Puig to the United States was always around:* From multiple sources close to Puig.

225: *One of them asked to borrow his Lincoln:* From a source close to Puig.

226: *"Two and a half billion dollars and two fucking runs":* A Dodger executive said this to me.

227: *"It's not over yet, we need you":* I heard Puig had gone missing from multiple players. I confirmed the details with the principal parties involved.

228: *"meep meep":* I observed this.

229: *So Nolasco took the mound in Game 4:* They almost started Kershaw but decided against it.

231: *poster comparing Puig to a squirrel:* I witnessed this bizarre scene and took a picture that wound up going viral.

232: *Ramirez finally acquiesced to the needle:* From two sources close to Ramirez.

237: *"They took turns high-fiving him":* From a person with knowledge of what happened.

238: *"In twenty years we can sit down":* I was the reporter Puig said that to.

CHAPTER 9: NO NEW FRIENDS

241: *Juan Uribe went first:* News of Puig's clubhouse meeting was widely reported. I got multiple players to fill in the blanks for me later.

242: *Puig secretly admired Schumaker and Punto:* Told to me by a source close to Puig.

244: *"But five years is the max for me":* Interview with Clayton Kershaw at his home on January 15, 2014.

247: *"Matt Kemp! Why you no talk today?":* I heard Ramirez say this. "Oh. So that's why he's do sad," Ramirez said to me.

248: *"you need to get your ass here on time":* This is what Gonzalez told reporters when he was asked what he said to Puig.

248: *Puig had changed his phone number:* From multiple team sources.

250: *they thought he put together tougher at-bats:* From a conversation I had with a member of the coaching staff.

251: *"It could be his last chance to prove us right or wrong":* From a conversation I had with a staff member.

252: *"He used to throw maybe ten pitches":* Interview with A. J. Ellis on June 18, 2014, after Kershaw's no-hitter.

253: *"I just want to get my four at-bats every day":* Hanley Ramirez said this to me in an interview on March 12, 2014.

254: *"When certain guys want to play":* Schumaker made these comments to the *Cincinnati Enquirer* on June 11, 2014.

256: *"It doesn't feel that way, though, does it?"* Interview with Stan Kasten on July 15, 2014.

258: *"He stated he's the best outfielder in the league":* From a CBS Sports article written on March 7, 2015, by Jon Heyman.

CHAPTER 10: THE BEST FRONT OFFICE MONEY CAN BUY

258: *Forty-eight hours later:* Greinke pitched the next day in Chicago, and looked out of sorts from the start. In the first inning he made his first error in more than four years, throwing the ball away on a failed pickoff attempt. He gave up four earned runs in five innings. I don't know whether what happened the night before was related to how Greinke pitched that day, but his performance on the mound was bad enough for me to text a team employee and ask if everything was okay with him. The staff member told me he had been in an altercation with Puig over rookie hazing. I asked players and other staff members about it later, and they filled in the details.

265: *Ned Colletti was angry:* From two people with knowledge of the incident.

273: *The Padres asked for $18 million more:* From a Dodger executive.

Acknowledgments

This book was a labor of love. My family has been in Los Angeles for five generations, and I grew up in the Top Deck at Dodger Stadium. I'd like to thank my parents for taking me to a zillion baseball games when I was little, and for allowing me to stay after my own Little League games to keep score at my friends' games, even though it was impossibly dorky and time-consuming. I'd also like to acknowledge my sister, Sarah, who came along to most of these outings and grew to love baseball as well.

As I sit here trying to come up with my list of people to thank I am overwhelmed. So many humans have helped me professionally, spiritually, and emotionally that I feel like I could write another book just to acknowledge them all. But here goes.

To my family: Toni Heyler, Beverly LeVato, Mary, Mike and Gini Frauenthal, Bryce Stowell, Lisa and Stephen Patton, Kathy and John Hollister, Christian and Locke Luhnow, Carolyn Knight, Janice Knight, Ginny Knight, Margaret Scott, the Kellys, the Blakemores, the Farias, Albert, Janiece, and Andrew Phillip, Gary, Sheri, Camden, Whitney, and Chandler Richards, and my grandfathers David Heyler, Joe LeVato, and Vick Knight . . . Thank you for raising me and for keeping me in check.

To my friends who stood by me, encouraged me to write this book, and/or handed me writing jobs or whiskey: Anne Hubert, Allie Ganz, Jessica Kumai Scott, Danielle Evans, Ali Calamari, Rahael Seifu, Tammy and Mark Murray, and everyone else in the Nerd Herd. Casey Newton, Dan Murtaugh, Tom, John, and Margaret Allen; Jordan Brenner, Shags, Karolyn Gehrig, Nicole Horton, Elyse Pasquale, Bill Magee, Gloria Hawa, Nikki Brien, Pete Olshansky, Jackie Sindrich, Angel Amitrano, Joy Hamabe, Worthy Havens, Rick Albano, Tanya Guzman, Natalie Montoya, Matthew Tolnick, Ethan Schiffres, Justin Givens, Ani Raymond, Ryan Ridings, Jorge Arangure, Matt Gelb, Chris Jones, Seth Wickersham, Alison Overholt, Matt Meyers, Gary Belsky, Hugo Lindgren, Jon Kelly, J. B. Morris, Jon Scher, Ed McGregor, Otto Strong, Scott Burton, Chad Millman, Jenn Holmes, Neil Fine, Ryan Hockensmith, Sue Hovey, Gary Hoenig, Anna Katherine Clemmons, Stacey Pressman, Mark Giles, Troy Cox, Liz Padilla, Erik Malinowski, Bruce Arthur, Old Hoss Radbourn, Jeff Passan, Jay Jaffe, Wendy Thurm, Jerry Crasnick, Joe Lemire, Jayson Stark, Jonah Keri, Michael Boor, Rachel, Ben, Marjie, Caryn Rose, Amanda Rykoff, Alyson Footer, Ken Rosenthal, Jon Heyman, Bob Nightengale, Michelle Beadle, Chris Tunno, Jeff Luhnow, Lana Berry, Lauren Bush, Phil Crandall, Neil Janowitz, Tim Kavanagh, Chris Diedrich, Ramsey Ezaki, Hiro Iwanaga, Jaison Robinson, Naveen Kabir, Patty Compton, Rachel Moore, Srinivas Panguluri, Vamsi Adusumilli, Brooke Sloane, Lindsay Sloane, Suzanne Wrubel, Alyssa Roenigk, Lindsay Berra, Jon Wank, Lee Berman, Dan Reilly, Adrian Perry, and everyone from the Welcome Back Jim Thome and OMG Girls Leagues.

Thank you to Bev, Mary, and Mike for always being my home away from home. To Lisa for teaching me about crosswords, and to Toni and Dave Heyler for the gift of a great education.

I drew from the work of many other reporters in writing this book, and you can find their cited works in my notes section. But this book would not have been possible without the hard work of those on the Dodgers beat, including: Ken Gurnick, Bill Shaikin, Mark

Saxon, Tim Brown, Dylan Hernandez, Bill Plaschke, Eric Stephen, Pedro Moura, J. P. Hoornstra, Mike Petriello, Chad Moriyama, Ramona Shelburne, Jill Painter Lopez, Bill Plunkett, Jon Weisman, Tony Jackson, Josh Suchon, Beto Duran, Roberto Baly, Arash Markazi, Diamond Leung, Steve Dilbeck, Dustin Nosler, Josh Fisher, Steve Mason, and John Ireland.

I also drew from the exceptional work of Derrick Goold and Jenifer Langosch in writing about the Cardinals, and Gordon Edes for my Red Sox musings.

Thank you to Marjie Blevins and Robin Oliver for looking out for me in high school, and for encouraging me to find my voice.

Thank you to Perry Passaro, Tara Brach, and Neda Shafaghi for keeping me happy and healthy.

Thank you to every journalist who has ever asked a good question. You know who you are.

Bill Francis at the Hall of Fame fact-checked this book. He is a true American hero.

Special thanks to Mason, Jori, Dan, and everyone from the Norton School of the Occasionally Employed for allowing me to sit on your porch to write the first four chapters of this book.

To all the Dodger players, family members, and staff who helped in my reporting of this book, and in everything I have written about the club over the years, including (in alphabetical order): Nancy Bea, Steve Brener, Yvonne Carrasco, Jon Chapper, Carl Crawford, A. J. Ellis, Cindy Ellis, Mark Ellis, Andre Ethier, Tim Federowicz, Adrian Gonzalez, Dee Gordon, Zack Greinke, Jerry Hairston, Orel Hershiser, Trey Hillman, Rick Honeycutt, J. P. Howell, Kenley Jansen, Jaime Jarrin, Stan Kasten, Clayton Kershaw, Matt Kemp, Davey Lopes, Don Mattingly, Preston Mattingly, Mark McGwire, Rick Monday, Mitch Poole, Nick Punto, Yasiel Puig, Hanley Ramirez, Josh Rawitch, Paco Rodriguez, Lon Rosen, Hyun-Jin Ryu, Skip Schumaker, Vin Scully, Charley Steiner, Josh Tucker, Juan Uribe, Tim Wallach, Mark Walter, Logan White, and Pepe Yniguez. Many more people helped with the reporting of this book who insisted on remaining anonymous. I can't name them, but I extend my deepest gratitude.

There are five people who midwifed me through this process and encouraged me when I thought all was lost. They are: Nick Piecoro, Keith Law, Tyler Kepner, Buster Olney, and Stephen Rodrick. My sanity would not have been possible without them, and this book certainly would not have been.

I want to thank my mother, Mandy, and my sister, Sarah, for providing the support I needed to finish this book, including mountains of Bagel Bites. You gals are the best.

I would like to thank my editor, Bob Bender, his assistant, Johanna Li, and my agents, Jared Levine and David McCormick. David: you encouraged me to start this crazy project, and then sold my collection of notes to Simon & Schuster. I cannot imagine a better fit for me. Bob: you held my hand through this process, and made this book infinitely better with your suggestions and judicious cuts. Your calmness rubbed off on me, which is no small task. I am forever in your debt for helping to make this dream come true. Any writer would be lucky to have you edit her. And to Jared: thank you for being my sounding board and my friend, as well as the captain of this ship. And thank you for loving the Dodgers.

Last but not least, thank you to Simon & Schuster for publishing this book. That was pretty awesome of you guys.

Index